Peggy,
Thank you so much!
Stay RIGHT always!

Eric aka the Tygrrrr Express

Ideological Bigotry

A Politically Conservative and Morally Liberal Hebrew Alpha Male Hunts Left-Wing Vipers and Sucks the Political Poison From Their (redacted)

eric aka the Tygrrrr Express

iUniverse, Inc.
New York   Bloomington

Ideological Bigotry
A Politically Conservative and Morally Liberal Hebrew
Alpha Male Hunts Left-Wing Vipers and Sucks
the Political Poison From Their (redacted)

iUniverse books may be ordered through booksellers or by contacting:

iUniverse
1663 Liberty Drive
Bloomington, IN 47403
www.iuniverse.com
1-800-Authors (1-800-288-4677)

Because of the dynamic nature of the Internet, any Web addresses or links contained in this book
may have changed since publication and may no longer be valid.

ISBN: 978-1-4401-3389-3 (pbk)
ISBN: 978-1-4401-3390-9 (cloth)
ISBN: 978-1-4401-3391-6 (ebk)

Printed in the United States of America

iUniverse rev. date: 3/27/2009

Eric is the brilliance (or lack thereof) behind the Tygrrrr Express, the 2007 Bloggers Choice Award for Most Passionate Fan Base.

"The Tygrrrr Express" has been published in the **Washington Times, Jewish Journal, RealClearPolitics Online, Commentary Magazine Online,** and on the Web sites of Hugh Hewitt, Mark Steyn, Patrick Ruffini, and Michelle Malkin.

A radio host himself since 1992, his radio beginning was a sophomoric hard rock music program entitled "Hard as a Rock." Maturation eventually settled in (some disagree), and serious radio interviews with Ward Connelly, the Vets For Freedom, and Evan Sayet ensued. On the flip side of the microphone, the Tygrrrr Express has been a radio guest of Hugh Hewitt and Armstrong Williams, in addition to being a frequent guest of Frank and Shane of "Political Vindication" on Blog Talk Radio.

The Tygrrrr Express has conducted print interviews of virtually every notable politician, although the Secret Service still will not allow a warm hug of President George W. Bush or Vice President Cheney.

Governors and gubernatorial candidates interviewed include Jim Gilmore, Christie Whitman, Ralph Reed, George Allen, Michael Steele, Linda Lingle, Tim Pawlenty, and Lynn Swann.

Senators and senatorial candidates interviewed include Rick Santorum, Dan Coats, Mike Dewine, Slade Gorton, John Thune, Trent Lott, Orrin Hatch, Harry Reid, and Susan Collins.

Other notables interviewed include Hugh Hewitt, Armstrong Williams, Evan Sayet, Mike Gallagher, Michael Barone, Larry Sabato, Mona Charen, John Podhoretz, Tony Blankley, J.D. Hayworth, Bob Barr, Michele Bachmann, Tom Tancredo, Howard Wolfson, Juan Williams, Donna Brazile, Ambassador John Bolton, Byron York, Newt Gingrich, Orson Swindle, Colonel Bill Cowan, Sir Charles of Krauthammer, and by the grace of the lord, Miss Texas.

Often referred to as a "typical white person," the Tygrrrr Express in the future will be editor of the yet to be created "Non-descript Caucasian Monthly."

A proud member of the leadership of the Republican Jewish Coalition (RJC), meeting everyone from Australian Prime Minister John Howard to Sean Hannity has been an honor and privilege. The RJC has published the work of the Tygrrrr Express and more importantly, been a source of lifelong friendships.

Rumors of being romantically involved with Shannon Doherty, Mary Katharine Ham, Andrea Tantaros, or Monique from *Showtime at the Apollo* are patently false. None of them are Jewish. These rumors must stop, as they dismay the author's girlfriend and shame his parents.

ABOUT: To learn about me, I fell asleep at my computer and clicked on my imaginary "about" page. For those who are Canadian, an about page is similar to an "aboot" page. Anyway, this is what the page said:

<u>2007 Bloggers Choice Awards Winner–Most Passionate Fan Base–The Tygrrrr Express</u>

The Tygrrrr Express is me. I am Brooklyn born, Strong Island raised, and currently living the good life in Los Angeles as a stockbrokerage and oil professional. I like politics, the National Football League, '80s hard rock music, the stock market, and red meat. Blogging is a shameless ploy to get what I really want, which is to impregnate a hot Republican Jewish brunette. There will be a ceremony several months beforehand since my parents are NRA members. Society will benefit if my kids end up with her loveliness and my last name.

The only political issue more important than killing taxes is killing terrorists. I do not sing "Kumbaya" with Islamofacists or leftists. Scorched Earth is my approach, with the grace and subtlety of a battering ram. The events of 9/11 fuel my emotions every day. Civilization must defeat barbarism, and my generation is up the challenge. We will win the War on Terror, because we are Americans.

eric, aka the Tygrrrr Express

www.tygrrrrexpress.com

To baby Daniel Goldberg: I love being your de facto Uncle Eric. One day I will have a son of my own, and you will be his de facto big brother. Your father and I have been friends a long time, and you are one special little dude.

Warning: Much of what was written was done so between March of 2007 and September of 2008. Therefore, it could very well be obsolete and quite wrong. I decided to leave it as is for the following reasons:

1. Laziness.

2. Honesty—Analysts are masters at predicting things after they have already happened. I am more than willing to get things wrong, and display that.

3. Like a blinking VCR, I am astonishingly accurate twice a day. If I wait long enough, things I got wrong now could be right one day.

4. You try writing a book in a rapidly changing world. That is a fancy way of reiterating reason number one.

I am now 40 percent qualified to write a Top Ten list for David Letterman.

Contents

Chapter 0:
A Backward Thinking Foreword

For those wishing to learn all about me, please buy my second book. This is my first book. I am not a celebrity, so reading about my favorite foods, junior high school heartache, or any other tidbits about my average everyday existence would be as pointless as it would be coma inducing. Talking about my family would be a mistake since they are alive and able to retaliate. Besides, they changed their addresses and last names again, so their whereabouts are not certain.

Besides that, I am a regular guy leading a mainstream life. I am just like you, only perhaps better. Sorry about that remark. I briefly became a liberal. I'm back now.

Conservatives can be arrogant gasbags just as liberals can, only we acknowledge it and try to make it the exception and not the rule. We conservatives also poke fun at ourselves and others. We can tell jokes because we do not have to apologize every five seconds to some interest group that wakes up in the morning and has a cup of victimhood with their copy of the "Jayson Blair" *Times*(*JBT*).

The only thing I want to communicate in this book is that without love and laughter, there is no life. Nothing I do will change the world, but if it gets a stiff person to lighten up and smile, I am pleased.

So whether your favorite charity is Save the Big Business Men or Lesbian Vegans for Libya, the political spectrum of life has space for you.

Relax, have a soda and a burger, and enjoy what I have to say. You already bought the book, so you might as well read it.

This book is a compilation of columns ranging from the serious to the senseless. This was done so that if you detest what I am saying, in two or three pages I will be on to something different. For those that abhor salaciousness and scandal, skip chapter seven. For those that want to avoid anything that may expand the mind, skip the first six chapters.

I do tend to wander far off of the reservation, but rumors that I started have described this as a fabulous ride.

So get on board and ride the Tygrrr's back to the finish line of this book. You'll be glad you did.

Welcome to the 2007 Bloggers Choice Awards Winner for Most Passionate Fan Base. Welcome to the Tygrrr Express.

eric

P.S. I sign my name with a lowercase "e." Let it go.

Chapter 1: Ideological Bigotry

Ideological bigotry is the hatred of people simply due to their political or ideological beliefs. Ideological bigotry is every bit as destructive as racial or ethnic bigotry, but receives far less attention.

Conservatives disagree with liberals. Liberals despise conservatives. They hate them. The reason why they hate them is because conservatives exist. It is not due to any policy disagreements. Liberals hate conservatives for merely existing and breathing air.

Ideological bigotry must be handled in the same way as all other bigotry:

With swift, loud condemnation and full throttled self-defense.

Ideological Bigotry

One benefit of being politically liberal is never having to apologize for being hateful.

First of all, I know several liberals who are good people who express principled (wrong, but principled) opinions based on noble beliefs and a deep love of America. Having said that, this reasoned approach that allowed Douglas to debate Lincoln and Kennedy to outpoint Nixon is not the norm for twenty-first century political liberalism.

Conservatives look at liberals and say, "I disagree with you." Too many liberals look at conservatives and say, "You are a bad person." When people are demonized for having differing opinions, we as a society are losing our way. Someone has every right to question my beliefs, whether it be Coke vs. Pepsi, the Whopper vs. the Big Mac, or Leno vs. Letterman (full disclosure: Coke, Big Mac, and Letterman). What someone does not have the right to do is question what is in my heart.

Questioning the legality of gay marriage does not make one a homophobe. Wanting to privatize social security does not mean I wish to see seniors bleeding to death on the streets. Questioning whether affirmative action succeeds in making things better does not make one a racist. Supporting the Iraq war does not make one an imperialist, a warmonger, or a Muslim-hater.

Are there people who express these viewpoints who are racists, sexists, homophobes, etc? Absolutely. However, most conservatives condemn those on our side that throw bombs. Liberals embrace their most hateful elements.

Michelle Malkin refers to these hateful individuals as "Moonbats." Now, I have my issues with Michelle Malkin. For one, she is a happily married woman to someone who is not me. Also, she is too dignified and classy to do a *Playboy* spread, insisting on dazzling us with her fine mind, gorgeous smile, flowing black hair, angelic ... (gimme a few minutes).

Back to my point. Michelle Malkin calls them "Moonbats."[1] Charles Krauthammer refers to a disease known as "Bush Derangement Syndrome."[2] I personally created the term "ideological bigotry" to explain these people.

Right-wing bomb throwers such as Ann Coulter get criticized by liberals as an example of all conservatives, even as conservatives are criticizing them for allowing liberals to do this. Left-wing bomb throwers, which pretty much includes most activist groups and most Democratic politicians, get invited to wine and cheese parties in places such as Boston, Malibu, San Francisco, and other areas where wealthy celebrities get to rail on about the evils of American capitalism and wealth.

It is one thing for private citizens to lob grenades. It is one thing for Hollywood celebrities to speak their empty minds. It is another for leaders of an entire political movement to resort to such discourse. Here are some great quotes:

"This election is a choice between good and evil. Do we want to be part of the forces of good, or the forces of evil?"

"He betrayed his country."[3]

"The president is a loser and a liar."[4]

"Republicans are basically a white Christian party. I hate everything they stand for."[5]

"This war is unconscionable."[6]

"This president misled us into war."[7]

"The Republicans ran the house like a plantation, and you know what I'm talking about."[8]

The first quote is Al Gore, accusing President Bush of treason and calling Bush supporters evil. Harry Reid, involved in a scandal in Nevada involving boxing tickets, insulted the president. Howard Dean attacked all Republicans. Robert "KKK" Byrd claims to be the conscience of the Senate Democrats. John Kerry and Hillary Clinton round out the quotes with slurs of lying and racism.

This is hate speech. President Bush and Vice President Cheney do not act this way. Class and dignity are values, not archaic concepts. It is possible to disagree with people without impugning their humanity. Conservatives, especially those in leadership positions, understand this.

I say this because as the son of a Holocaust survivor, I am shocked at how liberals do not see how dangerous the verbal hatred train can become when it rolls down the track. Once you dehumanize your political opponents, they are fair game for violence. This is how cars get keyed, newspapers get burned, and good individuals get destroyed. Black people who become politically conservative are referred to as "Uncle Toms" and must duck Oreo cookies being thrown their way. Jewish Republicans at Jewish parties are forced to hide their opinions in fear of verbal and physical attacks. Gay people are out of the closet, but Jewish conservatives live with "Don't ask, don't tell."

One Jewish liberal at a dinner party I attended expressed that she wished President Bush and his supporters were "flammable." Flammable! Setting people on fire is lynching. Except for Robert Byrd, I do not know anyone that has ever belonged to an organization that supported lynching. Replace "Bush" with "Jesse Jackson" and riots develop in the streets. Advocating the lynching of Republicans is treated as a joke, followed by sips of wine and a prayer service containing words such as "peace" and "tolerance."

Until mainstream liberals, who do exist, loudly condemn ideological bigotry, they will be lumped in with all bigoted liberals, and rightfully so.

Disagree with me. Disagree with my president. Heck, disagree with Michelle Malkin (daydreamy siggghhhh) if you have to do so. Calling Republicans "evil" or "moronic" (which are totally contradictory, but then again, hate speech is not logical) is pointless. Attacking Rush Limbaugh for being overweight, Michelle Malkin for being Asian, or President Bush for being an Evangelical Christian goes against the betterment of society.

The goal is to make the world a better place. Until liberals see conservatives as a noble opposition, they will continue to live in the intellectual, ethical, and political wilderness reserved for those who prefer rage, hatred, and anger to rolling up sleeves and creating solutions to improve the quality of life.

If it truly does take a village, then people should avoid the incendiary verbal devices that burn the village down, eventually emotionally killing those starting the fires.

I remain a happy, dedicated conservative, and I ask all liberals and conservatives to help me in fighting the scourge of ideological bigotry. Conservatives have already agreed.

Well, liberals? What say ye?

eric

MoveOn.org Needs to Just Move On

Moveon.org needs to just move on. So does the *Daily Kos*. I get your message. You hate President Bush, and anybody who supports him. You want to slap his vice president, humiliate his cabinet, and kick his dog. Just understand that blind hatred coarsens society.

As for Moveon and *Daily Kos*, let us be reminded of why they were created, or at least why they claim to have been born. Moveon came about during the Clinton impeachment hearings. Now while anyone who supports the rule of law should have found the impeachment of a corrupt politician the right thing to do, Moveon took a position that the impeachment was bad for America.

I have no objection to this. That is a position on an actual political issue. The problem with this is that when the struggle ends, so does the rationale for existence. When basketball fans wore "Free Kobe (Bryant)" t-shirts, confused people asked, "Isn't he already free?" The NAACP would look foolish if they marched down the streets today demanding that black people be given the right to vote. They already have this.

Rome fell because it conquered everybody and then had nothing to do. Moveon was victorious in the impeachment battle. They won. Unfortunately, the bored millionaires that created Moveon needed a reason to continue existing. People who start out with an actual philosophy don't have this problem.

When the 2000 election came and went, and Al Gore gave the least gracious concession since Richard Nixon in 1962, Moveon had a new reason to live. The problem is that they went from defenders to attackers. Defending somebody requires loyalty and a liking of them. Attacking somebody, especially somebody who did not attack first, requires a certain amount of rage. Otherwise, why attack anyone? Somewhere there is a woman living in San Francisco whom I have never met and whose name I do not know. She might disagree with me politically, but I have no rationale for hating her. It would make no logical sense.

Moveon simply defies logic. Once one accepts the premise of this cult that George W. Bush is evil, there is no reason to analyze things in a fair manner. President Bush has appointed some of the best and brightest individuals to powerful positions (in some cases they were holdovers that stayed), but Moveon never gave these people a chance.

Alan Greenspan, who former Senator Phil Gramm correctly referred to as "the greatest central banker in the history of the world,"[9] was deemed by left-wing wack jobs to be part of the "Republican controlled Federal Reserve Board."[10] Nobody controlled Greenspan, which is why he was so universally respected by everybody except those that had reason to fear positive economic news during a Republican administration. Instead of arguing that times were good despite the president (I would disagree, but it would be a legitimate argument), the left would attack Greenspan's reports as biased before they came out, and then state that the economy was bad.

Chief Justice John Roberts is an intellectual titan. Yet his decisions are often attacked as being part of a Bush administration cabal. Justice Roberts does not answer to the president. It is one thing to disagree with a report. It is another to impugn the integrity of a man who is decent and just.

Now General David Petraeus is being attacked. This is insane. The man is trying to save our lives, and civilization along with it, and he is the bad guy? The left has discredited his upcoming September report as being biased before he even testifies. Yes, he reports to the president. Yes, a positive report would benefit the president. However, is there any proof that this man has a history of lying or even sugarcoating the truth? His career has been sterling and spotless. Therefore, he deserves the benefit of the doubt.

I predict he will issue a mildly positive report that will show what we have done right, what we have done wrong, and what we need to do to do better. Under any circumstances, this is a normal process. So why would Moveon want to shoot the credible messenger of a reasonable message?

The reason is because the message does not matter. It is ironic that the same people who accuse President Bush of shooting first and asking questions later are doing this themselves. The same people that used phrases like "rush to judgment" are guilty of this. The left is simply guilty of having a predetermined opinion. It seems the one time that the left is ever in favor of a preemptive strike is when it is against a report or decision that might benefit Republicans.

Imagine if the left took all the anger they had at President Bush and directed it toward Al Qaeda. America is divided not because of President Bush, but because the left despises him. Politics used to stop at the water's edge. Republicans backed Woodrow Wilson, FDR, Harry Truman, and JFK on foreign policy, and were right to do so.

Moveon claims that they are being censored for disagreeing with the president. Nobody has censored them. They scream louder than everybody else combined. The problem is that invective is not a policy. Rage is not a program. Hatred is not a plan for governing or improving society. Moveon is still living in the year 2000. Every position they have taken since then stems from the fact that they believe George W. Bush stole the election.

The *Daily Kos* began in 2002 out of disgust for the president's popularity following 9/11. The left complains that we were unified after 9/11, and then Bush broke that unity. No, he did not. The *Daily Kos* began bombthrowing long before any war in Iraq took place. They were angry that a man who won a close election had sky-high popularity, and that the Democrats would suffer losses in the 2002 elections (which they did).

Winning elections cannot come at any and all costs. If losing one's soul is the price, then the price is too high.

In 2002, the Democrats failed to offer actual policy proposals to counter President Bush. In 2004, their governing philosophy was ABB (anybody but Bush). They won in 2006 due to Republicans running out of steam, but the Republicans were guilty of straying from their core beliefs and principles. The Democrats do not seem to have any of these. If they do, they will not articulate them.

Reasonable people look at men like Alan Greenspan, John Roberts, and General Petraeus, and they just do not see zealots, extremists, or partisan hacks. They see bright, capable men doing their jobs quietly and effectively. Normal Americans might not agree with every word, but they are willing to listen to what these men have to say before forming entrenched opinions. They understand that whether it be an economy, a court decision, or a military report, good news is not automatically bad news just because some people, mostly on the left, want it to be.

From a Machiavellian perspective, I want the Moveon and *Daily Kos* minions to keep speaking. They are the gift that keeps on giving to Republicans. However, from a human decency perspective, I want them to grow up and simply stop being terrible human beings who say vile things about good people they have never met.

Free speech is not free. Hate speech is not protected. Invective inevitably leads to violence, such as ecoterrorism. *Daily Kos* and Moveon have their leftist pit bulls so jacked up on the steroids of hatred and rage that they will have blood on their hands when a small number of their followers end up committing acts of violence in the name of some warped sense of righteousness (this has already happened).

In the same way that they say it is not fair to blame them all for the acts of a few, especially when comparing Bush to Hitler, this argument is merely a way of passing the buck. If I belong to a country club that is racist, anti-Semitic, or the like, I have the obligation as a human being to resign my membership or force internal change.

There might be people in *Daily Kos* and Moveon that are not cancerous, but until they weed out the cancerous elements, their whole organizations are one big festering area of bilgewater.

These organizations need to stop being against everything related to George W. Bush, because when he leaves office in 2009, they will again have no reason to exist. They need to be for something ... anything. Also, it has to be something positive.

Otherwise, they can just demand that the next president spend their entire term investigating the eight years of George W. Bush. Republicans could then hold hearings on Ted Kennedy at Chappaquiddick. The left would then say, "That is old news, just move on." Republicans have moved on.

Ted Kennedy killed a woman. We moved on. Robert Byrd was a Klansman. We moved on. Bill Clinton was a liar and a sexual predator. We moved on. If Hillary Clinton is defeated, we will move on. She and her supporters will not, but we will.

Moveon and *Daily Kos* have a right to exist. They just have a responsibility to find out why they should exist. I have a right to find them repugnant, vile entities.

These organizations need to do something to make the world a better place, and stop fighting decent people struggling to do exactly that just because of a disputed election several years ago. They need to get over it. They need to unite behind what is right, which is winning the War on Terror. They can disagree with the means, but not the end. They do not have the right to put the lives of good people everywhere at risk.

The left needs to regroup and become part of a civilized debate. They need to stop rejecting news that has not been offered yet. They need to form opinions and solutions after the depth of problems have been explained, not before.

They need to forget the anger and rage of the past, and move forward with a positive agenda for improving the world.

They need to become thinking, rational human beings.

They must, finally, move on.

eric

Light a Candle, Smack a Woman

Fresh from a ton of parties on one night of Hanukkah, I then prepare for partying on the next night. I love this holiday. Since I do not indulge in alcohol, tobacco, or drugs, I will enjoy my vice of choice—women.

Women dominate Judaism. One of the reasons Judaism is seen as "weak" by outsiders and why Jewish men are seen as "momma's boys," is because our religion emasculates men. Judaism is the Phil Donahue of religions. We call it "celebrating women," but it is out and out male castration. We have holidays specifically dedicated to the power of women.

That is another reason to love Hanukkah. It is pure male testosterone. We came, we saw, and we conquered. We kicked some rumpus. Pure military force allowed the Maccabees to just smack around the enemy like they were women in need of a good backside slap.

For those of you wondering why out of nowhere I am deliberately advocating the denigration of an entire gender, just relax; the twist is coming any sentence now.

Ever since the feminist mistake, women have been up in arms looking for ways to exact vengeance on the male gender. It was supposed to be about the right to vote and equal work for equal pay. Now it is about attempting to destroy men. Unfortunately for the radical feminists (redundant, I know), they are cannibals. They eat their own. They betray each other. They do more to commit violence against their "sisters" than men ever could.

Therefore, in the spirit of Hanukkah, I will describe eight situations where it is perfectly acceptable to abuse women physically, sexually, or psychologically, one for each night. You can take these women and paddle their backsides, and there will be no consequences, unless gratification is a consequence. Do not worry about the feminists getting angry, which is how they normally go through life. They will allow this abuse. So for those of you out there looking to abuse women, here are eight acceptable situations.

1) The male sexual predator has to be politically liberal. Ted Kennedy and Bill Clinton have carte blanche to abuse women. If the woman ends up dead, it is acceptable, provided that the abuser is pro-choice on abortion. Of course they will be pro-choice, because that way they can be irresponsible and be able to get rid of the evidence. If abortion is not the way to get rid of the evidence, driving over a bridge is plan B. Kathleen Willey and Paula Jones? Sorry, ladies.

The feminists do not care. Anita Hill? No evidence required. Republicans do not get this exemption, even if they are pro-choice. Sorry, Bob Packwood.

In fact, the NOW announced that Bill Clinton should be praised because after he tried to get lewd with Kathleen Willey, he did not try a second time. He took no for an answer. Therefore, every man in America gets one free chance to cop a feel.

2) The woman can be a beauty pageant contestant. They are fair game for being violated. Feminists hate beauty queens due to obvious jealousy. Angry women have more wrinkle lines. Desiree Washington alleged rape against Mike Tyson, and I do not recall any feminist groundswell.

3) The woman must be politically conservative. Radio DJs recently advocated raping Laura Bush and Condoleeza Rice. Stone-cold silence. I can advocate taking a paddle to Hillary's badonkadonk and believe you me the Secret Service will have something to say about it as soon as they find out what a badonkadonk is.

4) Poor and/or ugly women are not given the same protection as attractive women, provided the women are not too attractive as to be in a beauty pageant. If a woman is considered hideously ugly, a man can abuse her because nobody would believe that he would be interested anyway. If the man is considered handsome, then the case is closed. There is no way Bill Clinton could have raped Juanita Broderick. He is considered pleasing to look at, while she is not. Rules 2, 3, and 4 apply to Sarah Palin.

5) Muslim women can and should be beaten as often as possible. From Detroit to Dubai, from Afghanistan to Zambia, feminists condone the brutal beating of Muslim women. Feminists really struggle with this one, because they want to be against male violence toward women. Yet those who abuse the Koran for their own evil purposes also tend to hate Republicans, especially George W. Bush. Besides, if they succeed in destroying America and we become part of the Caliphate, there will be no Republicans left. If some women get beaten in the process, such collateral damage is part of a greater good.

6) Non-Muslim women in Muslim nations are entitled to forty lashes at a minimum. Any woman that allows a teddy bear to be named Mohammed should know better. The feminists of America will not speak up to save her. They will treat her as if she smoked tobacco or caused global warming. To get an exemption, one has to submit to Islam and denounce all Republicans, primarily George W. Bush. This how Nancy the Pelosiraptor escaped her

lashes. She wore a burka, sipped tea with Assad, and denounced the tyranny of an American president.

7) Prostitutes can be beaten. Feminists will go insane when some radio shock jock refers to women as "nappy headed hos."[11] Some feminists will even criticize music that refers to women as b*tches and hos. Ironically, these same feminists will not stick up for actual hos getting pimp slapped by ... well, pimps, I guess. It could be because prostitutes tend to be attractive, and feminists despise women who succeed by being pretty and offering sexuality, whether they be strippers, call girls, etc. Besides, many women have lost their men to these women. Once Hugh Grant cheated on Elizabeth Hurley (proof perfection exists), no woman was safe anywhere.

Before going further, all people are prostitutes. I am a corporate slut. I will not compromise my principles, unless there is money in it for me. I sold out to the establishment for money and got a decent haircut. The old joke is quite true. A man asks a woman if she will sleep with him for a million dollars, and she says that she would. The man then asks if she would for ten dollars. She responds that she is not a hooker. The man explains to her that, "We've already established that you're a hooker, now we're just negotiating price."

8.) Women can be beaten in the movies. After all, feminists cannot advance their agenda unless society is convinced that every white, conservative investment banker in the movies is busy sexually violating minority women in between drinking oil-flavored martinis at lunch and chopping down trees for sport. After all, if both genders actually felt life was getting better between them, the feminists would have no power. They are the angry, white liberal versions of Jesse Jackson and Al Sharpton. Exacerbating hostility between the genders allows these feminists to have something to do. Most women in Hollywood are liberals, but since Hollywood is about acting, the more liberal the woman on the screen, the more oppressed she is. Only in real life are liberal women protected.

I support women receiving equal pay for equal work, and for achieving full equality in society. After all, if radical feminists ever do shut up, men and women will be better off. We will not have to listen to women comparing marriage to slavery while secretly praying for flowers and a wedding ring from a strong, smart Adonis who will turn them into paddle queens.

It is very important that men do not try to physically or sexually abuse women who are politically liberal, the correct level of attractiveness, or the wrong religion or ethnicity. For those who are still unclear which women are fair game and which women are off limits, Barbara Boxer's office will be publishing a list of the women she has defended and ignored over the last three decades. The list will be available in Spanish, Braille, and Ebonics. Coincidentally, Ms. Boxer herself is the first woman in the protected column, meaning that conservative Republican men should not even think about spanking her liberal hide.

The world now knows the eight categories of acceptable abuse of womyn, one for each night of Hanukkah. May the men of this world enjoy this testosterone driven holiday, and as for the women of America, I suggest you join a protected group very soon.

Okay, off to find my tennis racket and go visit a certain Republican Jewish brunette. Don't worry, sweetie, I will bring some ointment for you after I finish. You may object to this, but you don't have a say. Feminists will not defend you, since your beliefs justify my misogyny.

Actually, I have no desire to hurt anyone, although I would not mind radical feminists having their mouths ductaped while I watch football. They could voluntarily shut up until the commercials, but that has never happened.

(Raw) Bottom line: either all women should get abused, or none of them should. I prefer none of them get abused. I also prefer to live in a world where feminists actually stop promoting a liberal agenda, and start fighting for all women to be treated with respect. Men and women would both benefit from this.

eric

Chapter 2: Jewish Ideological Bigotry

Ideological bigotry is running rampant in the Jewish community. Those that have been the victims of the greatest hatred and intolerance on earth are now among the strongest practitioners of such malice.

As the son of a Holocaust survivor, to hear liberals compare any conservative politician to Adolf Hitler is deeply offensive. To hear Jewish liberals make these comparisons is a disgrace.

I am not worried about airing the filthy laundry of my own community. I will not let my community immolate itself through left-wing rage and hatred.

Synagogues can keep their liberalism or their tax exempt statuses, but they will no longer be allowed to keep both. Until the Jewish community becomes a place where every Jew feels welcome, I will personally break out the unwelcome mat for the leftist bullies in the Jewish community. Otherwise, when they come for the Jewish leftists, I will not be there to speak up.

You are most welcome, Jewish America.

Ideological Bigotry Part II–How Many Jewish Liberals Continue to Make the Klan Proud

Ideological bigotry has got to stop. Now. This instant. Six million Jews died in the Holocaust, and many of their descendants resort to the same dehumanizing hate speech that led to those glorious summer camps of concentration.

What many Jewish liberals fail to understand is that dehumanizing anyone is bigotry. These "enlightened" and "tolerant" people would cringe if bad words were said about gays, blacks, women, or other "accepted" groups. Disparaging remarks about conservatives are said without the slightest regard for those people, who, shockingly enough, medical science has discovered are actual human beings with feelings and emotions.

Yes, I am one ticked-off conservative. Trying to make the world a better place can be trying indeed. Suggesting I just "let things go" is like telling a black man to just ignore remarks that the Klan make. They can continue with their lives, but silence is acquiescence. Ignoring bigotry is tolerating it.

A woman said to me recently that "The reason there are very few Jewish Republican women, because Jewish women are charitable, giving, loving, accepting, and believe in freedom of speech, equal rights, abortion rights, gay rights, etc. The GOP represents none of the things we hold dear. Sorry."

Who is this "we," Kimosabe? Only Democrats are accepting, loving, and charitable? Are you kidding me? As for "accepting," this woman does not seem to have much acceptance for Republicans. The word "accepting," is apparently like the word "unilaterally," or "is" is. It means whatever the liberal wants it to mean at any given moment.

As for the things "we" hold dear, I hold dear that we are fighting World War III against Islamofacists. That is my issue. Republicans are, according to this woman, against equal rights and freedom of speech. If we were, President Bush would have the publisher of the *New York Times* thrown in jail (not a bad idea, but that is for another column).

So, let me now teach Jewish liberals some manners. (At this point they will go find examples of conservative bad behavior since that is easier than taking an introspective look inside themselves and making actual human improvements.) It is okay to ask someone, "Why are you a Republican?" or "Why did you vote for President Bush?" It is *not* okay to ask someone, "How in good conscience can you be a Republican or vote for President Bush?" or, "How can you justify being a Republican or voting for President Bush?"

This is where I want to rip their liberal throats out to simply stop them from speaking this nonsense. Where does anyone get off questioning what is in someone else's heart? How in good conscience? Because my conscience is just as pure as yours. How can I justify? I do not have to justify.

Conservatives do not do this, especially not Jewish conservatives. We disagree with liberals, often fiercely and passionately. We do not despise them, or call them evil.

A rabbi of mine, who I consider a dear friend, will sometimes introduce me as his "Republican friend." On more than one occasion at dinner parties he has said to people sitting next to me, "This is Eric. He is a Republican, but he is a good guy." Those qualities are not mutually exclusive. Replace the word "Republican" with the word "gay" or "Mormon" and the point becomes clear. Now, this rabbi is not in any way a bigot. He is a very good person. Yet those types of remarks are insensitive.

Some people I know will introduce me to someone by stating my political views. This is either to warn the other person or start a conflict. This turns a potential friendship into potential acrimony.

So, let me describe who I am clearly. First and foremost I am a human being, a creature of God. After that I am an American and a Jew. Way down the list I am a Republican. I take pride in each association. I am also a football fan, a lover of rock music, and a stock market lover.

The point is I am many things, and to define me by one element is shortsighted, and yes, dehumanizing. If a homosexual likes football, does that make him less valid to watch the NFL on my couch on a Sunday? Of course not.

What Jewish liberals need to do is admit their biases, and that they are often insensitive, myopic, and sometimes downright vicious. They must change.

I will speak up when the rabbi of Temple Valley Beth Shalom states during a Hanukkah speech, "Forget your stressful day. Picture a calm peaceful existence. A world without problems and stress … a world without negativity … a world without Donald Rumsfeld being in the news."[12] The liberal Jewish audience chortled.

I will speak up when Sinai Temple, on Memorial Day, has liberal activist Ruth Messinger give an antiwar speech laced with references to Darfur. Darfur may be a worthy cause, but would it have killed Sinai Temple to reserve Memorial

Day for positive references to the soldiers? Instead they bring in perhaps the only woman too liberal to be elected in New York City.

Do liberal Jews have any spokespeople at all that are not arrogant gasbags? What is this Jewish community that they claim to speak for? My Republican Jewish friends and I would like to know.

The reason I continue to verbally club liberals over the head is because I cannot and will not sit back and allow 1930s German behavior to infect my religion. We have a Museum of Tolerance. It does not describe exceptions or say, "tolerance of those who are politically liberal."

So how can Jewish liberals change? Simple. Look in the mirror, think of how you view conservatives, and picture me knocking you upside the head saying "knock it off!" This would be the best way to deal with Klansmen, terrorists, and hatemongers everywhere.

So, dear Jewish liberals, I don't want to get to the root causes of why you hate conservatives. I could not care less. Just stop being hateful. Now. As for you liberals, especially Jewish liberals, who are honestly not ideological bigots, when you hear your friends being bigoted, insist they stop.

Edmund Burke stated that when good people do nothing, evil is allowed to flourish. He was right then, and his words are right now. All forms of bigotry must stop. Ideological bigotry must be defeated. It is my hope that the descendants of Holocaust survivors will change their ways and become better people.

I am a human being, and expect to be treated as one, especially by my own people. I will not give an inch on this. It defines me. It is my core. *Hineni.* Here I am. Jewish, conservative, proud, and here to stay.

eric

Ideological Bigotry Part XVI—Yom Kippur and Lesbianism

The other night, I began the celebration of the holy day of Yom Kippur. The holiday is about apologizing for our transgressions and promising to be better people. I have my private conversations with God and vow sincerely to try and do better.

One thing I am truly thankful for is that there are many synagogues within walking distance of my home. Like other religions, Judaism has various denominations.

I live near UCLA, which has a Hillel House. "Hillel" is the center for Jewish life on college campuses. Many colleges have Hillel. Given that Hillel is specifically a place for students to feel welcome, it is supposed to be nonpartisan. If you ask Hillel directors, they will claim that Hillel actually is nonpartisan. Then again, most liberals in the media think that they are fair as well, so perhaps Hillel truly believes its own leftist spin.

My goal here is not to bash Hillel. My goal is to reform it. I deeply believe in what Hillel is intended to do. I am even more deeply troubled by what it has become on many campuses, including UCLA.

I walked into the building to see some friends as the service was nearing conclusion. I had already been to services at the local Chabad House, where the closest that the rabbi came to political speech was to condemn the leader of Iran for wanting to kill all Jews.

Yet the Hillel guest speaker spent several minutes talking about gay and lesbian issues and how important it is that gays and lesbians be treated better in society.

I was not in the room. I stayed in the back, outside the doors. As the speaker continued talking about gays and lesbians, and the intolerance of some, I just shook my head in disbelief. The more she spoke, the more I shook my head.

I was shaking my head specifically because I do not believe that politics should be a part of a religious service. Politics should especially not be part of a synagogue service on Yom Kippur, the holiest day of the Jewish calendar. It is inappropriate. I would argue it is borderline illegal, and that UCLA Hillel is coming close to violating rules for a tax exempt organization.

Liberal activists do not understand that to preach the need for tolerance while lashing out at others as intolerant is simply wrong and hypocritical.

UCLA Hillel again showed that ideological bigotry is rampant in the Jewish community, and that diversity and tolerance apply only to liberal ideals.

I want to make it crystal clear that the speaker, at least while I was there, did not bash or lash out at conservatives or Republicans. She passionately pleaded for more love and acceptance of gays and lesbians. Had her speech been the only event that occurred, I would have considered the evening ideologically slanted, but not ideological bigotry.

Where the line got crossed was in my first and hopefully last meeting with an operations director for UCLA Hillel. I name names, since I know I am telling the truth. His name is William Calder.

I had never met Mr. Calder before and was shocked when he came up to me and said, "You need to leave."

I was stunned. Several minutes earlier he asked me if I wanted to pull up a chair. I stated my preference to stay outside the room. My rationale was that pulling up a chair would have made noise, and I do not like interrupting speakers.

I asked him very quietly why I had to leave. I was not bothering anybody. I did not even open my mouth. He explained that he "saw me shaking my head." He firmly stated that "this is a liberal service."

I told him that I was not shaking my head because of that. I was shaking my head for my own personal reasons based on my private thoughts. I told him I was pro-gay rights.

He then said, "Oh, okay. Well, your shaking your head could be misinterpreted."[13] He walked away and left me alone.

For those who do not understand how serious this is, I was asked to leave a synagogue. I was not asked to leave for saying anything. People who disrupt such speakers should be asked to leave. Freedom of speech does not give one the right to disrupt speeches. That is just rude.

I was asked to leave because Mr. Calder *thought* that I was *thinking* something that he disagreed with.

This is liberalism at its very heart. Actions are irrelevant. Deeds do not matter. Being politically correct is all that matters. This is why we have hate crime legislation, because liberals think that certain crimes should be punished more than others. All crimes are hate crimes. Yet people should be punished for the crime itself and the level of culpability based on intent. The gender, race, or sexual orientation of the victim does not make them any more or less dead.

William Calder made it clear that those not supporting the gay and lesbian agenda were unwelcome. He thought my head shaking was in disagreement with the speaker. Even if he was right, which as a liberal of course he was wrong, shaking my head in quiet disagreement is a patriotic form of dissent. I was not even in the room! I uttered not one word.

After the speech and service ended, I approached the speaker. She was very pleasant. I told her that I was pro-gay rights, but that I had a concern. I did not bring up the inappropriateness of her speech, since I did not want a hostile conversation devoid of common ground.

I pointed out that I belonged to a minority group that has faced much hostility. I quietly whispered (it disgusts me that I should even have to whisper, but such is the abusive nature of liberal Jews towards Republicans that we have to stay in the closet out of fear) that I was politically conservative.

She laughed and said that her father was a Republican. I let her know that one concern I had was that so many gay people were hostile toward Republicans, not giving them the benefit of the doubt. I told her that many Jewish Republicans are libertarian on social issues, but it is difficult to dialogue with gay groups when they see Republicans and say, "We hate you."

She was very nice and clearly understood. I requested in her speeches about tolerance that she include that everybody must be given tolerance, including Republicans. She agreed with me that by rejecting people out of hand, it could push them further to the right and away from supporting her issues.

The last thing I said to her was, "You never know who may be a potential ally. I want to live in a world where all people are free to live their lives and be treated with decency and respect, including Republicans."

I will again emphasize that she was warm and pleasant. She did not seem to contain the hypocrisy that infects so many on the Jewish left.

However, she does not run the Hillel. Mr. Calder is in a position of power, and had I not immediately professed my support for gay rights, I would have been subjected to left-wing bullying. Worse, it would have been for thoughts, not actions.

Mr. Calder is in a position to influence and mold students, and if his behavior was reflective of his typical disposition, then he is just another example of ideological bigotry in the Jewish community.

Some people have argued that in many Christian churches, the sermon is a politically conservative message.

This does not make it okay. The analogy of two wrongs and a right applies. Also, I am not a Christian. I do not go to church and am totally unqualified to evaluate how churches behave. I would say that a Catholic Church arguing against abortion is not political. It is in keeping with church doctrine. However, telling people to vote against a pro-choice candidate may cross the line.

I know only my own community. Left-wing bigotry is a cancer in the Jewish community, and I am mortified that the holy day was allowed to be perverted by such speech. No, I am not calling gay people perverts. I am referring to devaluing a religious holiday with political speech of any stripe.

Some will say that it is unfair to indict liberalism based on one unpleasant person.

It is not one person. This is a problem that runs deep. Mr. Calder is the norm. Left-wing bullies are what much of Judaism has become, and it must cease.

Even if I did not believe in gay rights, the God I believe in is the God of all.

Mr. Calder believed I was intolerant because of my supposed thoughts. I know Mr. Calder is intolerant based on his actions.

UCLA Hillel has a long way to go before it becomes a tolerant place free of ideological bigotry. A good start would be if synagogues around America took the Calders of the world and forced them to sit quietly and not judge people they do not know and have never met. Ductape can be very useful in these situations.

Hineni. Here I am … Republican, Jewish, proud, and tolerant of others. I wish those on the left that scream and rage about tolerance could understand that Republicans deserve tolerance as well.

eric

Why Young Single Jews are Totally (Censored)

Young single Jews in America today are completely (redacted bad word). I can honestly say that our plan at self immolation is working splendidly. What Hitler failed to do, we are doing to ourselves through intermarriage and remaining childless as long as possible. Yet if there is one thing that is decimating Jewish singles, it is their political activism. I say "their," because I am not an activist.

Personally, I think activists should be ductaped, strapped to a chair, and forced to watch video presentations of other activists. Then they would realize what it is like to listen to somebody ramble on about social causes that only the speaker cares about.

Animal rights activists could be forced to listen to somebody rail about illegal immigration. Environmentalists could be subjected to pro-life lectures. Feminists can be pilloried with NRA members trying to shoot boll weevils. Do you know how hard it is to put an AK-47 through a boll weevil? Also, they do destroy cotton crops, and if there is one thing that will keep people of all stripes enthralled, it is an agriculture video.

Yet Jewish liberals remain activists, or as I call them, "lacktivists," because they lack ... well ... everything.

This is not just about liberalism, although that is part of the cancer eating away at Judaism. The bigger problem is that if civilizations do not reproduce, they die. The only way to reproduce is for people to meet each other. Being in the same room is not enough. There has to be actual human interaction. A Jewish social event I attended is a prime example of the problem. The only reason I attended was because it was one block from my home, so I could walk there and back. Plus, even if I did not meet a potential romantic partner, friends of mine would be there, making it bearable.

First there was a prayer service. People cannot talk to each other while they are praying, which is fine. However, there is a meal afterwards, and at some point people at the same table should be able to converse.

Yet pre-meal rituals must take place. Again, understandable. Rituals are important, and I love my religion. However, this event had an environmental theme. All the food had environmental connections. I told my friend, "I think the potatoes are made of hemp. Wanna try and smoke them later?"

Then came the speeches. It is not that they were liberal, boring, pompous, and worthless. I have come to expect that out of liberalism. It is that I could not hear the people at my own table. Luckily they were friends of mine and not romantic prospects, but still, it was a nuisance. I tried to say hello to friends at a nearby table, but every time we reached a couple sentences, the next speaker would come on. Even my columns end faster, and I can be paused online.

The last speaker asked what we in the audience could do to be better based on what we had learned. This led to a speech about vegetarianism, at which point I began to pray that somebody would quote Howard Stern and recommend that we recycle toilet paper. Short of an oil tanker crashing into the room carrying scantily clad Republican Jewish brunettes bearing sodas and hamburgers, this night was not improving.

Yes, the event was environmental, but it was still billed as an event for young single Jews to meet each other. How can we mingle when we cannot hear each other?

After the speakers concluded, moments of conversation almost occurred. However, the organizers then had to do "introductions." Is every other person in the room a committee member? Apparently. After the introduction came "announcements." Trips to Israel, planting trees, blah blah blah.

By that time, dessert had arrived. After precious moments of mentioning how delicious the dessert was, it was time for after meal prayers. Then the head of the event announced that everybody was to take their chairs and form a circle. They would be passing around bongo drums, or drums of some sort.

As I waited for people to start singing, "May the circle/be unbroken/by and by Lord/ by and by," my friend asked me if I was joining in the drum circle. I replied, "Well, even though I love a good drum circle as much as any other straight man, I think I am calling it a night."

Some could fault me for not realizing how many true believers liked the evening the way it was. This was not the case. Even zealots cannot recruit new zealots unless they can talk to them on a more personal basis.

This is the Jewish community in a nutshell. Bleeding heart do-gooders are in synagogues, and they divide into two groups. The first group couldn't care less about the audience. The social cause of the week is all that matters, whether it be "save the homosexual mosquitoes" or "allow wildlife to have abortions." The "I hate evil Republicans Museum of Tolerance" is a very popular one.

The second group of people actually want young single Jews to meet. They are just too self-absorbed to understand how to avoid making things worse. My advice to these lactivists is simple.

Shut ... up ... just ... shut ... up ... for five minutes ... just ... shut ... up.

I am not saying they have to become conservatives. I doubt liberal Jews will ever embrace the NRA, but if the entire room was armed, they could have demanded silence long enough to have decent conversation. Liberals have every right to be boring and wrong, but pause for a few moments. Breathe. Understand that some people in the room are trying to scope each other out, and we cannot impregnate anybody and bring new life into the world if all we know about the person we may lust after is that they are equally bored and fed up.

Young single Jews today will remain (censored) until event planners realize that the event is secondary, and that attendees themselves are the primary focus.

The next time I have to sit through an evening of "Jewish transsexuals for peace in the West Bank," all I ask is that if there is a hot girl across the table from me, let us get to know each other before she rips her name tag off in disgust and goes home out of boredom.

I would prefer my community of Jews stop being leftist liberal lacktivists to begin with. That is asking too much. If they can just reduce their acid-base ratio to 95 percent useless mindnumbing, self-righteous zealots, and 5 percent quiet, docile, silent people, that would be a good start. Five percent is better than nothing. Babies can be conceived in a short amount of time.

At least have the girls wear hemp skirts that the guys can bury their faces in like a good bong if the event planners run out of earthy potatoes. Oh, who am I kidding? With my luck, the girls would be liberal in every way except one. They would be morally conservative.

Okay, off to buy ductape. My friends and I will chat with each other next time, lacktivists be d@mned. We are young, Jewish, lusty, and in need of less social justice, and more socializing.

eric

Chapter 3: Liberals Can't Govern

This chapter is self-explanatory, which means that conservatives will grasp it.

I do not worry when liberals win elections. For them, winning elections is the end result. I would panic if they actually did something while in office.

Liberals cannot govern because they cannot even admit they are liberals. I have never met a "modern progressive," but I suspect they are as legitimate as those that truly believe in "new Democrats."

Now by new, if they mean worse, I could accept that. Yet they imply that new equals better with the same zeal that Coca-Cola introduced New Coke back in the 1980s.

Watching liberals attack each other is like watching beggars in the town square fight over the last scrap of bread. It is like watching a pair of peace groups get into a fistfight over who is more peaceful.

All we as conservatives have to do is watch and enjoy the show.

Liberals are Right ... Just Not About Anything that Matters

When listening to the left (which is occasionally necessary to remind myself why I am right about being on the right), I do sometimes hear them say true things. The statements are useless and inconsequential, but nevertheless true.

"We should love our children more." Wow, I am glad people in Congress can remind parents to do that.

"It is wrong that some people go hungry while other live well off." Yes, it's terrible.

"If we destroy the planet, there will be nowhere for humans to live." This is brilliantly insightful.

These statements and others discuss problems, but like most accurate liberal statements, do not offer any solutions. Yet this is perfectly acceptable, because when liberals make untrue statements, those are usually followed by disastrous ideas for solutions.

What drives the liberals crazy (redundant, I know) is that no matter how hard they try, it is not possible to make someone corrupt if they choose honor. Bill Clinton was corrupt. His supporters concede this. They just believe the ends justify the means. He was a lovable rascal. Bill Clinton's background in Arkansas? "Oh, that's just Arkansas politics." Sandy Berger? "Yeah, he always was disorganized ... good old disorganized Sandy."[14] The list of scandals before Clinton came to office, while in office, and even after he left office ... I suppose it could be a right-wing conspiracy. Newt Gingrich held Bill Clinton at gunpoint and forced him to go mothballing or bobbing for apples between Monica. This is not about sex. It is about a pattern of corruption. Clinton was impeached because he violated the rule of law.

This brings us to George W. Bush. Democrats are not interested in governing. They are interested in vengeance. Clinton was impeached, so Bush has to be as well. Given that logic, one Democrat should resign from Congress for possessing kiddie porn to even out the Mark Foley scandal. One Republican should drive off a bridge and leave a girl to die so that Ted Kennedy will feel better. Equal punishments are only appropriate for equal results. Despite every effort to force President Bush to be corrupt, he simply has no interest in dishonor.

The first thing the liberals screamed about was the 2000 election. Bush stole the election. No, he didn't. His election was illegal. No, it wasn't. The Supreme

Court was partisan. Somehow the Florida Supreme Court was non-partisan. The butterfly ballot was confusing. A Democrat created it, and those who can't read a ballot should either stay home, be euthanized, or both.

Then Bush had an obligation to govern from the center. No, he didn't. He had an obligation to keep his word to those who voted for him. JFK did not enact Nixon's policies (Nixon, for all his flaws, spared the country the legal nightmare Al Gore created despite the fact that dead people put JFK over the top). Bush had an obligation to govern as a conservative. He kept his word and did so.

Then the non-scandals began. Enron? Well, Bush was from Texas, and so was Enron, which means I am responsible for the Gambino crime family misdeeds, since I was born and raised in New York. Halliburton? Cheney used to be CEO, which means that any contracts Halliburton gets are tainted despite the fact that no other U.S. company does what they do. In fact, ask liberals what Enron and Halliburton actually "do." They won't know. It has something to do with oil ... although it actually doesn't. I used to work for Morgan Stanley. Morgan Stanley had an office in the World Trade Center. I was laid off from Morgan Stanley. Therefore, I caused 9/11. See how easy it is?

Bush lied about the war. No, he didn't. The war was illegal. No, it wasn't. Resolution 1441 was explicit. We went to war unilaterally. No, we didn't. Liberals, buy a thesaurus. What about Valerie Plame? Joe Wilson badly wanted to go on a cushy junket and sip tea with dictators. His wife recommended him. She was covert, despite posing for *Vanity Fair*. No, she wasn't. Joe Wilson said Bush lied. So what? I could claim Bill Clinton rapes puppies and kittens. Does that make it so?

Yet the worst untruth of all is that Iraq is lost. No, it isn't. The surge is failing. No it isn't, although it very well could if liberals ever decide to actually govern. Luckily, this will not happen because they are incapable of governing. You cannot pass an agenda when you lack one. You cannot turn policies into law when your own side does not know what policies it should believe in. The truth is, Democrats need Bush to be corrupt, because they are bankrupt in terms of intellectual ideas.

Dick Cheney shot someone and covered it up. No, he didn't. An accident happened, and he quickly dealt with it responsibly. Karl Rove lied. No, he didn't. The list goes on and on. Bush fired U.S. attorneys. So what? He can. He did. Done.

From Robert Bork to Clarence Thomas to the next Bush non-scandal, Democrats need to distract Americans away from the real issue ... that Democrats are useless. They have no coherent philosophy, and even if they did, they could not implement it. When the only options are to stand for nothing, or stand for something wrong, the former seems preferable.

The Democrats had all the levers of power from 1992 through 1994, and they did such a fabulous job that they lost Congress. Two years was all they needed. Republicans ran out of energy after twelve years. Then Democrats did so after about twelve hours. It's not that they're bad people. Americans are just optimistic. Even if President Bush is unpopular, he is still more likable than Congressional Democrats are. Americans want him to succeed. They see a good, decent man who has made mistakes, as all humans have. He wants to improve the world. This is noble. The Democrats in Congress want to lose the war because defeating Republicans is more important than defeating global evil. They need Bush to be corrupt so they can get elected, so they can then do nothing and stay elected.

As we get closer to 2008, look for Democrats to make some startling announcements.

"It is wrong to hate people." "It is a tragedy that people are dying every day." "It is wrong to kill puppies and kittens for no good reason." "We have to love our children." "We have to love our neighbor (unless the neighbor is a Republican)."

I totally agree with the liberals on these issues. They are right. Now perhaps they might be right about something that actually matters.

eric

Al Sharpton, Colon Cancer, and Other Pains in the Rumpus

When playing chess, the white pieces get to move before the black pieces. This is racism. Call Al Sharpton immediately.

Good guys wear white. Bad guys wear black. Holy Selma, Alabama. This must stop.

Black people have white blood cells, but white people lack black blood cells. Nothing has changed since 1863.

Not since music group Hot Chocolate changed their name from Pure Vanilla (okay, I made that up) and sang, "You Sexy Thing,"[15] has America needed Al Sharpton so badly.

The man is a miracle worker. He is a reverend, yet nobody has ever seen his congregation. He is a civil rights leader, yet his followers were freed decades ago. Mostly, he is a colonoscopy gone bad, a proctological carbunkle that refuses to subside.

Long after James Dean died, Al Sharpton is a rebel without a cause.

Why is Al Sharpton losing his power? For the best of reasons, the one that many refuse to admit. Society is getting better. Not perfect, but absolutely better.

For every Abner Louima (who retracted his comment saying that the cops who abused him said, "It's Giuliani time"), there are many police officers of all stripes saving lives of all people, regardless of race.

Are we where we need to be? No. Has there been significant progress? Absolutely.

There are black billionaires in America. They are not basketball players or actors. They are investment bankers, corporate attorneys, government leaders, and CEOs of Fortune 500 companies. This is an overwhelmingly positive development, and it should continue. The reason this is not reported is because Al Sharpton, Jesse Jackson, and other excuses for "leaders" are more interested in lining their own pockets than in improving society. The problem is Al Sharpton is running out of causes.

Al Sharpton slandered Steven Pagones, labeling him as one of six white men who raped Tawana Brawley. This was a lie and a hoax. The jury found for Pagones, and Sharpton has never paid him.

Al Sharpton is now going after gangsta rappers. I have admitted before that I find Snoop Doggy Dogg incomprehensible (although I admit I like some of his songs, and think he is funny, and of course, a football fan), but he is not making his money by leeching off of other people. People buy his albums. He succeeds in the marketplace. Al Sharpton earns (if you can call it that) his success attacking the Dogg Pound.

Now Al Sharpton is continuing his jihad (or is crusade the politically correct word?) against Don Imus with help from a complicit media.

I condemned Imus's remarks. My objection was that the women's basketball team were private citizens. We can argue until the end of time whether calling them "nappy headed hos" was a firing offense, but the real issue is that private citizens not in the public arena are to be given significantly more privacy than public figures. This is why John Kerry and John Edwards got into hot water for bringing up Dick Cheney's daughter in a debate.

Yet this issue should have ended when Imus was fired. The problem with that is once Imus was fired, Al Sharpton had nothing to do. Agitators need to agitate. Al Sharpton did everything but speed down the highway drunk at two hundred miles per hour hoping that a white cop would pull him over. The problem is he cannot even get profiled because the cops know him and fear him. He can't win for losing.

Howard Beach is a fading memory. White students want to be like Mike, wear Air Jordans, and listen to gangsta rap. Maybe that is why Al Sharpton is going after gangsta rappers. If whitey likes it, it must be bad.

The thing is, unlike guilty white liberals, black gangsta rappers aren't backing down. They are not afraid of Sharpton. What can he do, accuse them of racism?

Al Sharpton was thrown a lifeline when Don Imus was given a severance package, in the sense that he settled his lawsuit over his firing. Then one of the basketball players decided to sue. Reverend Al came to the rescue, supporting the lawsuit.

This basketball player is on the verge of going from innocent victim to greedy profiteer, which is coincidentally what gangsta rappers are accused of labeling many women as. How is greed through frivolous lawsuits any better than greed through trying to hook up with a rich rapper because of his money? A parasite is a parasite. I am not in favor of calling women "hos," but the rappers that call them that are not attacking all women. They are attacking women that leech off of others.

For a person to have a legitimate reason to sue, they must have been injured. This woman claims that wherever she goes, she will be seen as one of the women humiliated by Imus.

This is insane. The reason why—again—that Imus's comments were so offensive was because these were unknown, anonymous women. Sorry to get Gloria Allred's granny undies all bunched up, but people still do not know who these women are, nor do they care! Yes, her name was mentioned on the news, and no, people do not remember it a few moments later.

Now to really enrage the Allrednistas and as many others as I can offend to make a point: nobody outside of a precious few people care about college women's basketball. Title IX forces schools to spend money on various sports so we can all feel good about ourselves. The truth is, at most schools, everything except men's football is irrelevant.

The only thing people care less about than college women's basketball is trying to figure out where colleges are located when the name of the school does not reveal this. I understand where Georgia Tech is. I can find Michigan State on a map. Does anybody really know where Rutgers is located? It turns out New Jersey, but what part?

An obscure woman in an obscure town living an obscure life was joked about in an inappropriate manner. The joker was punished. However, that same woman who was justified in being upset because obscure people should not be targeted cannot then turn around and say that she is ruined because everybody knows her.

These women were known as "the Rutgers women's basketball team." To find out who she is would first require that people care, and then know who she actually is from somebody besides herself going on television and telling us. This woman is the Valerie Plame of basketball, shouting at the top of her lungs that it is her right to remain anonymous.

This basketball player needs to have a colonoscopy to have a cancerous lesion known as Al Sharpton removed from her rectum. Like the parasite he is, he will then find another black host to leech onto and pretend to care about.

I predict he will then get involved in the Michael Vick case. If anybody can find a picture of one of the black dogs being attacked by one of the white dogs, Al will be there on the case, combining the rhyming of Johnny Cochran, the intelligence of Barney Fife, the ethics of Bill Clinton, and the purity of Tawana Brawley.

If that does not work, he can always try slandering some Jewish store owners as "diamond merchants"[16] until an angry mob burns down their grocery store and covers it in swastikas for refusing to sell Lean Cuisines. After all, there is a Zionist plot by Jews to kill overweight black agitators by murdering them through "cholesterol extermination."

Racism absolutely does exist in this country. Comparing every frivolous lawsuit about nonsense to Selma, Alabama, helps nobody. It devalues Selma. The way to end racism is to stamp out racists. That includes David Duke as much as it does Al Sharpton. Perhaps a Harvard educated black doctor can remove the mole on Mr. Sharpton's rectum—that being his head—and reattach it above his neck.

Now if this doctor can only give him black blood cells, all will be right with the world.

eric

Carbon Credits—The Next Liberal Lie

One person I have had the pleasure to get to know over the last couple years is Jonathan Hoenig. He runs the hedge fund Capitalist Pig Asset Management. As his name suggests, he is an unabashed, unashamed capitalist who worships at the altar of Ayn Rand and free markets. Like me, he is not a fan of carbon credits.

Carbon credits, also known as carbon offsets, are basically screw-up credits. It is equivalent to buying indulgences to get into heaven rather than actually doing good deeds. The way a carbon credit works is as follows. Many limousine liberals, or in this century, Lear jet liberals, use a ton of excess energy that supposedly hurts the planet. Rather than cut back on this energy usage, these gasbags purchase carbon credits, which are promises for other people to use less energy.

Why not have Hollywood celebrities throw lavish banquets with fancy food that goes uneaten and gets thrown away while people in third world countries eat less and starve to death? Actually that already happens, but if these celebrities gave food credits, poor nations and their people would be paid to not eat.

An even better example would be a murderer sitting in prison for life. The prisoner then finds out somehow that some innocent human eing needs a kidney transplant. The murderer donates a kidney, saving the innocent person. Newspapers love these feel good stories. Liberals hail stories of how a man could take a life, and then give one. He is now neutral.

How about being life positive? How about not murdering to begin with?

Why can't these leftist greeniacs just use less energy and convince others to use less energy and be carbon positive?

The reason is because then these people would not be liberals.

I am not against energy conservation. I am against others telling me how to live when they live in the very same way with greater excess. It's the hypocrisy, stupid.

Now comes the investment world getting into the act. We are living in exciting times, and virtually anything can be wrapped into some sort of financial product.

The other day, people had a chance to purchase shares in a carbon offset financial product with the simplicity of purchasing a stock.

So how many million shares traded on the first day of trading? One hundred.

Not one hundred million … one hundred. With all the money in this world, one hundred shares traded.

"If you think the market for crude oil is manipulated by powerful interests, then consider carbon finance to be the ultimate rigged game. Carbon credits trade, by definition, on the whim of a regulator. In reality, there is no limit to carbon-based economic activity and no economic purposes served by passing out worthless credits. 'Cap-and-trade' is simply a tax dressed up to appear like a free-market solution. But with the government behind the scenes pulling the strings for both supply and demand, there's nothing free market about it. Tree-hugging politicians, egged on by the environmental lobby, will make up the rules as they go along."[17]

Bottom line: the left knows they are wrong. They just don't care. Government regulation is not the means to policy. Regulation is the end result itself. Regulation equals power and control.

The left simply does not believe in the concepts of supply and demand. Liberals truly believe that governments function better at setting prices than free markets.

This is why liberals try to shut down conservative talk radio with the Fairness Doctrine. They tried competing with entities such as Air America. They failed in the marketplace. Liberals try to get the government to regulate the game because they have colossally failed at it themselves. Lose an election? So what? It only takes one left-wing activist judge to overturn most elections.

I am a conservative. I support big tobacco, big oil, big guns, big alcohol, and big red meat. I do not drink or smoke, but I support the right of companies to engage in commerce of legal products.

The problem is not that liberals want to ban everything. (Ironically, they do not want to ban abortion. Why bring a child into the world if it will be strangled by the government anyway?) Those people are bad enough. The problem is with liberals that want to ban everything for everybody else while partaking in the supposed sins themselves.

When a right-wing politician spends his life proposing anti-gay legislation and then is discovered to be gay, the wolves and jackals in the media exact their pound of hypocritical flesh.

Yet crickets chirp when a left-wing columnist is found possessing a handgun to defend himself while writing columns about why citizens should not own handguns.

The crickets chirp even louder when environmentalists gather on college campuses to bash President Bush, Dick Cheney, and big oil, right before leaving their signs on the lawn to ruin the grass as they head to their next rally.

Crickets chirp at the sound of a sonic boom when leftists at peace rallies shout anti-Semitic epithets and other obscenities linking President Bush to Hitler, in the name of peace.

Carbon credits are not the biggest liberal lie. After all, the Clintons did not create the idea. Yet it is the most current liberal lie. Luckily, once this investment idea fails, liberals will get bored and start wearing a new color ribbon to support the newest social cause that they know nothing about and will soon not care about.

The idea will fail because liberals don't actually care about these things when the cameras are off. The idea will also fail because people do not want to invest in a market unless it is a truly free market.

eric

Chapter 4: Liberals, Palestinians, and Other Warm Fuzzy Moonbats

Palestinians and liberals are a perfect match, and not just because they are both great sources of anti-Semitism. They both have group members that contribute positive things to society. I have just never met these people.

Palestinians are actually "modern progressives." They are a fictional creation invented out of thin air. They would be like unicorns if unicorns were genocidal rather than warm and fuzzy.

For those of you who as children may have had a stuffed unicorn that randomly exploded, chances are your toy was made in the Gaza Strip somewhere, with George Soros and Moveon.org funding the "toy factory."

I'll Have Gaza Strip and Eggs for Breakfast, Please, Sunny Side Down and Burnt to a Crisp

The Gaza Strip is burning. I do love dinner theatre. That reminds me, I need to stop at the grocery and pick up some Doctor Brown's Black Cherry Soda and Taco Doritos. Normally when the guys come over to watch sports, my cabinet and refrigerator are stocked. Yet between the NBA and NHL playoffs, I forgot that Gaza's version of the Olympic Games was taking place this week.

Ralph Peters, as always, writes more brilliantly in the *New York Post* than I ever could.

"We need to stop making politically correct excuses. Arab civilization is in collapse. Extremes dominate, either through dictatorship or anarchy. Thanks to their dysfunctional values and antique social structures, Arab states *can't* govern themselves decently.

We gave them a chance in Iraq. Israel 'gave back' the Gaza Strip to let the Palestinians build a model state. Arabs seized those opportunities to butcher each other."

Exactly. However, I no longer see this as a bad thing. If they want to educate their children with "Hooked on Eugenics," I say let them. Some feel the poor, innocent Palestinian people (an invented fictional creature similar to unicorns, except less friendly) are not to blame for their government. Nonsense. I blamed Republicans in 1992 who stayed home demoralized, and then were surprised at the Clinton years. I wish they remembered that in 2008. The Palestinian government is a government of, by, and for their people in every miserable way. Various polls over the years have reflected that between 70–80 percent of Palestinians support homicide bombers, which should lead one to be unsurprised when they get elected to government. Every once in awhile Palestinians look at their miserable, self-inflicted lot in life and decide that their strategy of indiscriminate murder is not helpful to their cause. The idea of being against indiscriminate killing because it is simply wrong would not occur to them. That would require valuing human life.

Ralph Peters correctly points out that the Gaza situation is a valuable tool in trying to educate American liberals about what would happen if America left Iraq today. I do not expect liberals to learn this lesson, since the killing fields of Cambodia would scare straight most rational people.

"The left doesn't care how many Iraqis die as long as President Bush can be humiliated. Now the Murthacrats insist that, once we bail out, Atlantis will rise from the Tigris and Euphrates.

Look at Gaza, at the orgy of self-destructive savagery, the macho idiocy, the junkyard-dog religion, and the murder-suicide cult sweeping Arab civilization."

My only area of mild correction is that this death cult is not sweeping Arab culture. It swept it centuries ago, and accelerated it one century ago.

"But for all that, it's the Arabs who failed themselves, again and again and again. When Lebanon tried to achieve a semblance of democracy, Syria embarked on a killing spree that, to this day, has had no tangible consequences for the Assad regime. When elections came to the Palestinian territories, the Palestinians voted for terrorists. And while Prince Bandar reportedly was raking in billion-dollar bribes between tennis matches with U.S. pols, our Saudi 'pals' were spending their oil wealth to ensure that no Muslims will ever live under a tolerant government that regards women as human."[18]

Shockingly enough, watching these people kill each other does not make me lose sleep. In fact, the only thing that would cause me to sleep better is if a pair of Jewish Republican brunettes were next to me. Heck, I would even let one be to my left in that situation.

The nations of Turkey, Afghanistan, and Iraq are more interested in seeing their people succeed than in causing their enemies to fail. Paraphrasing Golda Meir, they love their children more than they hate their rivals' children. This cannot be said about Palestinians, the only people on earth too crazy for even Arabs to deal with. For them, destruction is the goal, the ends, and the means.

Therefore, the only things left to do are perhaps fire up the balcony barbecue and relax on the sofa. It is not that I am delighted that Arabs are killing each other. I am merely thrilled, elated, and relieved that they are so distracted with civil war that they lack time to kill Jews. Not since the Iran-Iraq War in the 1980s have Jews had a tranquil moment. The best scenario would be if Palestinians decided not to kill off anybody and perhaps take up knitting sweaters or stamp collecting. So far those seem less exciting hobbies for these bloodthirsty individuals.

If Palestinians would ever truly opt for peace, I would welcome them with open arms. However, if the choice is letting them kill each other, or more Jews, I say let the war be civil, and yet very uncivil.

They did this to themselves, and I will do what is necessary ... thank them. For now, I will enjoy the Gaza Strip the way I enjoy my bacon strips (rabbi, they are beef based), burnt to a crisp with eggs sunny-side down. Actually, make them sunny-side up to reflect my optimistic mood. No wait, since we are dealing with Palestinians and their logical reasoning, the eggs should reflect them. Make them scrambled.

Now to enjoy some soda, some toast with margarine, and a good sporting event.

eric

Mr. Easter Bunny, Meet Mr. Moderate Palestinian Leader

Let me say this very slowly.

There ... are ... no ... moderate ... Palestinian ... leaders .... They ... have ... never ...existed.

There is growing talk that the world should come to the rescue of Mahmood Abbas, to protect his "moderate" Fatah party from the clutches of Hamas. For once, the world should turn a blind eye and let them kill each other.

For those unaware, there is no such thing as a Palestinian. A fictional invented people, they have a rich, deep history that goes back about fifty years. Jews have been around six thousand years. Their biblical claim to the land of Israel goes back a few thousand years as well. Arab Muslims (Yes, I am aware they are not precisely the same thing, but the overlap is significant) have existed since the seventh century. None of them were Palestinians.

The land of Israel was worthless until Jews arrived and created an agriculture industry. Yes, simple orange groves. Now Israel is high tech, a Middle Eastern version of Silicon Valley. What have Palestinians ever created? Only themselves, out of nowhere.

Yassir "That's my baby terrorist" was from Egypt. Palestinians are basically defective Arab rejects. They have been kicked out of everywhere they have lived. Given that they are Arabs, why would Arabs not embrace them? Simple. They cannot stay out of trouble! They are agitators. Instability follows them everywhere they go. These people are too crazy for Arabs to deal with. I did not know that was possible. Charles Manson was mad dog mean, but apparently not wacked out enough to blow himself up. He may not value human life, but he sure valued his own. He would never make it as a Palestinian leader with that cavalier anti-death attitude.

When Daniel Boone got lost, to cover up his mistake, he just announced to his group that "We are here." The town was called Boonesborough. This is basically what the Palestinians did. The problem is, if someone tried to move into my condominium, I would have a problem with that given that it is ... well ... mine. You can visit, and even stay in my guest room. That does not mean you may change the channel when I am watching television. You should not even spot the remote unless it is in my hand.

These fictional invented Arab defects announced their arrival and decided to help themselves to the oranges that the Israelis harvested. Then they decided to try and kill the Israelis, which would make sense if any of them knew how to grow food. They then, I assume, killed all the schoolteachers, so at least they could become number one at something, in this case illiteracy. They used to be number one in homicide bombings, but they ran out of enough people, temporarily slipping behind Hezbollah in the rankings. At least they are trying to be number one again. I give them their due.

There is no Palestine. There is only Israel. There are no Palestinians, only Israelis, aka Jews, and Arabs.

The Palestinians managed to immerse themselves by simply having more unprotected sex than their Jewish counterparts. If that is not the best advertisement for condoms, then I do not know what is. They bred and we did not. That is the fault of Jews everywhere.

Then the argument became that biblical and legal claims to the land were irrelevant based on realities on the ground. The Palestinians were already here, so they had to be acknowledged. Apparently, mass deportations are only for Jews … the lucky ones, anyway. So Jews are cheated out of land everywhere, Arabs kick them out of their nations (when not murdering them for existing), and yet Israel has a 20 percent Arab population. Now Israel is supposed to add several million Palestinians as well? Are you kidding me, world?

So first these people invent themselves. Then they try to claim land. Then they decide that not only should they own the land, but that all the Jews should be driven into the sea, aka killed. Enough already!

Here is where we get the politically correct drivel about their being many Palestinians who do not hate Jews and just want to live in peace. Polls show around 80 percent of Palestinians supporting extremist positions. 80 percent lunatic is enough for me. The other 20 percent are collateral damage. Where are the Palestinians in Western democracies like America standing up and loudly condemning such evil? They are hanging out with the Easter Bunny on Noah's ark. Try and find them.

This brings us to the nonsense that Abbas is a moderate. Abbas is the public face of Fatah, which was Yassir Arafat's terrorist organization. Saying Fatah is moderate compared to Hamas is like saying paraplegics are healthy compared to quadriplegics, or that Charles Manson is moderate compared to Jeffrey Dahmer because Manson did not eat people.

Those who need to learn about Abbas should listen to Walid Shoebat. Mr. Shoebat was trained to be a homicide bomber, but at the last moment lost his nerve and found something deeper … his humanity and his soul. He now lectures around the world, surrounded by security. I have met him, shaken his hand, and asked God to bless him. He has pointed out that Abbas is a terrorist, just not a respected one by other terrorists.

Why should Abu Mazen (Abbas), be any better than Abu Allah (Arafat) just because he smiles on camera? For all I care they could be led by Ali Baba, or the guy in the Bugs Bunny cartoon who chases him and Daffy Duck while brandishing a sword and yelling "Hasssan Chop!"[19] Just because Abbas is the Inspector Clouseau of terrorism does not mean he is a good guy. An incompetent murderer is just as bad as a successful one.

There is nobody that speaks for the Palestinians that has any value of human life, especially not Jewish life. Saeb Ekarat is a terrorist with a microphone. Like all Palestinian leaders to date, he only renounces violence when it is deemed "not helpful" to the Palestinian cause. How about renouncing senseless murder because it is just plain wrong? When violence is helpful, it is the first option of these people.

At least with Hamas the world knows what Israel is dealing with. They are ethical terrorists, honest and upfront about their murderous zealotry. Fatah is more stealth. Therefore, Israel and the world should let these factions kill each other. Then after one side wins, Israel can go in and smash the weakened remaining Palestinian faction.

That is on the verge of happening now. Maybe all the self-inflicted pain will finally cause the Palestinians to change their culture of murderous hatred. Of course it will. They want to frolic and play with their fellow Jews in Candy Land. The Easter Bunny would join them, but he is afraid they would go Glenn Close *Fatal Attraction* on him and burn and eat the furry critter. How could this happen though? The Easter Bunny is fictional.

So what? So are Palestinians, every one of them, from their poor, innocent, misunderstood, Jew-hating citizens to their poisonous homicidal leadership. The entire lot of them needs to be dealt with. Jews and other peace-loving citizens everywhere should be relieved if not delighted that people who want to kill us are killing themselves instead.

eric

Burn Gaza Burn ... Disco Inferno

Burn Gaza burn ... disco inferno ... burn Gaza burn ... disco inferno ...

I am not sure what is worse: the fact that I am delighted by the carnage in the Gaza Strip, or that I just quoted disco. I profusely apologize for the latter. Thanks to this Middle East inferno, I actually remembered the lyrics to the Thelma Houston song from the movie *Studio 54*. "Baby ... my heart is burning like a Ketushah rocket for you."

It actually does tie in together. Mike Myers played the main villain in that movie, and also was Dr. Evil who, like the leaders of Hamas, are just misunderstood children that want to love and be loved. Um ... no. Genocidal lunatics are killing each other, and frankly, the timing could not be better. With hockey and basketball done, and football not until September, the only thing to do is enjoy a nice summer of love. Like Jan and Dean, those crazy Gaza kids "are out there having fun ... in that scorched earth Gaza sun."

The main reason this trivial matter is treated as such is because unfortunately, it has taken comedians to offer hardnosed and hard-edged common sense this week, while politicians were busy clowning around. Dennis Miller nailed it perfectly in discussing the differences between the political parties. "Democrats are worried about the earth. Republicans are too busy worrying about the world."[20] Translation for the intellectually impaired: global warming is an abstract concept that may or may not happen one day in the future. Islamofacism has been happening for three decades and must be dealt with right now.

Dennis Leary, refusing to be the second-best Dennis this week, took on the concept of Bush Derangement Syndrome. "President Bush is supposedly not smart enough to end the Iraq War, but he was smart enough to conspire to create 9/11."[21] As I have pointed out, liberals need every successful conservative to be either evil or imbecilic. Their inability to decide on President Bush has led them to contradiction, declaring him both.

Before returning to the glorious age of disco (God help us all), I want to offer a pop culture reference: the television show *Scrubs*. This show is fabulous not just because Zach Braff reminds me of my alter ego, "El Dorko," but because a brilliantly and wickedly funny character named Dr. Perry Cox, when confronted with this young fellow (after one of his sweet but effeminate comments) said to him, "I am going to write you a prescription for a brand new pair of testicles."[22]

In real life, that message was given by Tony Blair. Hopefully, it will be delivered to Republicans everywhere. We could give it to Democrats as well, but the mommy party would probably prefer *Vagina Monologues* tickets. Dear Republicans: grow a pair. Instead of being put on the defensive for making the wrong decision, try pounding the table with clenched fists and reaffirming that the Iraq War was right then, and right now. Ideological bigots will remain unchanged, but supporters will be pleased with the gonads transplant. One cannot win everybody over, but spinelessness demoralizes supporters. Thank you, Mr. Tony Blair, for reminding us what is at stake. So what if he is being forced out over the war? Winston Churchill was fired after World War II. He remains one of the all-time greats. Abraham Lincoln and Ronald Reagan were ridiculed. History will vindicate those who never wavered about this war. Why should they? We are right.

There is a time for negotiation (Russia in the 1980s), a time for overwhelming brute force (Afghanistan, Iraq, and hopefully Syria very soon), and there is a time to say "Screw it. Who cares? (Gaza ... now and forever)" Despite Gaza being hotter than Hot Chocolate (I believe in miracles/where ya from/you sexy thang), no amount of stripper poles and blacklights will be able to put a bow tie on this pig of an area. Heck, Gaza people (not citizens, just people) are trying to flee to Israel for safety. Are you kidding me? Aren't Jews the enemy, and the cause of all these Gaza problems? I mean, once the Jews get out, Gaza will be a land of peace.

"Palestinians of Hamas ... and Fatah ... join hands ... start a love train ... love train." When the O'Jays sang that song, Palestinians were killing everyone around them, and as Hall and Oates did the remake, nothing had changed (and no, Earth Girls are not Easy). "It's just an old fashioned death song ... whether it's Hamas or it's Fatah ... It's just an old fashioned death song ... nothing's changed since Oslo '93 (or the seventh century)."

To bring everything full circle, the song "Disco Inferno" was in the bowling movie *Kingpin*, with a brilliant cameo by Bill Murray. Camper Van Beethoven once sang a bizarre song called "Take the Skinheads Bowling."[23] Strange as it was, the point was that if people took up hobbies, war and fighting would stop. So if we turn Iran and Syria into 50 thousand hole golf courses, with miniature golf as well, Gaza can be one giant bowling alley, with Palestinian leaders Fatah and Hamas representing both gutters. How appropriate. We can even drill holes in the Palestinian leaders' heads so they can be used as bowling balls.

Why bowling? For anyone who has gone "cosmic bowling," it is a lot of fun. That is where there are swirling disco lights and loud music, often disco music, playing in the background. It is like trying to bowl blind. Given that Palestinian leaders in Hamas and Fatah are blind (and deaf and dumb come to think of it) to their constituents' concerns, I think cosmic bowling should be the official sport of Palestinian lunatics everywhere. To torture them (another reason to support torture), we should pipe Israeli music over the loudspeakers. Perhaps those old Yeshiva kids from the 1980s, the Beastie Boys, should be played. Given how ill Palestinians make me (and the rest of the civilized world), the album "Licensed to Ill,"[24] should be the official Palestinian cosmic bowling album.

Then again, one cannot go wrong with disco. So as I watch Gaza, all I can think is "Upside down … boy Gaza you burn me … inside out … and into the ground…" "Gaza you can do it, take the time, burn it right, you can kill all day, and burn all night."

Okay, off to watch Palestinian porn. There's nothing like "Debbie does the Gaza Strip."

eric

Chapter 5: The Jayson Blair Times

Hateful, boring, and virtually always wrong? Yes, that sounds like a liberal newspaper to me. The *New York Times* is to journalism what Palestinians are to world peace.

Luckily, nobody of any relevance reads the (New York Times) *Jayson Blair Times*.

If only Judaism was like Catholicism, we could have excommunicated their Jewish leftist publisher. I would like to apologize to normal Americans everywhere for another Jewish liberal disgrace. Just know that I do not read his paper.

Judging by the quality of the writing, neither does their own editorial staff.

The Jayson Blair Times Needs a Hug

Okay, I confess. When I need to crank out a quick column, I find somebody who writes something idiotic and give them their deserved dressing down. When my list of idiots gets too big, I just go with my favorite bastion of worthlessness, the *Jayson Blair Times*. I can't help it. They simply do not know how to say anything positive, unbiased, reasonable, or accurate. Being liberal, shrill, and wrong may offend some, but as a conservative columnist, I delight in their intellectual deficiencies. The Gray Lady (New York Times) is the main reason I support euthanasia. Somebody kill this old bag already.

JBT columnist Thomas Friedman is your standard Jewish liberal, which means I often have to apologize for him to the normal Americans who lump me in with the 80 percent of Jews that need cranial-glutial extraction surgery. If I dealt with the *JBT*'s idiocy every day, I would have to ignore other topics. However, today the mercury on the *JBT* ridicule meter is sky high, deserving them a heaping of scorn.

The title of the newest debacle put to print is entitled, "9-11 is over."

Really? I took a nap. Perhaps I missed it. Did we win the War on Terror? Did all the terrorists surrender? Or did we all join hands and start a love train?

Mr. Friedman takes umbrage at the fact that Rudy Giuliani is running partially on his leadership on 9/11. First of all, he is also running on his spectacular record of turning around New York City. What the heck is he supposed to run on? An imaginary record with empty promises for the future with nothing in the past to provide a credible track record? If you're a Democrat, sure. Thankfully, the *JBT* bullies don't get to decide Republican platforms, keeping with their tradition of not writing anything worthwhile.

Friedman laments that, "How much, since 9/11, we've become 'The United States of Fighting Terrorism.'" Yes! We have become that! What the heck else should we become? Oh I know … we could just politely ask the terrorists to stop it and play nice! Mr. Friedman "does not know whether to laugh or cry" at what is happening to America. That is how I feel about the *JBT*.

Like the cancer of liberalism itself, this *JBT* article spread stupidity and insincerity with each passing sentence. Friedman wrote, "*Times* columnists are not allowed to endorse candidates, but there's no rule against saying who will not get my vote:"

The *JBT* has its head so far up the Democratic Party's hide that to say that the lack of an official endorsement means they are open-minded and unbiased is insane. In the cases of Mondale, Dukakis, and McGovern, the *JBT* was the only entity supporting these people outside of their own families.

Now who is not getting Mr. Friedman's vote? Let's find out. "I will not vote for any candidate running on 9/11. We don't need another president of 9/11. We need a president for 9/12. I will only vote for the 9/12 candidate."

In the real world, a 9/12 candidate is a person who witnessed 9/11, shook their fists in a state of rage, and wanted justice. This was not bloodlust. It was human decency demanding that our leaders honor our right to life, liberty, and the pursuit of happiness.

In the *JBT*-Friedman bubble, 9/12 is a post-modern world where intellectuals sit down and rationally deal with all that ails us. We dialogue with people, because if we could all just learn, love, and understand each other, we could communicate better.

I am not in any way, shape, or form advocating violence against Mr. Friedman. Yet liberals truly are conservatives waiting to be mugged. Does somebody have to break into Mr. Friedman's multi-million dollar mansion, take a crow bar to his winery, and smash an expensive bottle of Chablis over his family's skulls before he realizes that some people are just bad? What is he going to do, defend himself with the gun that he doesn't own because only criminals should have them?

Yes, I am stereotyping and trivializing this guy (with help from him), but the issue itself is far from trivial. To turn a phrase on a famous left-wing hate group, no we cannot just "move on" to a 9/12 world without 9/11. Saying it does not make it so.

"9/11 has made us stupid." Speak for yourself and the dozen people who read your paper. I have an advanced degree, I disagree with you, and my brain actually works.

"You may think Guantánamo Bay is a prison camp in Cuba for Al Qaeda terrorists."

Yes, because it is.

"A lot of the world thinks it's a place we send visitors who don't give the right answers at immigration."

Are there twelve million people at Gitmo? I thought it was closer to three hundred.

"I will not vote for any candidate who is not committed to dismantling Guantánamo Bay and replacing it with a free field hospital for poor Cubans. Guantánamo Bay is the anti-Statue of Liberty."

A free what?????? Can we please send the Gitmo detainees to this man's home? If some wealthy Republicans are willing to build a sanctuary for Gitmo and homeless people right across the street from this fellow, I would support it. Also, since there will be strict gun control laws, he will be safe because these terrorists would never break the law. Firearms are against the rules, especially if they want parole.

"I'd love to see us salvage something decent in Iraq that might help tilt the Middle East onto a more progressive pathway. That was and is necessary to improve our security."

It's called the surge, you left-wing horse's hide. It's working.

"I still can't get uninterrupted cellphone service between my home in Bethesda and my office in D.C. But I recently bought a pocket cellphone at the Beijing airport and immediately called my wife in Bethesda—crystal clear."

Yet this fellow lives in the United States of America. "Love it or leave it" is not perfect, but "change it or lose it" mistakenly believes that all change is good. America must do a lot right, because billions of people, including many from China, want to come to America, inferior cell phone service be d@mned.

"We need a president who will unite us around a common purpose, not a common enemy. Al Qaeda is about 9/11. We are about 9/12, we are about the Fourth of July—which is why I hope that anyone who runs on the 9/11 platform gets trounced."[25]

The only thing getting trounced is the *JBT*'s financial well being. What Al Qaeda contributed to infrastructure, the *JBT* contributed to quality writing.

I have a right to life and liberty, despite Friedman's desire to live under a Caliphate. He never stated that he desired this, but it's a logical inference. Anyone can say that fighting is wrong. Wanting peace is easy. The problem is not that peace is wrong, but that the way peaceniks try to achieve peace does not work, cannot work, will not work, and has never worked ever ever ever!

Winning the War on Terror is more important than every other political issue combined. Maybe if we spent more on health care and prescription drugs we could get Friedman and his ill ilk the care they need. Yet if America is blown to kingdom come, there will be nobody alive to administer anything to anybody anywhere.

To every normal civilized foreigner, I want to say that I am a normal New Yorker, a mainstream Jew, and an intelligent American. The people at the *JBT* may have certain traits in common with me, and I will repeatedly apologize for all of them if need be. However, these post-modern 9/12 imbeciles do not represent me.

I want to live. I support people that want me to live. I will only vote for a candidate who will repeatedly remind voters why 9/11 matters.

Yes, I am willing to support killing terrorists, even if it means keeping the *JBT* headquarters and all its worthless inhabitants on this planet where they will continue to detract from what is right in this world.

Maybe I should try to just understand the *JBT* and give their people a big hug. Or maybe, what they really need is a kick in the hide.

I am willing to put aside my own disgust with their stupidity to save their lives. If only they valued mine—and their own—the same.

eric

Waterboard Palestinians and the Los Angeles Times Editors

Since I am not sure whether Arab terrorists or the liberal media that enable them are a bigger scourge to the world, I will deal with them both today. As decent and literate folks everywhere know, the *Jayson Blair Times's* illiterate cousin, the *Los Angeles Times*, has a soft spot in its bleeding heart for warm and fuzzy Palestinian terrorists.

On December 21, 2007, an *LA Times* headline thundered, "Israeli raids into Gaza leave at least six dead."

Yes folks, those horrible Israelis are killing poor, innocent Palestinians.

In smaller print, the paper then stated, "The military responded after Palestinians fired rockets, one of which exploded near a school; no one there was hurt."

The headline should have read, "Genocidal Palestinian lunatics tried to murder innocent Israeli schoolchildren."

Does the fact that no Israeli children were hurt mitigate what these Palestinian animals tried to do? Does anybody that has ever believed in anything decent and right actually believe that the *LA Times* headline cares about truth?

Buried deep in the story is who actually died. If it was poor, suffering Palestinian children, it would be on page one.

"Israel said its forces killed seven Palestinian gunmen in four clashes. Palestinians confirmed six dead and twenty wounded."

Yes, Israel had the nerve to retaliate against people that tried to murder their children. How many people in this world, after seeing an attempt on the life of a family member, would not want those people dead in return? Isn't the killing of child killers a good deed? Of course it is. Reasonable people can understand this, which exempts Palestinians and *LA Times* editors.

"Hamas floated the idea of a truce this week."

So what? The only reason Hamas ever seeks any kind of truce is when they are getting destroyed militarily. They then use the truce to regroup and rearm themselves.

"Israel rejected the advance, saying there was no need for a truce because Israel would have no reason to attack if the rocket fire stopped."

In plain English, I want every Palestinian wack job all over the world to understand a simple concept. If you stop trying to blow things up, there will be peace.

At this point a Palestinian might ask, "How can we be sure of this?"

The civilized human being should ask a different question. "Have you ever tried?"

"Israel refuses to deal with Hamas because the movement calls for the destruction of the Jewish state."[26]

Nobody else in the world has to negotiate for their right to exist.

Here are points to commit to memory.

There is no such thing as a Palestinian. They are a fictional invented people. They are the Easter Bunny without lucky feet, Santa Claus if Santa was a homicide bomber.

Palestinians are Arabs. More precisely, they are defective Arabs. In America, we have product recalls, and defective products that blow up around children are removed from shelves. Shelves in this case are Arab nations, where these poor, sweet, murderous fuzzballs are removed. They have been kicked out of other Arab nations because they are agitators, not victims.

There has not been a successful Arab nation since Mesopotamia. Israel flourished because a bunch of hard working Jews turned orange groves into worldwide beauty. Arabs took beauty, such as the Cedars of Lebanon, and destroyed it. In the Middle East, Jews build beauty while Arabs spread poison and hatred.

There is nothing that Arabs in the Middle East contribute to this world that is positive.

So yes, the Arabs in the Middle East are the worst people on earth, and the Palestinians are the worst Arabs. They are a defective, recessive, cancerous element in a body that is not that emotionally healthy to begin with.

There is no Palestine or Arab East Jerusalem. There are no occupied territories. There is one Jewish state, and Arabs that are trying to seize Israel as the twenty-third Arab state because they have already screwed up and made themselves unwelcome in the first twenty-two of them.

The solution is simple. Every Palestinian that at some point somehow decides to act like a normal human being will be allowed to exist, and nothing more. Israel created something out of nothing, and they will have to do the same. Perhaps Jordan and Syria will take them in, especially if the threat of force is applied if they do not. I am sure Jordan and Syria would be delighted to welcome their black sheep brethren if they were the ones on the verge of being told that they soon would not have a right to exist.

As for the Palestinians that continue to act like ... well ... Palestinians ... they need to be broken. They must be broken financially, emotionally, physically, and psychologically. I would recommend that we waterboard them, but waterboarding is not torture. Since we do not torture, and sterilization is considered cruel, the only answer is to kill them humanely in the same way we sacrifice animals in a kosher manner. Either way, bullets to the heart will prevent them from breeding any more than they already do, preventing future screwups to enter the world.

Killing can be done humanely, despite the fact that Arabs in the Middle East have been beheading infidels for centuries. Palestinians need to go before Jewish schoolchildren, who actually grow up and contribute positively to the world, are all murdered as the world sits silent and leftist newspapers cheer for the murderers.

For the cheerleaders of murderers, beheading might not be a bad idea. No, I am not advocating the physical murder of the *LA Times* editorial board. They can be beheaded financially. Money runs the world. A conservative billionaire needs to buy the paper, fire everyone, and create a quality publication.

Otherwise, we can scare the editors with some harmless techniques, far less dangerous than anything the Palestinians do.

Somebody please waterboard the *LA Times* editors. I am tired of them. Decent human beings everywhere should be.

eric

Support Terrorism—Buy the Los Angeles Times

While the *Washington Post* is firmly entrenched as the ugly kid sister of the *Jayson Blair Times*, the *Los Angeles Times* has decided that it is now qualified to be the retarded family cousin that nobody talks about.

Once content to be a badly written paper that was simply less awful than its East Coast counterparts, the *LA Times* has now officially declared itself an enemy combatant. Take the editors to Guantanamo Bay. There is no turning back. This is not about free speech, or even disgusting speech. This is about expressing support for terrorists.

The *LA Times* wants American Taliban John Walker Lindh to be set free.

The headline "Free our Talib," is eye popping. Talib is short for Taliban, which could be fine if the *LA Times* were communicating to their childhood friends on MySpace or FaceBook. Lindh is not "our" or "my" anything. Perhaps the headline can be redone so it properly reads: "San Francisco liberal killer defended by Los Angeles liberal rag."

This might be the first time in history a Southern California entity has so fiercely defended someone from Northern California. Perhaps if John Walker Lindh was accused of cheating in baseball, there would be more outrage from their editorial staff.

The first paragraph reads like something only an imbecile suffering from Bush Derangement Syndrome could write.

"The president's power to grant clemency—in the form of either a pardon or a commutation—is much maligned and occasionally abused, as was the case when President Bush used it to keep his colleague, I. Lewis 'Scooter' Libby, from facing even a day in prison for lying and obstructing justice. But the power has its appropriate uses as well, and the case of John Walker Lindh calls out for it."

The obligatory left-wing cheap shot at the president is laughable. Unless the *LA Times* was not paying attention, which based on the quality of everything they say and do is easily within the realm of plausibility, Scooter Libby did not kill anybody.

"John Walker Lindh broke the law. He pleaded guilty to the one crime of which he was guilty—aiding the Taliban—and to carrying a gun and hand grenades in the service of that regime's war against the Northern Alliance. For that, he deserved to go to prison."

No, he did not deserve prison. He deserved two bullets to his heart, and it should have been broadcast on live television, and not pay per view either.

"Lindh, who converted to Islam as a teenager, joined the Taliban before Sept. 11, not after; he did so to fight the Northern Alliance, not the United States. Lindh never took up arms against this country. He never engaged in terrorism; indeed, his commitment to Islam leads him to oppose the targeting of civilians."[27]

Belief in Islam prevents targeting of civilians? Who on Allah's green earth is beheading people? Has it occurred to these *LA Times* terrorist supporters that just because somebody says they are Muslim, that maybe they do not obey all the rules of their own religion? Some Jews eat pork. Some Catholic priests molest young boys. Some Islamists murder people for sport.

The other claim that San Francisco Johnny should get the equivalent of a get-out-of-jail-free card is the ludicrous notion that he did not directly attack America.

Let's see. Al Qaeda attacked America. The Taliban protected Al Qaeda. San Fran John fought for the Taliban. These dots are only possible to connect if one keeps their eyes and minds open and functioning, which apparently disqualifies the severely mentally retarded and *LA Times*' writers.

When *The Onion* wrote, "ACLU defends Nazi's right to burn down ACLU headquarters,"[28] it was satire. The *LA Times* seriously wants to free a man who supported enemies of America.

It is one thing to argue wrongly for the release of enemy combatants at Gitmo because there is some mistaken belief that they might be innocent (until they are freed and go back to terrorism), but the *LA Times* is advocating freeing a man that pled guilty!

Do *LA Times* editors have to have their own children kidnapped and beheaded before they realize that the enemies are the kidnappers and beheaders, not George W. Bush? Is their hatred of President Bush and the Iraq war that much that they need to free people out on the streets who want everything American dead?

I have said on more than one occasion that until San Francisco gets bombed, they will not get it. If I did not live in Los Angeles, I would absolutely add LA to the list. This is not hypocrisy, because I am one of the Californians who was not raised here, and I am willing to loudly condemn those who want to blow my city to kingdom come. I am not willing to send them home to the wonderful parents who raised this monster.

Maybe this is what Hillary Clinton means when she uses the term "Modern Progressive."[29] It is her way of distancing herself from San Francisco liberals. No, I am not blaming them for what John Walker Lindh did. However, can anybody doubt that an environment of absolute hatred for President Bush can lead to violence when carried one step further?

After September 11, 2001, President Bush stated that people were either with us or against us. If you harbored a terrorist, you were a terrorist. The Taliban was against us, and Lindh was with them. He was against us.

The problem with the *LA Times* is that it only recognizes terrorism when the person committing it is right of center. Animal rights activists who break into testing labs and free animals are seen as rescuers, not terrorists. Environmentalists that commit violence at trade summits and burn down buildings because they dislike construction are not just tree huggers ... they are ecoterrorists. Leftist rebels that try to overthrow right-wing governments, or take over schools with children inside ... yes, they are actually terrorists. The men that defeat them, be it Vladimir Putin, Ariel Sharon, or Alberto Fujimori are not the terrorists.

Some will say that being raised in Northern California had nothing to do with Lindh's descent into evil. Yes, real evil, not the kind of evil described about people who merely want to cut taxes and give businesses incentives to make profits. Perhaps his conversion to radical Islam had something to do with it.

The bottom line is that it is not the fault entirely of his parents, radical Islam, or even radical San Francisco. The fault is with him. A young man chose to fight alongside America's enemies. His doing this is less tragic than the fact that he was taken alive, an act of mercy he not only did not deserve but would not have shown an American soldier.

John Walker Lindh should spend the rest of his life in jail. He is entitled to his Koran and his *Los Angeles Times*. While it would be a civil rights violation to ban him from reading his Islamic holy book, nobody is entitled to read a fourth-rate newspaper with horridly written editorials by equally contemptible human beings.

Somebody give this kid a *Wall Street Journal* or *New York Post* so that he can be reprogrammed. Unfortunately, he will be reintroduced to society again, where by the standards of Nancy Pelosi's district, he will be considered normal. Perhaps if he gets rewired in jail he will be less disgusting than his defenders upon his eventual release.

As for the *LA Times*, I simply wish Angelenos would stop buying it. It will not go out of business, since I am sure there are plenty of people in terrorist sponsoring nations that would be happy to import it while enjoying their morning Jihad and Java.

eric

The Jayson Blair Times Descends Into Madness

The *Jayson Blair Times* is descending into madness. It is now officially the equivalent of a drug addict unable to get clean. It is in a downward spiral, determined to drag everybody down until nothing good in America is left. We can argue whether it takes a village to raise a child, but it seems that it takes only a newspaper to burn the village.

For the sake of full disclosure, for those who truly do need to be hit upside the head with a bar towel to know they are in a bar, I find the paper formerly known as the *New York Times* to be a contemptible piece of trash run by disgusting individuals that long ago gave up on concepts such as honor and integrity.

My objection to this paper is not political. I disagree with liberals. I detest the *JBT*. I detest the fact that they allow blind partisan hatred to get in the way of making America happier, healthier, and safer.

I am a conservative blogger. Yet if you are a liberal, you are welcome on my blog. You will not be castigated. I will treat you politely. We will disagree, but you will be welcome as would any guest in my home. When watching football on Sundays, some of the guys sitting on my couch are liberals. They have a friendly place to watch the game. I want my blog to be equally welcoming.

The *JBT* would rather destroy than reach out. They are sinking in readership because they have taken so many repugnant actions that only their most ardent ideological warriors will read them.

Some people will bemoan the state of politics today. They will say it has gotten coarser. We were better off before Fox News, Rush Limbaugh, and the blogosphere lit up society. Things were so much more peaceful "back then."

No, society was not more peaceful. There was not harmony. Debate was merely stifled. When a liberal says, "Be bipartisan," what they really mean is, "Shut up and agree with me." The *New York Times*, ABC, NBC, CBS, and NPR ruled with iron liberal fists. Conservatives were not allowed to speak. The debate is coarser today because liberals have not been able to silence and bully conservatives back underground.

Yes, there are strident conservatives out there. They will argue that they were bullied, so they have every right to get down and dirty. This is wrong. This is how entire groups of people who have been victimized in the past seek vengeance rather than justice. Some people run for president fueled by this vengeance. What conservatives should do is what most of them are already doing. Do not get in the gutter, but be a worldwide group of ombudsmen that expose every liberal lie. This is a full-time job when it comes to the *JBT*, but examples abound of how they have sunk.

They became the *JBT* by promoting Jayson Blair himself. He was unqualified and incompetent. He continued to rise in the ranks, passing over better qualified and longer tenured Caucasian employees.

Affirmative action is a sensitive issue. I have enraged many conservatives myself by not being rabidly against it. Yet at the same time, promoting Jayson Blair hurt everybody. Critics of affirmative action made him the poster boy in an attempt to destroy an entire structure meant to help people. Where the *JBT* went wrong is that they sacrificed quality in favor of ideology. There are plenty of capable black people in America, a majority of them liberals. Instead of picking somebody who happened to be black, they picked somebody because he was black.

Yet the Jayson Blair imbroglio was a molehill among other mountainous scandals.

In 2004, Mary Mapes and Dan Rather used their power at CBS to try and bring down President Bush. In conjunction with the *JBT*, memos that were "fake but accurate" made the airwaves. If the new media did not exist, John Kerry would have triumphed. That in itself is not the tragedy. Many people wanted Kerry to win. The real horror would have been when the scandal erupted after he was sworn in. His presidency would have been paralyzed, making Monicagate seem like child's play. America would have been irreparably harmed.

President Bush being reelected does not mean we can all say, "no harm, no foul." Attempted murder, while not murder, is still awful. Whether or not President Bush shirked his military duties would have been a legitimate story if there was hard evidence. CBS and the *JBT* let ideology trump quality, and let emotion override facts. They continued to hasten the destruction of their own brands.

If trying to rig an election was sinister, then trying to get innocent Americans killed was bordering, if not crossing over, the line separating good and evil.

The *JBT* has gone beyond reporting the war in Iraq and the War on Terror. They have openly cheered for America to lose. This is treason. It is sedition.

Some may ask how an inanimate object can hurt or harm anything. This inanimate object has a flesh and blood owner. His name is Arthur "Pinch" Sulzberger Jr. Pinch Sulzberger has a long history of despising his own nation. Like all rich children of guilty white liberals, he joined the counterculture. Unlike others who took part in that wretched movement of drug loving hippie excess, Pinch never grew up. His father, Arthur "Punch" Sulzberger Sr. was a liberal, but even he had limits. He asked his son who he would want to die in a conflict between an American soldier and a Vietnamese soldier. Pinch replied, "The American soldier should die because we invaded his country. The Vietnamese soldier is just defending himself."[30]

One does not have to support a war to wish that our soldiers come home safely. Pinch has continued his warped thinking to this very day. On the day that Iraqis voted in their third democratic election, The *JBT* chose to break the wiretapping story involving the Bush White House. Reasonable minds can disagree on whether this was a story to begin with. Yet the story could have been reported one day earlier or one day later. It was not time sensitive. The day of the Iraqi election was historic. To give it short shrift was horrifying.

Yet even more horrifying was the *JBT* giving away secret troop movements, endangering the lives of American soldiers. This is not about right vs. left. It is about right vs. wrong. Our troops may overwhelmingly vote Republican, but they conduct their missions with honor regardless of who at any moment in history is their commander in chief. Those who say they "support the troops" cannot condone this activity. These young men and women should not be blown to kingdom come because one man is against war in principle and American victory in practice. Ideology has blinded him. There is no decency left.

2008 brought three more big black eyes at the Gray Lady.

The first is mild in comparison. It involves the furor of the paper in general for hiring commentator Bill Kristol, who happens to be a conservative. Notice I did not refer to him as "conservative commentator Bill Kristol." He is a human being first, and I do not recall the *Wall Street Journal* referring to "liberal columnist Al Hunt" when he was there. That is because the *WSJ* placed quality above ideology, allowing it to export both.

London Times Editor Daniel Finkelstein wrote a brilliant article questioning why a movement obsessed with diversity would object to a columnist offering ideological diversity.

The reason is because ideological diversity is frowned upon.

"A quality newspaper should have columns reflecting a wide variety of opinions, even those uncongenial to the majority of its readers. While the bulk of a paper's columnists may reflect the publication's character and view, there must always be space for an alternative opinion."

Apparently Mr. Finkelstein believes the *JBT* is reasonable.

"Considering that Kristol represents a large strand of American opinion (even if it is a smaller strand of *NYT* reader opinion) it is entirely unremarkable that his columns should be commissioned."

This is because ideology is what they want. Quality is irrelevant. Expanding the readership is only irrelevant for people wanting to grow their business. Judging by the collapsing stock price, Pinch does not care about increasing circulation.

"The job of a reader's editor surely is to defend the rights of its readers, all of its readers. It is not to start picking a 'Fantasy Columnist' team to reflect his own politics. What of people who agree with Kristol? Do they not deserve the protection of the reader's editor?"

JBT ombudsman Clark Hoyt did not want Mr. Kristol hired because he had the nerve to criticize the paper in the past. Internal dissension is healthy. It avoids groupthink. Ironically, the very things that the *JBT* accused the Bush administration of being guilty of is what has affected the *JBT* itself.

Mr. Hoyt stated, "This is not a person I would have rewarded with a regular spot in front of arguably the most elite audience in the nation."

Mr. Finkelstein's reply was brief, to the point, and deadly accurate.

"Isn't this the most pompous sentence you have ever read in your life?"[31]

This is the *JBT* mindset. They have between one and two million readers and think that seven billion people agree with them. Even for liberals, this is arrogance overload.

The second black eye is 2004 redux. Many people feel that Rudy Giuliani is the strongest Republican candidate (Disclosure: I am supporting Rudy Giuliani for president). While many on the left and right are not Rudy fans, he was the frontrunner in the polls for some time. Then a scandal broke about Secret Service protection for his mistress (now his wife), Judi Nathan. In the end, there was no scandal. The expenditures were legal and charged to the appropriate account.

So no harm, no foul, right? Wrong. The scandal was on the front page. The retraction was on page thirty-seven. Rudy Giuliani might still become president, but if he does not, that scandal is what sent him down in the polls. The *JBT* failed to get President Bush in 2004, but they fired their guns on Mayor Giuliani and derailed a strong Republican … and more importantly, a staunch advocate of an aggressive continuation of the War on Terror. Ideology reigns supreme, and any man further to the right of President Bush with regards to the Bush doctrine must be destroyed.

Yet if attacking one man falsely is disgusting, continuing to disparage our troops is vile.

The newest story slandering the troops came in the form of the *JBT* claiming that 121 murders have been committed by American troops returning home. This is to show returning soldiers as shellshock induced, crazed, murderous lunatics. The story has already been debunked. As a percentage, American civilians who have not served in the military are five times more likely to commit murder. Soldiers are better behaved, more disciplined, and less violent. They are not "killing machines." They are humanitarians who love America and defend our citizens. Portraying the entire group as murderers is to hate the troops.

It is not the *JBT*'s liberalism. It is that they are pernicious, wrong, and unapologetic. They get the story wrong, issue mealy mouthed apologies, and continue to make the same mistakes over and over again. Sometimes honest mistakes happen. More often than not, the paper engages in deliberate smears.

It is no wonder that the *JBT* and its ever dwindling number of readers despise Fox News, Rush Limbaugh, and their less popular brethren. The *JBT* repeatedly lies. They have always lied. Only in recent years are they getting caught.

The *New York Post* and *Wall Street Journal* avoid this problem. It is not that they are conservative, but that they obsess with getting news right. Not right politically, but right accurately. On the rare occasions they err, they issue loud mea culpas. They have liberal columnists, or to be more accurate, columnists that happen to be liberal. They are not token hires. They simply write well.

My blog will succeed because my strong belief in conservatism is secondary to my obsession with integrity. I will be periodically wrong and blow a story. Yet I will place the value of my brand above my pride.

I will not allow myself to become the conservative equivalent of the *JBT*, because conservatives have to be thrice as good as liberals to survive. The mainstream media loves to show conservatives fouling things up, so they can claim equivalence. I will avoid that trap.

The *JBT* will continue to rot from its arrogant liberal head. They prefer madness to goodness. Quality is job zero. They will burn the village, and yes, some decent Republicans will get singed. Yet the *JBT* will be burning right next to them, their own reputation burnt to a crisp, tattered, and charred.

Conservatives will be better off when the Gray Lady gets euthanized. Liberals will not realize this until later on, but they will also be better off. Society will be better.

The *JBT* is the politics of personal destruction. Politics will be less coarse when the JBT expires worthless. This will not eliminate liberalism. Another liberal publication will take their place, obsessed with avoiding the same mistakes. They will choose honesty over treachery, and a rich, deep national debate can continue, free from hatred and lies.

I hope there are enough liberals that value integrity enough to prove me right.

eric

Chapter 6: Greed, aka Trying to Make a Decent Living

When bank robbers steal, it is called a crime. When liberals in government confiscate, it is called "investing" and "fairness."

I would love to have an enterprising attorney file a class action lawsuit against the Social Security Administration. This ridiculous pyramid scheme should not be compulsory. I want my money back.

If I ever win the lottery, I would sue the public schools to get my dollar back. I refuse to play the lottery because I will not contribute one dollar to anything as worthless as public schools.

So what happens to people who want to destroy society but are unsuccessful at becoming dictators? They become schoolteachers and social workers. That way they get the best of all possible worlds for themselves. They have a platform to rail against productive citizens, by educating and coddling the next generation of failures.

It is bad enough when people decide to travel down a financial dead end road. Just don't drag me down with you. Call it greed, but I will embrace it, bathe in it, and fornicate with it if it will let me.

A Violent Bear (Stearns) Market

While I do not believe the sky is falling, and have lived through people panicking hysterically before, I have to confess that I was taken aback by the violence and ferocity and speed with which Bear Stearns was brought down.

This was not some fly-by-night company or Internet stock without revenue. This was Bear Stearns, an established, white shoe, blue chip Wall Street firm. This stockbrokerage and investment banking powerhouse has collapsed.

In 2007, the stock was at $160 per share. On February 27, 2008, it closed at $87.30. On March 12 it closed at $57. It then plummeted 47 percent on March 13 to close at $30. On March 16 it crashed another 84 percent. J.P. Morgan offered to buy it at $2 per share.

Disclosure: I do not own stock in Bear Stearns (thank God). I do own stock in J.P. Morgan. Despite my being a part owner of the company, I am not on the board of directors. The CEO has never solicited or accepted my opinion on anything.

Fuller disclosure: I worked at Bear Stearns for one day in 1994. Fresh out of college, I was hired as a cold-caller. The broker felt I was fabulous on the telephone, but the manager was angry that the broker hired me without his knowledge. Plus, my hair was past my collar, and my shirt was dark red instead of white. The manager had a military background, and over the vehement objections of the broker, I was told to leave. I was not fired, because I was told I was never hired. Thankfully, soon after that, the manager was fired. Several years later I did some temp work at the same office. They did not remember me, and the week I spent there was fine. I even saw people wear jeans on Friday.

Lastly, in the department of too much disclosure, my best friend growing up worked at J.P. Morgan. He did not know a stock from a bond, so I wondered how he ended up on Wall Street when 50 million people would kill to work there. He explained that he worked in the firm's gym as a personal trainer. He told me that if I sent him my resume, he could see about getting me an interview. When I asked if he knew anybody in equity research, he replied, "No, but I know everyone at the gym." I laughed, thanked him, and decided not to ask him to flex his (gym earned) corporate muscles.

As for this violent Bear (Stearns) Market, there are certain things that require perspective.

The United States is not in free fall. Yes, the dollar is low. The downside is people do not want to invest in a weak dollar. However, a strengthening of the dollar would exacerbate the trade imbalance and deficits we have with many nations. I will be the first to admit that the dollar must stop weakening, because unless we remain an economic superpower, we will not be a military superpower.

This is not 1929, or even 1987. Yet this unfortunate situation was equally completely avoidable. In the 1920s, people bought stocks on margin. Margin is leverage. When you buy something outright, be it a car, a house, or stock, you own it, lock, stock (as in market), and barrel (as in oil). It cannot be taken away. Purchases on margin mean liquidation upon default.

As cruel as this sounds, those that lost money in the stock market got what they deserved. The speculators went wild and eventually lost. The expression, "Don't confuse brains with a bull market" is still apropos. In an irony that should not be lost today, it was J.P. Morgan himself who stepped in and saved the country during an early twentieth century financial panic. The private sector did have its positives.

In the 1980s, leverage became the issue again, this time in the form of derivatives, mainly options. People thought they were buying "portfolio insurance" to keep their portfolios safe. There is nothing safe about financial markets outside of bank CDs and U.S. Treasuries. Attempts to smooth out markets and minimize risk usually lead to bigger risk and more volatility. Portfolio insurance did not work. The options went against those using them, and the stock market crashed over 500 points, a 22 percent loss in one day in 1987. Quick and decisive action by Sir Alan of Greenspan prevented what could have been a financial breakdown.

The situation today is no different. People can blame greedy and crooked lenders to make themselves feel better, but at some point personal responsibility has to take over. Speculation is as old as the hills, and whether it be tulips, paper, gold, porkbellies, Internet stocks, or real estate with "cheap" loans, the bottom line is that bubbles burst and unlucky gamblers lose.

Given my fifteen years of Wall Street experience, I offer sound advice for many.

Buy only what you can afford. I drive a 1987 Oldsmobile Cutlass Sierra. Yes, this *is* your father's Oldsmobile. The owner took good care of it, and I bought it with only seventy-four thousand miles on it. I live only a few minutes from my office, and put less than ten thousand miles per year on a car. This helps from a quality of life standpoint as well. The car is not sexy. Who cares? I have seen guys drive $200,000 cars that get repossessed. I bought mine for $2,000 and own it outright.

I do not own my own home. I rent. I would love to buy my condo, but prices are too high. Besides, people should not buy anything without doing research. I know nothing about real estate. I know stocks, which is where I invest.

People are in debt today for different reasons than in the 1920s. Many had to buy a big screen TV on an installment plan. I went "factory refurbished," after determining that this was safe as long as I had a warranty. My fifty-five-inch TV cost me $800 and has lasted several years. Yes, I will cry when it dies, but it was worth the purchase. My black leather sofa set seats nine people. Two of the chairs fold out into lounge chairs, and the other side opens up to form a bed. It costs over $2,000 in stores. I bought it on eBay for $600. The seller was too rich to care. One person's trash is another's treasure. Someone in my building was throwing away a lovely marble table. I think they were insane. I quickly (okay, slowly, it was heavy) brought it back to my condo. It is gorgeous, and I am stunned that it was undesired.

As for investing, all investing … let me repeat, all investing … is gambling. Eschew buying something unless you understand it. Your friends know nothing, unless they are financial professionals. Their needs may differ from yours. Mutual funds are not "safer." Mutual funds are merely collections of "things." If individual things are risky, combining them may not equal a diversified portfolio. It could reduce diversification and add risk.

Also, public companies issue reports. Those reports are public information. Everything about the financial health of the company is listed. Even situations like Enron can be avoided from an investor standpoint. I have gotten many things wrong, but this one I got completely right. By reading that the company had a significant amount of "off balance sheet financing," one could see the company was debt laden. I read the footnotes.

Additionally, 401k owners should ensure that their 401k is not heavily invested in the stock of their own company. It does not matter how large or solid the company may be. Bear Stearns was ""blue chip."

Some people claim they are too busy to do research. Even if they hire a financial planner or money manager, they must do research on that professional and oversee them. Being too busy is not acceptable. If your life is at stake, you do what is needed to survive. Financial health should be no different. It is your money.

eric

My Interview With Dr. Walter Williams

I had the pleasure and privilege of interviewing Professor Walter E. Williams.

Dr. Williams has served as an economics professor at George Mason University for over a quarter of a century. His syndicated column can be read in 140 newspapers and locations as diverse as Townhall to *Jewish World Review*. He is often asked to testify before Congress on economic issues due to his expertise on such matters. He is also an occasional guest host for Rush Limbaugh, blending lighthearted humor with a serious and principled conservatism. He announces to his audience that he is "Black, by popular demand," which fits in perfectly with Limbaugh's over-the-top humor.

I interviewed Dr. Williams by telephone on Presidents Day, and the conversation lasted for about twenty-five minutes. I shared with Dr. Williams that in the early 1990s, Rush Limbaugh was looking for a potential guest host. One of Rush's stagehands suggested a brilliant conservative thinker, but got the name wrong. The stagehand mentioned "Juan Williams," a liberal radio host on National Public Radio. This led to a comedy bit where Rush roasted his stagehand for committing an act of heresy by confusing liberal Juan Williams with conservative Walter Williams. That mistake led me to research Walter Williams. I recommend that any person desiring a brilliant analysis of economic and political issues spend a significant amount of time on his site.

With great pleasure I bring the words and wisdom of Dr. Walter Williams.

1) Does government do anything right? What should government do?

WW: "The federal government should be bound by the U.S. Constitution. Article I, Section VIII of the Constitution lists about twenty-one things that the federal government is authorized to do. Today, two-thirds of our spending is unauthorized, whether it be justified by misuse of the commerce clause or the general welfare clause.

In 1794, James Madison was against spending $15,000 to help French refugees. Madison stated, 'I cannot undertake to lay my finger on that article of the Constitution which granted a right to Congress of expending, on objects of benevolence, the money of their constituents.' Today the federal government spends on benevolence from everything from crop subsidies to prescription drug benefits. It should spend money specifically on what the

Constitution authorizes it to spend, such as providing a national defense and providing post offices."

2) With regards to the stimulus package ... you have come out against it, decrying it as economically insignificant. Yet what about psychologically? Does that matter, and should it? Can bad policy be good policy by merely being seen as good policy?

WW: "There is no evidence that such stimulus packages work. In terms of actual dollars the stimulus package is a drop in the bucket. With most stimulus packages, studies show that two-thirds of the money given out is either saved or used to pay bills. What would be far more helpful would be to make the Bush tax cuts permanent."

3) What part of the conservative message should appeal to black America, and so far why is the Republican message not being received by 90 percent of black voters?

WW: "This has always perplexed me, since blacks have suffered the most from the failures of government. The government failed to end slavery in a timely manner. The government is responsible for the rotten state of public education today. The government has failed to protect people in their neighborhoods. The Democratic Party propaganda has been believed, yet the Democratic Party has been in power where blacks have suffered the most whether it's the Jim Crow of the past or the major cities of today. Part of the problem with the Republican Party is that the Republican Party is not for limited government either. However, it was Republicans that ended slavery. The Democrats would not have passed civil rights legislation without the massive support of Republicans. Black Americans, like all Americans, would benefit from less government intrusion."

4) Poison Ivy League universities recently did their version of *Tea with Mussolini*, in this case Columbian Coffee with Armageddonijad. Should sanctions be levied against universities that invite terrorist enemies to speak on their campuses?

WW: "It might be debatable if President Ahmadinejad is a terrorist. Iran is a terrorist nation. It is not worth the argument. If anything, the visit showed what leftist universities really are. It exposed them. After his visit, Columbia University professors trekked to Iran to personally apologize to President Ahmadinejad for the rough treatment he received on campus."

5) The *Jayson Blair Times* has been accused of giving away troop movements. Does freedom of speech allow for this? If not, should media outlets that engage in such behavior face criminal sanctions?

WW: "Absolutely. I'm seventy-one years old. In World War II, people who gave away secrets were tried for treason. Treason is not treated seriously anymore. In earlier days people were shot for treason. People accused of treason should be given a fair trial and a good defense, but if they are found guilty, they should be punished."

6) Chris Rock says the same things in his comedy routines that Bill Cosby and Juan Williams express regarding concerns facing black America. Yet Chris Rock gets a pass because it is comedy. Do you believe that most black Americans truly disagree with the issues being discussed, or are they just keeping silent due to fear of repercussions?

WW: "People who the media focus on disagree with the average black person. Black Americans living in bad neighborhoods are worried about being mugged, the sounds of gunshots, and having their property destroyed. Polls show that a slight majority of blacks are in favor of the death penalty, against abortion, and in favor of prayer in schools. The black so-called leadership express other values.

Jesse Jackson and Al Sharpton have more in common with white hippies than with the average black person. Black people, according to survey polls, actually have more in common with Jerry Falwell. Most black voters are supporting Barack Obama, while the Congressional Black Caucus is supporting Hillary Clinton. This is another example of black leaders not reflecting black people. Also, the term 'black leaders' is a strange term. Go to any other culture and ask who their leaders are and you will get strange looks. Who are the Irish leaders? The Italian leaders? The Jewish leaders? The Chinese leaders? Why do we alone as blacks need leaders? Are we too dumb to think for ourselves that we need leaders? Again, black leaders appeal to white hippies, but most black Americans are closer in thinking to Jerry Falwell."

7) Who are your three favorite USA and non-USA political heroes?

WW: "My favorite American political hero is President Grover Cleveland. He was known as the 'Veto King.' His total number of vetoes exceeded the total number of vetoes of his predecessors combined. He understood that charity is not part of the U.S. Constitution. In vetoing a charity bill, he stated, 'I can find no warrant for such an appropriation in the Constitution, and I do not believe that the power and duty of the general government ought to be extended to the relief of individual suffering which is in no manner properly related to the public service or benefit.'

I also admire former presidents James Madison and Thomas Jefferson. As for world leaders, obviously there is Margaret Thatcher. In addition, I admire Golda Meir and Winston Churchill."

8.) Outside of Milton Friedman and Dr. Thomas Sowell, not many economists are achieving legendary status today. Has the age of the "superhero uber-economist" passed? If not, who are the rising economists we should all know and admire? (When Dr. Williams expressed that he was not sure he would call either Milton Friedman or Dr. Thomas Sowell "legends," even though he had befriended both of them, I stated to him that I was arbitrarily bestowing that title on them. He laughed.)

WW: "Milton Friedman was a good friend of mine. Thomas Sowell is a good friend of mine. The problem with economists is that we haven't made the tools and thinking of our profession accessible to the ordinary person. There is too much jargon and technicality. Also, economists tend to be the skunk at the picnic. When politicians are talking about free this or free that, economists point out that nothing is free, and in order for government to give to one person it must take from another. People don't like to hear that. This prevents economists from being seen as rock stars. The average person does not relate to such a dose of reality."

9) Mutual fund manager Bill Fleckenstein uses a slogan, "Often wrong, but never in doubt." With that in mind, do you have any predictions for the Democratic primaries and the general election? Do you have any personal preferences? Also, as a follow up question, G. Gordon Liddy has referred to Ann Coulter, Sean Hannity, and Rush Limbaugh and other harsh critics of Senator John McCain as "suicide bomber Republicans." Should we fall in line behind Senator McCain, or is it reasonable to just stay home, or even vote for Hillary to teach Republicans a lesson?

WW: "I have no predictions, and I condemn all of the remaining candidates on domestic policy. John McCain is the best among them on foreign policy.

As for teaching Republicans a lesson, that would not be smart, to stay home. It is all right to criticize Senator McCain. To take it a step further, it is also perfectly all right for Republicans to criticize President Bush when he is wrong, such as with the prescription drug benefit and "No Child Left Behind." If Al Gore had been president and done half of what President Bush did, conservatives would have been all over him. We can hold Senator

McCain's feet to the fire and still vote for him. Domestically, he is the lesser of three evils."

10) How would you like to be remembered? One hundred years from now, what would you want people to think about Dr. Walter Williams the person?

WW: "While my primary job is teaching economics, my goal is to sell Americans on the moral superiority of personal liberty, whose main ingredient is limited government. If liberty dies in America, it is dead in all places for all times. I would hope people would remember that I tried to teach people about the importance of liberty."

I would like to thank Dr. Williams for his generosity with regards to his time. He mentioned to me that he does not take days off, and that he works seven days a week. He has the energy of a man half his age, but the brilliance obtained with the wisdom that age delivers. His intelligence is beyond dispute, but his humility was refreshing. He clearly understands that great concepts are meaningless unless they can be communicated effectively to the average person. He is not afraid to take on the flaws in his own profession, and he puts principles above sacred cows.

If Rush Limbaugh needs to take more time off, his show will not miss a beat as long as Dr. Williams is filling in. The only people who would suffer for this would be liberals having their arguments dispelled and students at George Mason University, who would miss out on top-notch economics lectures on those days.

I wish Dr. Williams the best of everything, and look forward to reading his next column. After all, as he reminds us, he is black by popular demand.

eric

Destroying the Jewish People One Schoolteacher at a Time

As the son of a Holocaust survivor and a proud Jew, I genuinely want the Jewish people to exist. As the son of two retired schoolteachers, I see the Jewish people on the way to slow disintegration one schoolteacher or social worker at a time.

For the sake of full disclosure, I always hated school. School is jail. Junior high school is maximum security prison, high school being medium security, and college being minimum security. You can play tennis, but conjugal visits are not common enough. Graduate school is like probation.

Having said that, it is one thing to attend school when it is mandatory. It is another to voluntarily choose to teach others. When I speak to young Jewish individuals, I beg them not to become schoolteachers, social workers, or entertainment industry personnel. I explain to them that the survival of the Jewish people depends on their avoiding these professions. There are three reasons for this.

The first reason to avoid these professions is economic. The pay is dreadful. Jewish people have political power in this country because they have economic power. Jews gained this economic power by being successful businesspeople. We were bankers, and more importantly, merchants. Whether it be agriculture, textiles, or precious metals, Jews excelled in import-export and other trade-related professions.

Jews nowadays, especially Jewish women, gravitate toward professions that may be noble but are disastrously low on the socioeconomic scale. I doubt these women grow up dreaming of life with economic insecurity, longer hours, frustrating bureaucracy, and powerful supervisors enforcing rigid routines where creativity equals rebellion. The era of the creative teacher is long gone. Teachers spend hours working on lesson plans that must conform to a central plan approved by their high commanders.

Schoolteachers often complain that star athletes can make millions while they struggle. This is because only several hundred people are qualified to play professional sports. Every year the players get stronger and tougher. The standards get higher. In education, standards keep getting lower. This allows more people to become teachers, lowering the market value of the entire profession. Supply and demand works. If enough people would simply refuse to become teachers, shortages would occur, raising pay levels.

College professors can earn six-figure salaries, but professors are not teachers. They spend several hours a week teaching and the rest of their time engaging in self-aggrandizing pursuits designed to enhance their own portfolios. It is publish or perish. I have zero objections to people devoting their lives to their own selfish causes, but for some reason college professors refuse to admit that they do this, offering pabulum about noble pursuits and greater goods. Going into research or on the lecture circuit is lucrative. Actual teaching is not.

Then again, schoolteachers are financial geniuses compared to social workers. Some people find fulfillment observing families on the verge of destruction twelve to fourteen hours a day while earning very little pay in exchange for much emotional heartache. One cannot pay bills or feed a family on emotional agony.

Entertainment industry people are the worst. Yes, actors can make millions per movie. Lottery winners exist. The many who get destroyed in pursuit of a dream few ever attain get washed away by the celebration of the few who succeed. Unlike sports, Hollywood is not a meritocracy.

Jewish moms still pray that their daughters marry doctors and lawyers. Prayers would be unnecessary if their daughters would become doctors and lawyers themselves. Not legal aid lawyers … corporate lawyers. Hired guns willing to defend tobacco companies, gun makers, fast food companies, alcohol manufacturers, etc., earn lucrative salaries, corner offices, and healthy bonuses.

Jewish women must start acting like men, only with breasts. They need to become investment bankers, stockbrokers, international trade merchants, corporate lawyers, and accountants. They need to become salespeople, be it life insurance or automobiles. They need to learn skills that allow them to charge whatever they want. How many Jewish women become plumbers, electricians, auto mechanics, or carpenters? Jewish moms may find these blue collar jobs to be beneath their daughters, but we give hundreds of thousands of dollars to these people because we can't change our oil, fix a sink, or install any system. The plumber not good enough to be the son-in-law earns more than the schoolteacher because the plumber's income is not limited.

The second reason for the education-disintegration link is also economic, but it is the cause, not the effect, the means, not the end. The concept is risk. America was founded by risk takers. The pilgrims had to succeed. Failure meant death. Through wars, famines, pestilences, or bad harvests, they learned skills. They lacked Harvard MBAs, yet were educated. The founding fathers risked everything when they declared independence from the French (just checking to see if you were paying attention ... lord knows what your teachers are teaching you).

America is about entrepreneurship. America is where risk takers can be rewarded, often quite handsomely. Yet Jewish people, again primarily the women, are risk averse in their professional choices. Teaching is risk aversion personified. Teachers receive a safe paycheck, have a safe work schedule, and are condemned to a life of safety, or what the business world calls mediocrity. Truly blessed teachers can become an assistant principal, then a principal, and even a superintendent. This is rare. Those decisions are political, and cronyism does exist. Education is not a meritocracy, because so many people are qualified to be teachers. When athletes succeed, they get bonuses and rich contracts. When good teachers succeed, they are rewarded with the worst students, because they can handle it. The worst teachers get the best students, because that is all they can handle. This hurts teachers and students.

The Internet age has been a godsend for everyone. It has allowed entrepreneurship to flourish. Home-based businesses are booming. Startup costs are low, and barriers to entry are even lower. From eBay to Craigslist to anythingyoucanimagine.com (go ahead and use it), the options for people are limitless, as is the income potential. The only thing required is the ability to take an ounce of risk, much less than the Pilgrims needed.

Social workers are not risk takers unless you count showing up at the home of each case, or as I call them, potential death threats. So, yes, there is risk, but financially where is the reward? It is all the downside with no economic upside. The entertainment industry does have an element of risk, but it is not a calculated risk. It is a lottery. Skill is outweighed by luck. This is not taking risks. This is jumping off a bridge in the hopes of flying.

When Jews become teachers and social workers, they force their own limited world view on their innocent victims, known as students or families. My teachers did not influence me to try and succeed on Wall Street. I had to do it on my own. They taught us about how safety and security were important, and that being part of a successful collective will lead to happiness. Successful individualism is discouraged. Bright students are forced to slow down so that the dumb students do not have their feelings hurt. How can children learn of careers that make money if no one teaching them knows anyone who actually does?

The third reason why Jewish people need to stop going into the education and social work fields is political. These professions are overwhelmingly politically liberal. Jewish people are angry at how little we supposedly contribute to education. Why should we? If somebody brought me an investment that they guaranteed me would cost more money while giving me worse results, I would hide my wallet quickly. The solution is not to give more money to education. The solution is for people to stop going into these professions to begin with. Then when America becomes desperate, the system will be improved. Colleges and universities in America are the envy of the world because of competition and the free market. Colleges fight for top professors. They offer financial incentives to do what would otherwise be a thankless job. It works. Despite professors being liberals and/or socialists, they benefit under the capitalist/conservative system.

When liberals take over education and social work, they have people dependent on them: students and families. This then creates liberals creating more liberals, where these new liberals learn that equality and collectivism are good, making money is evil because profits are greed, and sugar and spice and everything nice is the way to live. Safety and security are paramount. Wall Street works because conservatives teach those who enter it conservative business values. The question then becomes, why are the conservative values better to teach? Because in real life, they actually work. Liberalism talks of noble intentions. Conservatism brings results. Kids need to develop a cold-blooded reality that the schoolteachers will not share with them … that life is ruthless and cutthroat, and if they expect anyone in life to save them they will get swallowed up by life. Ask European Jews in the 1940s the benefits of trusting your neighbor to help you enjoy a good quality of life. The tough Jews that relied on themselves, that escaped to the USA, knew that survival, even in America, costs money. So they began the task of making a lot of it, risk by risk, dollar by dollar.

Some of you in this world might say that there is more to life than making money. If making money is not important, that is commendable. Go to Africa and help blind kids learn to see. Travel to a poor nation and help feed the homeless. Run a soup kitchen in a poor neighborhood. You will barely subsist yourself, but you will feel good and get into heaven well before most people, myself included. However, a carpenter would know how to build the soup kitchen. The investment banker can raise the money to make the soup kitchen a larger and better shelter. The electrician can set up the lights. Rich people can give more money to charity than poor people, because they have it.

Jewish people, particularly women, gall me with how their faces light up when they help people. Tikkun Olam is their guide. (A good orgasm makes my face light up, and I can't feed myself on sex. My face lights up because I make enough money to afford the things that cost money but allow my face to light up.) They would rather be happy than make money. This would be taken seriously if their mothers were not demanding that they marry an actual achiever so that their kids do not eat snow for dinner (or grass and dirt if you live in Los Angeles).

Wake up, Jewish America. The best way to help people and live a quality life is by getting wealthy. Wealth can be used to create more wealth. There are a billion Christians in this world, many who believe that Jesus commands them to help the poor through labors of love. Let them spend their lives on the downtrodden. We do not have the manpower. There are too few of us. We need to help ourselves, or we will cease to exist as a people.

Until Jews are on the streets panhandling en masse, this will not be taken seriously. We are one step away. Mortgages are getting expensive. College tuition is skyrocketing. Vacations are a thing of the past for many. Living paycheck to paycheck is becoming the norm. So stop becoming schoolteachers, social workers, or entertainment industry dreamers. Get high paying jobs. Our future survival depends on it.

Lastly, remember the words of Jewish entrepreneur Norman Lee, who used his money to build a university. In 1993, in finding out I was a graduating business major he said, "Never be ashamed of making money. It is easier to give back when you have money. Live life the right way, make money, and be happy. I'm rich … and I'm very happy." This was less eloquently but still brilliantly expressed by Ben Affleck in *Boiler Room* when he said, "You think money doesn't make me happy? Look at the f*cking smile on my face."[33]

God helps those who help themselves. So please, my fellow Jews, quit ruining the lives of the young and downtrodden who don't appreciate you. Enter the business world, build an empire, and live happily ever after as the Jewish kings and queens used to live.

eric

Chapter 7: Politically Conservative and Morally Liberal

The first rule of scandals is to release the most damaging information immediately. Everything else then pales in comparison, and the scandal becomes boring. Had Bubba Clinton just told America that he was really George Clinton, and it was just the dawg in him, everybody outside of Hillary would have understood.

Republicans get in trouble by preaching values and living salaciously. I will never have that problem. I am a giant walking peccadillo. I warned America in advance. Expect little from me morally, and I will fail to disappoint.

Now that I have admitted my sins, I am prepared to go commit more while you read this book. Now if I could just get a tax cut, I would have more money to spend on that gender that has been wrecking good decent male society since Adam.

Such is the life of a happy hedonist. I am politically conservative and morally liberal. Financial freedom and licentiousness … may God bless America.

Snuffalupagus, Michigan J. Frog, Unicorns, and Republican Jewish Women

From the Easter Bunny to Santa Claus to the adorable tiger in the "Calvin and Hobbes" comic strip, the line between reality and fantasy is often the difference between an imagination and a lack of one. On *South Park*, Kyle Brovlovsky is committed to a mental institution when nobody else is able to see his friend Mr. Hankey.[34] Decades earlier, a man discovered a talking frog named Michigan J. Frog. The frog sang "Hello my Ragtime Gal"[35] in front of the man, but nobody else. Again, the room with white walls was his destination. On *Sesame Street*, Big Bird saw Mr. Snuffalupagus, [36] but nobody believed him. This always surprised me, because they believed Big Bird existed. If a ginormous yellow creature could exist, why not an equally ungraceful, ginormous orange one? Unicorns are also a myth, except to those who have seen them. According to Al Gore, Republicans and their big business friends destroyed the environment, killing the unicorns (No, not really ... but perhaps the last unicorn mated with several animals and became the elusive "ManBearPig"[37] that Al Gore hunts for on *South Park*). Bigfoot and the Loch Ness monster should be mentioned only to belabor the point. There. Done.

This brings me to the elusive Holy Grail. No, not the one that tormented Sir Lancelot and Sir Galahad succeeded in finding. (I say Lancelot got the better of the deal. That Guinevere was a hot piece of fictional tail. Drinking from her Holy Grail beats drinking wine out of a goblet or chalice any day.)

The Holy Grail I refer to is the nectar that is tasted from that rarest of creatures ... Republican Jewish women. I have seen them. They do exist. My search was a long and exhausting one, but I have traversed this land of the red, white, and blue, and I found some. It was not easy.

This quest became important because my initial option of pursuing every woman on the planet was limited upon my entering the world. As a Hebrew, over 99 percent of women were forbidden. Although I figured Jews were united under a common cause (trying to avoid getting killed by about 2–3 billion enemies), apparently the majority of Jews in the 1960s became hippies, took tons of drugs, and produced a generation of liberals. (Debate rages as to whether the drugs caused liberalism, or whether being liberal led to taking drugs.) Jewish Republicans were to be viewed suspiciously, an enemy within.

For awhile on dates I hid my ideology in the same manner as a guy concealing drug use or felony convictions. Eventually I figured that if homosexuals could come out of the closet, I could as well. I began traveling America, determined to find Republican Jewish women. Every once in awhile, I would run into one, and it was a nightmarish occurrence that kept repeating. These women were Jewish, Republican, and boring.

No, God. Anything but boring. Ugly people can get plastic surgery. People can gain or lose weight. Being boring is forever. These women could talk politics, but little else. They were humorless. Could it be that as the children of hippies, liberal women were more—dare I say it—fun? Every girl I had ever dated was a Democrat, and a lot of them were fun to be around when politics was not discussed. They appreciated things such as Jacuzzi-romps, tantric massages (the Japanese call it "Reiki"), and other interesting actions/ positions that only non-uptight women could appreciate.

I then realized that even though I am a conservative, I believed in a liberal dose of sex and carousing. (I actually realized this when I was eleven, but my allowance could not foster that lifestyle.) It was not just about sex, though. It was about stimulating conversation. It was about fun. One Jewish Republican woman was concerned on the telephone when I referred to her as "straitlaced." She said that while she was a serious person, she was not stuffy. When a person has to announce that they are not stuffy, just call them Stovetop and serve them on Thanksgiving with giblet gravy.

So what is a Jewish Republican male who detests hippies but likes their spirit and immorality supposed to do? Finding a Christian Coalition woman was not the answer. A lot of them are even more straitlaced. Finding a Jewish leftist and sparring every day ... too stressful. Then I saw an advertisement for the Republican Jewish Coalition. I knew Republican Jewish women existed, but many of them were scared of being attacked. (Go on JDate and read the profiles where under politics it says "unspecified." They are often Republicans.) The Republican Jewish Coalition was a place where people proudly expressed themselves. (Some people want to form a Democratic Jewish Coalition, but that is as necessary as going to Libya and forming a Muslim club.)

The RJC has allowed me to meet top political leaders and make business contacts. Most importantly, I have had the pleasure of meeting Republican Jewish women that are smart, fun, and totally drop-dead gorgeous. One of these women resides in New York. She is taken, but I bet she has friends. One woman from Florida actually liked football. Beyond the stereotype about tight pants, she understood the game itself and watched it weekly. Another woman from Pennsylvania was so stunningly, blindingly beautiful that I briefly forgot my own name. Luckily her name was similar to mine, so by staring at her nametag I was able to refresh my memory. None of these women were vegetarians or yoga cultists. They did not wear tie-dyed t-shirts. They were funny and intelligent.

Other people there had daughters, nieces, and other Republican Jewish women that I should meet. Like Norm Peterson on *Cheers*,[38] when asked to watch the bar, I allowed my arm to be twisted repeatedly.

I left the RJC conference with my faith revitalized. My religious and political faiths were always strong. My faith in my quest to pursue the Holy Grail is now stronger than ever.

Upon asking one Republican Jewish woman in Los Angeles to join me for a Jacuzzi soak, she replied that it sounded overwhelmingly tempting. My response to any woman thinking this is, "Well then get tempted for crying out loud!"

My next New York business and pleasure trip involves a smart, corporate, funny, and gorgeous woman (who is a flaming liberal) wanting to dine with me. I have crossed over to the dark side before, but am relieved knowing that this is now a pleasant option and not a necessity for survival.

Steven Tyler of Aerosmith in the song "Full Circle" sings, "If I could change the world/like a fairy tale/I would drink the love/from your Holy Grail."[39] I realize that the Holy Grail is within reach. So to all the Republican Jewish women of the world, I say this: asking you to rip off your clothes instantaneously may be premature, but at least rip off your masks. Be as proud to be Republican as you are proud to be Jewish. Let the world know you are politically brilliant and fun.

I desire one of you ... and only one. I know how to cook and am trained as a masseur. The Jacuzzi water is perfect tonight. I am alcohol, smoke, drug, and liberalism free.

Hineni. Here I am (Rock You Like a Hurricane). *Hineni.* You are Jewish, Republican, and ready to be kissed like the chalice that rejected Sir Lancelot and Sir Galahad died for.

eric

Help Me Rabbi! I Am Desiring (Mary Katharine) Ham

I have to stop watching Fox News. It is numbing what little remains of my brain. Not since Shannon Doherty spoke at the 1992 Republican Convention have I faced such a crisis of faith.

I now know what Stevie Nicks means when she sings "Rooms on Fire."[40] A blazing hot woman appeared on my TV screen. Stunning beauty is not a rare commodity, but this woman is also a Republican. To quote Sting, "My logic has drowned/be still my beating heart."[41]

I have a craving for ham. Now before you all call my rabbi and give him another reason to wish that Judaism allowed for excommunication rights, this is not an issue of Black Forest ham. It is something much more tempting ... Mary Katharine Ham.

For those of you anticipating a borderline X-rated tribute disguised as harmless lustiness, sorrow awaits. First of all, Ms. Ham is one of the top people at Townhall.com, and I would rather not be banned from the site. Secondly, when she reports back to Bill O'Reilly to report on Internet Web sites that are destroying Western civilization, I would prefer she not give my parents another reason to change their last name and address again.

So I am asking my readers to help me get a date with Mary Katharine Ham. She is the belle of the Townhall ball, and I ... oh, heck, I'm so googly-eyed I cannot finish the analogy. I hate when that happens. My train of thought is boarding at the station.

Anyway, time for a plan. I do not want my readers contacting her, flooding her with e-mails, and agitating her. However, I want everybody to contact my blog and vote on whether or not she should go out with me. I know this is a useless nonbinding resolution, but with congressional Democrats gaining a point in the polls to 15 percent, it seems like a good idea, or at least less awful than my other bad ideas.

Now I know some of you are seeing this as a ploy to increase traffic on my blog, but women like powerful men. As a kid, my dad could beat up your dad. Then I had the better place to live, the biggest blankety-blank, and now have a larger TV set than most guys. If I can show her that my blog gets more hits than my rivals, she may swoon. (Does an eyeball roll count as a swoon? I hope so.)

I will deliver the results to her on July 5, after which point my MTV generation attention span will be focused elsewhere. Perhaps I could sacrifice a liberal in her honor. No wait … human sacrifices do not get the girl. This is difficult!

I could write something brilliant. That takes too long. Where the heck is the cut and paste function on my keyboard? This is so complex.

Okay, will everybody please just let her know through my Web site that I want her to swoon in my presence? No, she is not a soccer beauty. That is Mia Hamm. Sheesh, people, work with me here.

You as my readers have a role. Somebody please find out if she is single. Then find out if she is heterosexual. This is not an either/or proposition. (Oh lord, I just used the word proposition … what is wrong with me? I am so disrespectful sometimes.) She must be both. Also, please dear readers, find out if she is a member of the Hebrew faith. If not, she can convert. Problem solved.

I have so many political issues to write about, and this is delaying the process. I cannot have the whole political process held up just because I desire Mary Katharine Ham.

Dear Ms. Ham, just know that I am alcohol, cigarette, drug, and liberalism free. I have even been known to use utensils and dress nicely when forced to do so. I have had all my shots and am not afraid to be not afraid of whatever people are not supposed to be not afraid of. My phone number is (redacted). Please do not give it to college frat boys. I hate getting calls from oversexed freshmen asking if I am the "Saturday night special." Perhaps they desire a gun control debate, but I cannot chance it.

My email address is (redacted). Furthermore, every time I hear your (redacted) voice, listen to your brilliantly expressed (redacted), see your (redacted) body, and envision your (redacted), I want to (redacted) your (redacted) beautiful (redacted) all over your (redacted) until we are both (incredibly long redaction covering everything).

There. I am glad I got that off of my (redacted). (Wait a sec … why the heck would I have to redact the word "chest?" Then again, a chest is like a breast, so it should remain redacted.)

I am a Republican, for crying out loud. According to fictional character Bree Van De Kamp on *Desperate Housewives*, Republicans are not supposed to even think about (redacted), much less act on it.

The downside is possibly getting shot down in front of the entire blogosphere. Thank heavens the Internet did not exist when I was in junior high school. The good news is my parents have given up.

Okay everybody, get to work. I have until my self-imposed deadline of July 5 to get this woman to notice me, and not in a way that would make her call the bad taste authorities.

Write to me early, often, and repeatedly. The fate of my (redacted) with Mary Katharine Ham hangs in the balance. She is Jewish until irrefutable evidence that I try to deliberately ignore (wow, now I know how liberals exist) proves otherwise.

Do not worry, rabbi. If I get shot down, I will never lust after ham again.

eric

The Top 120 Political Yummy Bouncies

When high finance meets high society, we get finance movies such as *Stocks and Blondes*,[42] where the woman is covered only in the ticker tape. Yet even more powerful than the cocktail of sex and Wall Street comes in the mixture of sex and politics.

It is in that spirit that I have compiled the list of the top 120 political yummy bouncies.

Technically this is not much different from listing the top thirty hottest political women, except that the focus is on their T and A.

From the front, I dream of playing sexual volleyball, bouncing them vigorously. From the backside, I hope to play Sir Mixalot's "Baby Got Back" while giving them the ketchup bottle treatment.

I have a fulfilling life, which basically consists of uncontrollable sobbing knowing that the women on this list are not mine. To the best of my knowledge, I have had sex with none of them.

Compiling the list was more difficult than I expected. I thought the trouble would be narrowing the list. The reverse was the case. To even find that many women that caught my attention was rare. Politics is mostly powerful bald white guys, and I have never been attracted to the cue ball look.

The list has been divided into the top ten liberals, centrists, and conservatives. Given that they were all anatomically correct, this added up to twenty breasts and twenty backside cheeks for all three political denominations.

I excluded pictures of the women because they were all fully dressed, making the exercise pointless.

Several of these women are over forty, and in a couple cases over fifty. So what? Hot is hot.

Nevertheless, I now bring the top 120 political yummy bouncies.

Liberals/Democrats: I left out Senator Barbara Boxer because she is older now, although she was a hot piece back in the day. I left out Obama Girl because she was too lazy to even vote for him. Patti Davis, despite a *Playboy* spread, should be off the list because her father, the great Ronald Reagan, deserves to rest in peace. Al Gore's former campaign manager Donna Brazile almost made the cut, due to her salacious appearance on the *Colbert Report* where she offered to have sex with him in a Kansas City hotel room. This list was written before I saw Washington State Senator Maria Cantwell on television. She will absolutely make future lists.

With that, the official list is below.

10) Rachel Sklar—She is affiliated with the *Huffington Post*. Providing a link to promote that site is a non-starter. However, with her, just hit the mute button and enjoy.

9) Julie Roginsky—She is a hot Democratic strategist. She speaks as well, but I remember not one word.

8.) Sarah Gore—Her father tried to steal an election, but she used to steal the loins of men with pulses. She recently got married. I am green, but with envy, not environmentalism.

7) Lisa Lange—She is associated with PETA, and was behind their naked marketing campaign. She is proof that no matter how awful an organization, guys will listen when a woman promotes nakedness.

6) Alexandra Kerry—I really wanted to be between her legs in 2004, but not enough to vote for her father.

5) Segolene Royal—The former French Socialist candidate for prime minister is so regal. She was sleeping with the party chairman, and they had kids. The French election was a coin flip, since my head supported Nicolas Sarkozy despite her being a hot piece of tail.

4) Julia Allison—She used to date a Democratic senator. Every aspect of her life is on the Internet. She is like Jim Carrey in *The Truman Show*,[43] only with a much sexier body and much more granola lifestyle.

3) Jackie Clarke—She did an entire play dedicated to the movie *Showgirls*.[44] She likes football, cursing, and talking about her female body parts. She is equally frightening and ketchup bottle worthy.

2)(tie) Norah O'Donnell—She is an impartial analyst on MSNBC, meaning she is a liberal. Again, this is a visual contest, with the less auditory aspect being the best. She is stunning.

2) (tie) Naomi Wolf—Yes she has become part of the lunatic fringe that believes in 9/11 conspiracies and compares President Bush to the evil in this world. Who cares? This is a subjective beauty contest, and she is a hot piece of

Jewish rumpus. Plus, one of her sex books helped me get more than my fair share, which proves that even feminists can be useful from time to time.

1) Jane Fleming—Recently married with two children, those pouty lips of hers are a perfect fit for her constantly angry television appearances. I think she actually has a Hillary Clinton nutcracker that she keeps on her kitchen counter. She is the reason pool tables were invented.

Centrists/Independents: Entertainment reporter Shira Lazar would have made the list, but she rarely discusses politics. She is a sweet girl and easy on the eyes. Sarah Silverman frightens me to death, and her comments are barely political. She is proof that hot women can say anything at any time for any reason.

10) The women of Poland—Women in Poland are stripping naked to protest against politics being dominated by men. I support their freedom of expression.

9) Alison Rosen/Michelle Collins—They are both commentators on *Redeye*,[45] and I have never seen them on at the same time. They might be the same person. I hope they have eight yummy bouncies instead of four.

8) Gloria Estefan—Yes, she is a Cuban singer. She also got very political during the Elian Gonzalez fiasco. I would do the Conga if I was in bed with her.

7) Tammy Bruce—I am pro-gay rights for everybody except her. We should donate ugly women to the lesbian community in exchange for her. She curses like a sailor, and the fact that I am completely intimidated by her is a turn on.

6) Ashlee Dupree—Any woman that destroys Eliot Spitzer and appears in a *Girls Gone Wild* video is a goddess. I normally do not endorse drugs and prostitution, but she is why the lord created spring break.

5) Campbell Brown—CNN would have much higher ratings if she was allowed to moderate presidential debates in her undies. She is smart, but this column could care less. She reigns supreme at the Cheesecake News Network.

4) Kiran Chetry—She is also a Cheesecake News Network girl. She was not the hottest woman at Fox News, but at CNN, where the journalistic standards are lower, her legs fit in perfectly.

3) Dagan McDowell—Scarlett O'Hara made it to Wall Street. Her accent melts butter, and her brilliance is overshadowed by her beauty.

2) Mirthala Salinas—She is the news reporter that slept with the mayor of Los Angeles with a name that is hard to spell. I give the mayor credit. He has excellent taste.

1) Carla Bruni—She is the first lady of France. Nicolas Sarkozy understands that the only reason to gain power is to bed models. Between Bruni and Royal, the French have all they need for a primetime Jell-O wrestling special.

Conservatives/Republicans: I left Barbara Bush off the list. I am referring to W's daughter, not his mother. Barbara is adorable, but out of respect for the Dub, I will say no more. George W. Bush, just know I want to be her Secret Service bodyguard. Please do not waterboard me, I voted for you twice. Michelle Malkin is not on the list because I am beyond intimidated by her. When she goes on television and flares her nostrils in anger, I want to hide in the corner and cry. I am a sissy. Patricia Heaton, who played the wife on *Everybody Loves Raymond*, is one hot mom. She has contributed to Republicans, and I wonder if she was naked when she wrote the check. Fred Thompson's wife, Geri, is stunning, but out of respect for the Alpha Dog, I will leave it at that. I met them and liked them. The blogosphere has a Republican Jewish blogger named Spree. When she becomes more famous, I will make sure the world knows that I was the one who made salacious comments about her when others ignored her body and insulted her by judging her blog on the quality of the writing.

10) Jeanine Pirro—She may not have defeated Hillary Clinton in New York, but this prosecutor would easily win a contest over Hillary in terms of who guys would want to paddle. She also appears on *Redeye*, where she pops out opinions and her cleavage.

9) Amanda Carpenter—This Townhall.com political reporter is an incredibly sweet person. I almost left her off the list out of respect, given how dignified she is. However, I needed one more name, and she is lovely.

8.) Sarah Palin—She is the governor of Alaska, and a candidate for vice president. Her 91 percent approval rating may be because men outnumber women in Alaska by twenty-five to one.

7) Kate Obenshain—She claims to have four children. Some women never age. She is deep into Republican politics, and I am deeply into her, albeit from afar, given the restraining order.

6) Michele Bachmann—This congresswoman from Minnesota is smart as a whip. She is not into whips, preferring family values. She was never in Bachmann Turner Overdrive, but she turns me into overdrive. She should reprise the role of underwear model made famous by Teri Garr.

5) Angie Harmon—She is married to retired football star Jason Sehorn. As a hot Republican prosecutor on *Law and Order*, her first episode was fabulous. When she thundered, "Hang 'em all, no deals for anybody,"[46] I realized that there is nothing sexier than a tough hot woman in charge of the penal code.

4) Mary Katharine Ham—I met her in real life, and she is incredibly classy and dignified. She is a sweet, cool person. She was the subject of the worst blogging four-part trilogy in history, which began with "Help Me Rabbi, I Am Desiring Ham."

3) Julie Banderas—As for why I want to paddle her, it might be because I have a pulse. College students may not get *Playboy* in the dorms, but viewing her on Fox News is the next best thing.

2) Andrea Tantaros—This Republican strategist has a devastating piercing tongue, and men around America want to experience it. She was the spokeswoman for Jeanine Pirro, and they would rival any mother-daughter Jell-O wrestling tag team.

1) Shannen Doherty—Her speech at the 1992 Republican Convention captivated men. So did her *Playboy* spreads. I have met and spoken politics with her. I wish I had taken her on top of the jewelry table, but I was moderately less tactless back then.

Well, all these women will have to live with the fact that my focus is now on the current sexual administration. They are simply too late. Now I need to take a midday nap. Time to count sheep, or in my case, the current romantic administration's apolitical yummy bouncies.

4 … 8 … 12 … zzzzzzzzzz

eric

Republican SEX Scandals

I wish I was a liberal. Yes, I said it. I am a conservative Republican, and I wish I was a liberal. That way I could get entangled in as many sex scandals as possible with no consequences.

First of all I want to make something crystal clear. There is nothing funny about sex with underage citizens, or even pursuing it. Mel Reynolds is in jail, and Mark Foley resigned in disgrace, as he should have.

Secondly, I do not condone adultery. As Ted Koppel stated, "The Ten Commandments are not the ten suggestions."[47]

Having said that, it is unfair that Republicans have to be held to higher sexual standards. If I was a liberal, I would be expected to lack moral boundaries and be free to run wild like a drugged-out hippie (redundant, I know).

As a single male, there is nothing contradictory about wanting to sleep with every hot Republican Jewish brunette while also wanting lower taxes and dead terrorists.

The following is a conversation that I never had, because I value money and want to avoid getting slugged.

"Ms. Finch, you did an excellent job on this report. Well done."

"Thank you, Eric. Is there anything else?"

"Yes, Ms. Finch. I really want to paddle your hide. I know it is a sensitive area in more ways than one, but I want to play table tennis with your backside until you are red raw. After that, I need to see paperwork on the new account we are seeing next week."

I am not implying that to do the above behavior is appropriate, but thinking about it should be fine. Republicans are so conditioned to be straitlaced that we are pegged as boring. Family values are for families, but why should single people be straitjacketed?

For those claiming the above scenario is sexual harassment, how do you know Ms. Finch is the subordinate? Isn't thinking that sexism? She could be the boss.

I thought about this when Spree at *Wake up America* interviewed Melanie Morgan.

She did an excellent job with the interview, which I never could have done. Melanie Morgan is smart, Republican, and hot. She would think I was an imbecile within five minutes, especially if my first question was a marriage proposal.

After seeing her picture, I was determined to have a Morgan before bed. I could not convince Melanie Morgan, so I decided to settle for Captain Morgan. I figured if I finished the entire bottle, I would not be able to distinguish them. Actually, I don't drink, but I need an excuse for my behavior.

I know a gorgeous Republican Jewish brunette who has experimented with some mild girl-on-girl action. I can talk to her about Nicholas Sarkozy and Angela Merkel, but why should that stop me from admiring her physically and wanting to be reincarnated as a pillow that she hits her friend with? When did lust become acceptable only with liberals?

Senators are soliciting prostitutes. So what? Whether it is gay or straight, they are guys trying to get laid. Again, forget they are married. If they are single, how is that different from a surf-and-turf date? Does any woman in her right mind really think that a guy takes her out to steak and lobster for handholding? We have an agenda, and that involves using our teeth to claw through your underclothing. This does not mean we would do so without permission, but within the laws of decent society, we have every right to make an attempt.

For the Milli-Vanillionth time, one can respect women and want to sleep with them. One can respect a woman's mind while wanting to devour her body. Men are hunters, women are the hunted, and we have every right to adhere to the laws of nature and biology.

There is nothing in the Republican Party platform decreeing that men be repressed until we go crazy.

Bill Clinton lied under oath. That was my objection with him. He should have just gone on television and said, "I can't help it. It ain't nothing but the dawg in me. I bounced her like a volleyball and might do it again."

So where is the line? If believed, Juanita Broderick was a rape victim. That is totally unacceptable everywhere, always. Letting them die in a river like Ted Kennedy did is certainly unethical. Yet fear of approaching a woman out of desire? Are we that puritanical?

We are all flawed. We all make mistakes. Yet Republicans are seen as pious, and therefore, hypocritical.

Some say the war on drugs is lost, and others argue the same for the War on Terror. They are wrong. However, let's declare the war on sex lost. We can kill drug lords and terrorists. Sex cannot be killed. It is too powerful. It will always be there.

Rather than trying to humiliate every politician that tries to play pinkbelly with a hot woman, why not simply accept this as normal? If the guy is married, it will be his fault when his wife gets the shotgun and exacts Texas Justice. Actions have consequences.

Larry Craig is being forced to resign. Why? For being gay? Isn't that gay bashing? Jim McGreevey and John Corzine put their lovers on the payroll. Yet only McGreevey resigned. Wasn't Corzine's sexual crime, although heterosexual, just as bad? David Vitter is not being pressured to resign. Is it because his prostitution was heterosexual?

Why is a 535-member club filled with drunk drivers, tax cheats, and other reprobates so puritanical when the issue is sexual?

Rape and sexual harassment are wrong. Prostitution is legal in some parts of America. Doesn't it seem strange that Senator Craig was arrested in Minnesota for a crime that would have been legal in certain parts of Nevada? Perhaps if Harry Reid let loose, he would actually smile. That dour look on his face is probably due to his frustration at attacking every Republican less repressed than he is.

I will never preach family values, yet when I marry I will still live by them. Until then, I want my taxes cut so I can have more money to spend on women who will dance provocatively in my condo like Tawny Kitaen in Whitesnake's "Here I Go Again."

Should my being a conservative Republican mean that back in college, I should not have found Barbara Boxer a hot piece of (redacted) just because she was a liberal? Flaming fiery liberals are kinda sexy. It doesn't mean they are right about taxes or Iraq.

We should stop focusing on sex scandals. Sex is a privilege, not a scandal. Either Republicans defend their right to go buck wild, or we will all end up either repressed or worse … liberals.

eric

Eva Longoria and Other Reasons I Am Not a Social Conservative

I am so tired of being told that I should be an optimistic, happy conservative in the mold of Ronald Reagan. I am not a happy conservative. Sometimes I am an angry, ticked-off conservative. So what is the cause for this? Not abortion, illegal immigration, or the War on Terror. No, the issue that still sticks in my craw … Eva Longoria.

That's right, you read correctly. This whole Eva Longoria thing is getting to me. It doesn't compute. Why would a woman who could have any man in the world—as if God descended from the heavens and created a perfect flawless woman—why would this woman choose a Frenchman? If basketball player Tony Parker was Italian or Spanish, I could live with that, but French? It is just plain wrong. The Spurs lost in the playoffs to the Dallas Mavericks. I predicted that one. Let's face it. The star player on the Mavericks is Dirk Nowitzki, who is German. The Mavericks did not beat the Spurs. The Spurs just surrendered.

I tried being a social conservative, but then Eva Longoria started prancing around in her undies on *Desperate Housewives*. I almost engaged in self-love, but Republicans don't do that, especially not social conservatives. Besides, given all the diseases running around, I don't like to touch myself because I don't know where I've been. Also, like the business expression goes, the left hand doesn't know what the right hand is doing. If being a Republican means giving people a cold dose of painful reality, my friend summed it up worst when we were watching the NBA All-Star Game. As I booed Tony Parker every time his froggy hands touched the ball, my friend reminded me about Eva Longoria and said, "Let me explain this to you. You … have … no … shot."

I blame her because I would make a good social conservative, except for my immoral lifestyle and inability to even pay lip service to improving. It's not that I want the big G (God, not Greenspan, for those of you in finance) to shove a flamethrower up my hide. I just want all of heaven's benefits without doing any good behavioral deeds to earn them.

There was a brief period when I leaned toward the social conservatives. I was listening to some feminists say that they had full power to make decisions over their own bodies. They were liberated, and were going to have sex whenever they pleased. As a social conservative, this could be troublesome for society, but as a young single man, and forgive me reverends, priests, rabbis, imams, and miscellaneous religious dudes, this was an overwhelmingly positive development. Do you know how hard it is to even get a kiss goodnight sometimes? If a woman wants to engage in licentiousness, I will be supportive.

Then the feminists wanted the right to an abortion. So let me get this straight. Not only do these modern women want to have the right to screw whoever they please, but they want the right to let the guy off the hook guilt free by having an abortion, freeing him of any responsibilities for his actions? Where do I sign up? This feminism stuff rocks.

Then the feminists went too far. They totally had my support, and I was embracing their newfound freedoms. They had to ruin it and cross the line. Since it was their bodies, and they could choose to have sex, they could also choose to not have sex. This was not part of the plan. These women had to be stopped. It was time to call the Christian Coalition and get some good old-fashioned paternalistic body regulating.

I ended up calling Phyllis Schlafly, partly because I like saying "Schlafly." I told her that I was outraged at the way young society was behaving today, and I was ready to join the Christian right. She was delighted.

The conversation started out fine. She told me that part of her organization and other Christian organizations was about helping spread the word of loving one's neighbor. I found that a very noble sentiment indeed. She told me how important it was to get kids off drugs. I totally concurred. She explained how important it was to feed the homeless and help those less fortunate. I was ready to declare this woman a saint (Although she did not wear big shoulder pads, and might not have made a good New Orleans Saint). I was totally ready to be a social conservative, and then Ms. Schlafly crossed the line. She stated that one way of improving the schools was to teach girls about the importance of abstinence.

Abstinence? From what? Apparently sex. At that point I screamed at Ms. Schlafly and called her the zealot that she is for having the nerve to tell young women to not live up to their God-given sexual potential. These social conservatives need to keep their laws out of my bedroom now.

I make no apologies for rational (sometimes irrational) self-interest. Old people know that Social Security is a pyramid scheme, but it benefits them, hence their support. Schoolteachers know the educational system is disastrous, but given indifference toward the kids, they refuse to adopt standards. I am a young, single male, so I vote based on what matters to me. I look at every political issue and think, "Will this increase or decrease my chances of getting laid?"

This brings me to the issue of gay rights. Men should not have homosexuality as a choice. It should be mandatory. Criticize gay men? Heck, straight men should send them thank you notes for reducing the competition for women. Any man that is taller than me, drives a nicer car than me, and makes more money than me … be gay! I will march in your parades, show solidarity … anything you need. The only condition is no switching back. You must remain gay, and convert all your male friends.

This does not apply to lesbians. Jesus hates them. If the women are not gorgeous (being gentle) it is acceptable. Rosie O'Donnell can be as gay as she wants. Tammy Bruce needs to be straight immediately. My people (young single men trying to sleep with hot women) have suffered enough. Ms. Bruce is stunning. Why torture the entire male gender? The movie *Bound*[73] is an example of why lesbianism should be illegal.

I have come to accept that I have libertarian leanings, which means I am a conservative Republican who believes in liberal doses of physical contact with gorgeous women. It is no coincidence that the word gorgeous starts out with the word gorge, further proof that beauty was meant to be ravished and ravaged.

I refuse to apologize to social conservatives for my Chasidic (Orthodox Jewish) adult videos. Every time I rent *Oy Vay Three Way, Debbie Does Menachem Mendel*, or my favorite Chasidic bestiality video, *Rabbis, Rabbits, and Radishes* (don't ask what the radishes are for), I realize that I would rather blame social conservatives than examine my own shortcomings. So what if I have an adult video with Bea Arthur entitled *Golden Showers with the Golden Girls*? (My political career just went down the toilet with that one.) The Christian Coalition should stay out of my private life.

I want my government to cut taxes and kill terrorists. Lower taxes means more money in my pocket to spend on women like Mistress Evil, who for only $200 per hour will turn your hide the color of the devil herself. Killing terrorists is important because most of them are young single men, reducing my rivals even further.

Before social conservatives start complaining about diseases resulting from sexual misconduct, it is a known fact that embryonic stem cell research has found the cure for AIDS. Okay, so it hasn't, but maybe if the researchers would work harder they could figure it out already. Then again, between Viagra and Rogaine, men have it pretty good these days.

The bottom line is I am tired of social conservatives telling me to take responsibility for my actions. They should stop judging me. Perhaps if they would just lower standards and be as immoral as everybody else they would not be so high and mighty. Would it kill the local pastors to publicly get jiggy with it once in awhile? (I still have no idea what that means.) As long as I am not coveting my neighbor's wife's @ss, or coveting the @ss of my wife's neighbor, does it matter if the local clergy think my brain is up my @ss?

Social conservatives have to stop being so incredibly intolerant of everybody around them. If they believe we should love our neighbors, who am I to say that love should not begin with a Marvin Gaye or Barry White CD and end with a Jacuzzi romp?

I tried being a social conservative. It didn't work. If God wanted me to be chaste, he would not have brought Eva Longoria into this world. It is not my fault she prances around in her undies. Oh, and spare me the morality lecture about me being punished for my sins. I have already been punished enough. It is bad enough Eva Longoria is not sleeping with me ... but her lover is French. If social conservatives truly care, they should shame her into being chaste. Then maybe after I won the lottery financially, I can win the female lottery of her as well.

As I pray to God before bed, I say to him what I say to social conservatives. The phrase sounds meaningful when women say it to men, but idiotic in reverse ... what about my needs?

Okay, so I only have one need. As for true social conservatives ... perhaps I have been too hard on you. After all, I should like you. Given that you are true believers, that means you practice chastity, which eliminates some of my competition.

I have changed my mind. All men should become social conservatives and become chaste. Ladies, I am the only deviant left. Women, do not even think of becoming devoutly religious. Religion is evil. Let the men practice it. It is good for them.

May God bless us all, and may hot, barely legal Catholic schoolgirls continue to rebel. If God truly supported chastity, people would not call out his name when having sex. Amen.

eric

Chapter 8: The National Football League

The only reason God does not watch the NFL is because he already knows the score. Some ask if God can make a rock that even he can't lift. I want to know if God can create a game where he cannot know the score. After all, what is the point of absolute power and authority if one cannot enjoy their own creation?

I thank God for making me Jewish. Let the Christians be in church during kickoff. This Hebrew knows that the Lord wanted me to rest on Sunday watching football.

For those who do not know their Old Testament stories, the NFL actually proves God's existence. Those who disagree are either ignorant of God or football. Either way, they are heretics.

The National Football League—Why Football Matters

In April, the National Football League reveals its schedule for the upcoming season. Shortly after that comes the drafting of players, and several months later an actual game is played. At some point an 0-6 team will go on the road and shock a 6-0 team in front of their home fans. ESPN uber-announcer Chris Berman will look into the camera and say "That's ... why they play the games."[48] On any given Sunday, competitive balance provides hope for thrilling upsets.

Thrilling as those moments are, the real NFL is the one that contributes to the betterment of society as a whole. On September 11, 2001, life was temporarily brought to a standstill. The stock market had to decide when to reopen. Television comics had to decide when to go and be funny. (Jay Leno and others all waited for David Letterman to decide how to proceed.) The sports world turned to Commissioner Paul Tagliabue to decide when and if games should be played. Former Commissioner Pete Rozelle claimed that his worst decision was allowing NFL games to be played two days after JFK was shot. Paul Tagliabue gave the league one week off and then had games resume a week later. What transpired was sheer beauty.

American flags were everywhere. Fans cheered players from opposing teams. Yet despite their being thirty-two teams in the NFL, many fans were fixated on the New York Giants. The Giants (and Jets) had to pass Ground Zero every day on the way to practice. Yet instead of feeling guilty for playing a game while the NYPD and FDNY were suffering, they felt emboldened. This was mainly because New York's bravest and finest wanted the Giants to play, and play hard. The Giants went into Kansas City (a difficult stadium to play in for road teams) and beat a good Chiefs team 13-3. It was the emotion of their defense that won that game. As the players knelt in prayer after the game ended and hugged each other, the New York Giants for three brief hours carried an entire state on its backs and across the goal line. While not a victory over Al Qaeda, it was a victory for the American spirit that the game was played. As every NY Giant defender pounded the KC quarterback to the ground, one wondered if the FDNY and NYPD heroes pictured Al Qaeda getting sacked.

When Hurricane Katrina struck, New Orleans was devastated. The NFL came to the rescue. First they donated $1 million right off the bat. Then they realized that the players in New Orleans who lost their homes could be a force for good. One player took residents of the city on shopping sprees. One gentleman who had a job interview the next day bought $250 worth of clothing, including a nice new suit. People were given a sense of hope. In the first week of that season, the New Orleans Saints traveled to Carolina to play the Panthers, a team many (correctly) regarded as a Super Bowl contender. Before the game, a blood drive was held, and the people of the Carolinas donated in abundance to their Louisiana brethren. On the last play of the game, the Saints won 23-20. It was the upset of the year. It did not fix the city, but for people trapped in the Superdome, it was a three-hour respite.

One year later, the Superdome used to house those devastated by Katrina was finally ready to host a football game again. The Saints were hosting the Atlanta Falcons, at the time regarded to be an elite team. Before the game started, a preacher gave a fire and brimstone speech of determination and resolve. "In spite of flood waters, in spite of plumbing that doesn't work, in spite of it all … we are still here. We are still here. We are still here." This was followed by a rousing rendition of "When the Saints Go Marching in."[49] The crowd went crazy. This was not just a football game. It was a city announcing to the entire nation that they were ready to compete, and compete hard. Then the game started. Ninety seconds into it, the Falcons lined up to punt, and the Saints smashed through the line and blocked it for a touchdown. Just like that, 7-0 Saints. Before that moment, guys named Gleason and DeLoach would not be recognized on the street. Then in a flash, they had created the best blocked punt in football history and one of the greatest moments in all of sports. The Saints won the game 23-3, but the real victory was after the game. For an hour, the fans would not leave the stadium. Neither would the players. The players did laps around the field high-fiving as many fans as possible. The Saints came marching in, and they were here to stay.

To see a good, decent man like Tony Dungy win a Super Bowl so soon after suffering the worst tragedy any parent can face (the suicide of his son) makes me believe that somewhere out there, a lot of what is good and right in this world does matter. To see glowing obituaries of Eddie Robinson (May God bless you in heaven, Coach) for his fifty-five years at Grambling shows that when done right, teaching football can be a way of teaching the values that make for a better life.

Football is more than just hard hits. It is about loyalty, teamwork, and getting up after repeatedly getting knocked to the ground bloody, battered, and bruised. One feminist writer said that to understand men, one had to understand football. To understand life, one had to play football.

At some point in the future of America, there will be more tough times … perhaps even tragedies. As long as there is a National Football League, I believe that a very small percentage of that pain will be reduced for enough people to make it a relevant healing. While the Super Bowl is for the championship, and the Pro Bowl showcases the best players, it is the games after 9/11 and Katrina that give the NFL, and football in general, its noble legacy.

I eagerly await the schedule of the next season. With even greater eagerness, I await the first kickoff of the first game in September. No matter what challenges we face in life, we can meet them. We are Americans. We are led by real heroes, such as firefighters, police officers, and EMTs. Those heroes, in their darkest days, turned to football.

THAT is why they play the games. That is why I watch the games.

May God bless the USA and the NFL.

eric

Successful Socialism

For those who do not know, I have always preached that socialism is a colossal failure, and that capitalism is a spectacular glorious success. Capitalism creates and spreads wealth, and socialism creates and spreads misery.

The pilgrims experimented with socialism in the 1600s. It failed. They then tried capitalism, and lo and behold, it worked. This has been the case with both philosophies in the ensuing four hundred years.

Yet I am forced to admit by the overwhelming evidence in front of me that there is one aspect of society where socialism has succeeded. The National Football League is a socialist model, and it works.

Former Cleveland Browns and Baltimore Ravens Owner Art Modell once remarked that the NFL owners were "Thirty-two Republicans who vote socialist." He also ruefully remarked that, "The president can bomb a nation with a simple majority, but NFL Owners need a three-fourths majority to go to the john."[50]

One does not need to understand anything about football itself to understand the NFL business model.

First of all, the league has a unique revenue sharing arrangement. Revenues from the ticket sales to games are split equally between all thirty-two teams. Additionally, the NFL makes most of its money not from game attendance, but from television. The NFL has a multibillion dollar television contract. That is also split thirty-two equal ways.

The ramification of revenue sharing is that small market franchises such as the Green Bay Packers can compete with large market franchises such as the New York Giants.

There are some chinks developing in this model, but they are being dealt with. Revenue from luxury boxes is not shared equally, but in due time every franchise will have luxury boxes, nullifying that advantage. Also, some franchises, such as the New England Patriots and Dallas Cowboys, have owners who own not only their teams, but the stadiums those teams play in. This is critical with regards to advertising revenue. If the NFL has an official contract making Coca-Cola the official league beverage, no team can promote Pepsi. However, while Jerry Jones as the owner of the Dallas Cowboys cannot promote Pepsi, Jerry Jones as the owner of Texas Stadium can.

However, even if some owners make more than others, the NFL has one other element of socialism that works: a hard salary cap. Each team is allowed to spend the exact same amount on players. There is a minimum that must be spent, since some owners would prefer to field losing teams in order to line their pockets. The minimum forces them to try and compete. The maximum forces teams to make hard choices. Individual players can still earn astronomical salaries, but at the expense of their teammates. The term "capanomics" refers to teams that try to temporarily circumvent the cap using creative accounting methods. When that credit card bill comes due, teams have a fire sale known as "salary cap hell."

Major League Baseball is raw capitalism. Several years ago, the New York Yankees had a player payroll of $200 million. The Montreal Expos had a player payroll of $9 million. You read that correctly. Why should someone play for $1 million for the Expos when the Yankees would pay $20 million? The result is that the Yankees are perennial contenders for a championship, and the Expos now cease to exist.

The main issue then becomes why this is all relevant. How can one endorse capitalism in business yet endorse socialism in professional sports? Isn't this hypocritical?

No. The ultimate goal is successful ventures. One cannot have liberty and equality. They directly conflict. In American society, especially in business, liberty is the key. The profit motive is a powerful incentive. People do not want to work harder unless they believe they will be rewarded more. If I can get the same pay as my neighbor for doing less work, perhaps personal pride or ego would allow me to work hard. However, if I choose the lazy route, my neighbor has no recourse.

In professional sports, equality is the key to success. Some mistake the NFL for being obsessed with parity, aka mediocrity. The correct phrase is competitive balance, not parity. Parity would mean having each team finish around 8-8. This is the type of socialism that destroys most societies. Competitive balance is what brings the phrase "any given Sunday" into the American lexicon. An 0-6 team can go on the road and defeat a 6-0 team. Every week in the NFL something like this happens. The 1998 Rams went 4-12. The 1999 Rams won the Super Bowl. The irregular becomes the regular in the NFL. Mismatches on paper become shocking upsets, as ESPN uber-announcer Chris Berman reminds us that, "That's why they play the games."

So why can't the rest of the world take socialism and make it work the way the NFL has?

The answer is that the world does not have an undisputed governing body to enforce regulations and punish cheaters. It is why the Kyoto treaty went down in flames, and why the European Union, filled with socialist nations, is failing. Stronger nations do not want to be dragged down by weaker nations. One can argue that stronger nations could lift up weaker nations, but if even socialist countries do not believe this will work, what does that say about socialism itself?

The NFL has two powerful elements. The first is labor peace. The unions and management work together on many issues. There has not been a work stoppage in two decades. Gene Upshaw, the (late) head of the NFL Players Association, often testified side by side with the NFL commissioner on league matters. They socialize together. Brinksmanship is rare, and getting a deal done to ensure labor peace is paramount. It helps that the revenue sharing agreement forces owners to be united. Contrast this with baseball. The owners have incentives to cheat each other, so they do. Negotiations between players and owners makes Fallujah look like a walk in the park.

The second element of the NFL is a strong commissioner. For the last four decades, from Pete Rozelle to Paul Tagliabue to Roger Goodell, the NFL has had a commissioner whose word was and is law. Any player or owner that breaks the rules is punished, often severely. Michael Vick was one of the greatest players in the league. He broke the rules and was suspended from the game. Bill Bellichick is one of the greatest coaches in the league. He broke the rules and was fined and docked draft picks. Nobody is above the game of football itself. Some would consider the commissioner authoritarian, but the leader of the NFL can be fired. Also, the leader of the NFL cannot use the military to crush dissention.

The main reason socialism fails is because for it to succeed, everybody in the collective must buy into it. Money and other perks are given up in the present for brighter future days. Since past experiences prove this brighter future to be a fraud, skepticism sets in as people begin to see the benefits of cheating. Collectivism failed in the past, so people believe it will fail in the future. Therefore it is sabotaged in the present. To try and ask people to ignore history and have blind faith in a system that has never succeeded is to ask people to go against human nature.

However, the NFL has a history of financial success. Owners may grumble from time to time about sharing revenues, but deep down they all believe in the system. There is simply so much wealth that the idea of jeopardizing that golden goose is heresy to owners that even briefly consider it.

The only criteria in judging a system should be results. Intentions are worthless. Results, in the form of metrics, are what matter.

The world should embrace capitalism because it works. It is often described as the worst system except for every other one. It is why France, Germany, China, and virtually every other nation previously mired in economic stagnation, bureaucracy, and mediocrity wants to try some form of American-style capitalism.

Capitalism should be the order of the day in business because it has succeeded where socialism has failed, which is virtually everywhere. Where liberty is paramount, which is again virtually everywhere, socialism should be reduced to the ash heap of history.

May the National Football League be the one place on earth where socialism is allowed to reign supreme, because it is the one place where equality is the desired result, rendering the universally disgraced philosophy a complete success.

eric

Tony Romo—Pay Attention, Children

I have said on many occasions that every life lesson a parent could teach their child can be gleaned from football. No, it is not life and death. Yes, it is a game. Yet in terms of inspiration, I want children one hundred years from now to watch a copy of the Monday Night Football game between the Dallas Cowboys and the Buffalo Bills. I want them to learn about a twenty-three-year-old kid named Tony Romo, the Dallas Cowboys quarterback.

The Cowboys were on the verge of defeating the Seattle Seahawks in a playoff game. All they had to do was kick a twenty-three yard field goal. Then the unthinkable happened. Tony Romo fumbled the snap. He tried to pick the ball up and make a play. He almost did. Yet he didn't. Seattle won the game, Dallas was done, and sports had a new goat. Anybody can have character when times are good. Romo showed character. He went to the press conference rather than hide from the media. He promised to erase the memory of this blunder.

Fast forwarding several months, Romo brought the 4-0 Cowboys into a Monday Night Football game against the Buffalo Bills. On a national stage, Romo had one of the most nightmarish games in NFL history. He had four interceptions in the first half alone. Two of them were returned for touchdowns. A kickoff return for a touchdown had Buffalo up 24-13 in the fourth quarter. After cutting the gap to 24-16, Romo had a golden opportunity to redeem himself. Deep in Buffalo territory, he then … threw a fifth interception.

Yet Buffalo failed to capitalize. So Romo was given yet another chance. He drove Dallas down the field. A touchdown pass with only twenty seconds left cut the gap to 24-22. A two-point conversion would tie the game. Yet it didn't happen, and it appeared Dallas was done. However, a perfectly executed onsides kick followed by a couple perfect Romo passes led to a fifty-two yard field goal as time ran out. Two scores in twenty seconds resulted in a 25-24 Dallas shocker.

I hope that people who never grasp football can teach their children why the result of this game is relevant. The lessons are so obvious, but even the obvious can be obscured in a world of negativity.

Lesson number one is that failure is acceptable. Human beings fail. It is what makes us human. Accepting failure is what is not acceptable. Yes, this game had a happy ending, but if it did not, Romo would try again next week. He failed last year, and he came back.

Every person I know has either failed at a job, a marriage, rearing a child, or trying to do what they were simply not able to do. They were not losers, but they lost. For those who lose a job, it is bad, but not as bad as losing a marriage. For those who have lost a marriage, it is horrendous, but not as bad as losing a life.

When we wake up in the morning, we are not dead. By definition alone, we have life. We have a chance. We all lose sight of this. I know I do. Heck, I lose perspective when a slow driver in front of me causes me not to beat a traffic light that turns red. I get angrier when that one car at that one light causes me to get to work at 9:01AM instead of 8:59AM.

Yet life is a series of knockdowns. Some people are blind. Others are deaf or confined to wheelchairs. Yet I worry about being short and wearing glasses.

My father is a Holocaust survivor. He spent the first four years of his life being shot at. Needless to say, my having trouble in social studies class was not the end of the world.

This should not minimize others who feel pain. Telling paraplegics to be happy that they are not quadriplegics is not the answer. The solution is to lift people up, and give them the ability to lift themselves up.

Although I am not a baseball fan, two games stand clear in my mind. The Yankees had their season end at the hands of the Cleveland Indians. Yankee Manager Joe Torre, who is about to be fired after every game for twelve years, might be fired for real this time. One of his last gestures was to tell the losing pitcher that losing one game did not invalidate all the great things that happened during the season. The team lost, but they were not losers.

Another game had an ending that should never happen. In 1986, the California Angels were on the verge of defeating the Boston Red Sox for the right to go to the World Series. Angel pitcher Donnie Moore then threw the pitch that the Red Sox turned into the winning home run. The Red Sox won the Series, and the Angels were done. Then the nightmare scenario developed.

Donnie Moore was soon out of baseball. He fell into financial trouble. Within three years of almost reaching the pinnacle of success, he committed suicide.

Life should never have to be that way. Human beings ... all human beings ... are too important to have even one of them waste away. We are creatures of God. A piece of God dies when we do.

Life can leave us black and blue. Sometimes we feel like there is nothing but pain and misery. Yet some of my best moments in life have followed those black clouds. Losing a job and being nearly broke was followed by getting an even better job. A painful breakup was followed by meeting a woman I was much happier with.

I have said many times I have been lucky. Yes, being lucky helps. Yet so does digging deep down inside of us. Human beings often have time to pick themselves up. Football players do not have such luxuries. A quarterback that gets belted to the ground has about forty seconds to be ready for the next play.

Yes, Tony Romo led a heroic comeback. However, had his comeback attempt failed he would still be a human being that matters. Romo said last year that if the worst thing to ever happen to him would be losing a game, he would have led a good life.

If he means that, he is luckier and more well-grounded than most.

I know that in the future, I will fail at things. I also know that I have a great family and great friends. I will try not to let them down, and hope they do not let me down. Yet if any of us do, the lifting back up will be vital. If we do not, our children will suffer.

Children already have it rough. For one thing, public schools are a haven for making sure that children suffer. Some kids are fat, others are funny looking. They are all one bad experience away from slipping through the cracks. As time goes by, to quote rocker Bret Michaels of Poison, "It just makes me wonder why so many lose and so few win. Give me something to believe in."[51]

I do believe in something. I believe in the dignity and resilience of the human spirit.

I also believe that lessons can be learned in unlikely places. One motivational speaker took a $100 bill, crumpled it up, stepped it on it, and mashed it. He then asked the audience if anybody still wanted it. They all did. Why? Because even crumpled up and nearly tattered, it still had value. It had worth.

So do we.

Tony Romo did not save the world. He did not win the War on Terror, cure cancer, or save a drowning animal.

What he did was fail repeatedly and refuse to allow his failures to define him. He got up off of the mat and eventually flourished. Beyond the score of the game, if one child gives one last extra effort in anything, whether it be a school paper or a sporting event, Tony Romo will have given a life lesson worth emulating.

Somebody buy Tony Romo a beverage. Then somebody make as many copies of this football game as possible, and let young kids know what they are capable of when they dig down deep and reach their God-given potential.

eric

Detroit—Arabs, Automobiles and Awful Football

When a relative of mine told me they were going to Detroit en route to China, they expressed concern to me about arriving to an unknown place filled with crime, lawlessness, and danger. When I replied that China is the most capitalist communist country around, my relative shot back, "I am not talking about China, I am talking about Detroit. We will feel safe once we get to China."

When I look at Detroit, I see a city that represents successes and failures that are directly related to the human condition. As a Jewish person, I see Detroit as a city filled with Arabs. It is impossible for me to see Arabs without seeing the Arab-Israeli conflict. My religion is a powerful lens that I look through. No viewing glasses on the world stage are rose colored. I say this because like many, I want to know why Arabs in the Middle East are such a colossal failure when their brethren in Detroit are such an overwhelming success. In seeing why Arabs are a Detroit success story, a parallel can be made to Detroit's biggest spectacular failure … a once proud success … the automobile industry.

In the 1980s, the Japanese were supposedly buying everything in sight. Despite the fact that American television shows such as *Dallas* and *Dynasty* reflected an American mentality that was often mimicked on Wall Street by Michael Milken and Ivan Boesky, somehow Japanese people were not supposed to have the same desire to buy, sell, and spend as we Americans did. As GM, Ford, and Chrysler began bleeding dollars, Toyota and other Japanese carmakers began thriving. Politicians spoke of tariffs, quotas, and other protectionist measures. As a fourteen-year old I enraged a room when I meekly asked a simple question. "Why don't Americans just make better cars?"

That was a day when the idea of "free speech" was a myth. I uttered the unthinkable. I have never thought that Americans were stupid, lazy slackers. We are not French. We never will be. Yet if we are consistently losing in a battle we used to win, isn't it healthy to reevaluate where we slipped off track?

This brings us to the Middle East. Arabs are at the bottom of many world categories, and they used to be at the top. They were the best and brightest. They made valuable contributions to mathematics, science, medicine, and literature. They had the strongest military. Then everything changed. The Arab empire fell. Why? Well for one reason, all empires fall. The Crusades happened. The European Christians beat the Arabs, and beat them decisively. The Arabs were humiliated. They then had two choices: (1) How can we fix ourselves and get back to number one again? (2) Who can we blame?

Regrettably, the Arabs chose option two. For the last thousand years, they have blamed others. America is the "Great Satan." Israel is "Little Satan." Some Arab nations treat beating their women as a spectator sport. Non-Arab Muslims are "Infidels." Education is reserved for the rich and powerful, and almost never for women. Beheadings are practiced routinely.

This brings us back to Detroit. The Arabs in Detroit are the best and brightest. They are educated and successful. They have strong, thriving communities and are gaining political influence. Spencer Abraham, a proud Arab-American, became a U.S. Senator before becoming the U.S. Secretary of Energy. They prefer living under U.S. law to Sharia law because they see the difference in results.

This circles back to football. Football works because it is based on results. Nobody cares about race, religion, or ethnic backgrounds. The bottom line is winning on Sunday. The NFL has thirty-two mini-empires, and they rise and fall as all empires do. In 2002, the Oakland Raiders were in the Super Bowl, and the Chicago Bears were near the bottom of the barrel. By 2006, the Bears were in the Super Bowl, and the Raiders were in ruins. Most teams make adjustments. Yet the Detroit Lions are consistently NFL cellar-dwellers. Is there something in the uniforms that makes them significantly worse? They play by the same rules as the other teams. Yet year after year, the losses mount.

I do not know, nor do I care, how to fix the Detroit Lions. What I do know is that if everyone around you is doing better under the same system, then you are doing something wrong. Admitting weaknesses and flaws is not weak … it is a sign of strength, which leads to prosperity and growth.

If we combine the best of Detroit with the best of the Arabs, we see that anything is possible. Middle Easterners are not inferior to Americans. Americans are not inferior to the Japanese. Once people stop focusing on excuses and start focusing on results, positive change can occur.

The Arabs have a billion spots of human capital. India and China have leveraged theirs, and improved their world standing. If the blame game would stop, Arab Muslims in the Middle East could join the family of nations. The United States can be number one again in the global automobile market.

Dare I say it … the Detroit Lions could … well, one dream at a time.

eric

My Interview With Lynn Swann

I had the pleasure of interviewing NFL Hall of Fame wide receiver and Pennsylvania gubernatorial candidate Lynn Swann of the Pittsburgh Steelers. I asked him several questions about politics, before shifting to football.

1) What are the most important issues of 2008?

LS: "Leadership, the economy, the environment, and the capability to lead the defense of our nation. John McCain has the leadership experience."

2) Who are your three favorite political heroes?

LS: "Martin Luther King Jr., Ronald Reagan, and Governor Tom Ridge."

3) How would you like to be remembered one hundred years from now? What would you want people to say about Lynn Swann the person?

LS: "I'm honestly not sure. I don't know."

4) Mike Tomlin is doing a solid job as coach of the Steelers. Art Rooney (the late Steelers owner) created the Rooney rule (mandating teams interview minority coaches) that has helped the NFL discover talent like Coach Tomlin. Do you support the Rooney rule?

LS: "I do support the Rooney rule. I support it for the right of all in the league to have equitable opportunities. It has served the NFL well."

5) Regarding one of the biggest scandals in American history ... isn't it true that Frenchy Fuqua touched that football and not Jack Tatum? Can we finally get to the bottom of the Immaculate Reception?

LS: "Even with instant replay, that call would still stand today. There is simply not enough evidence to overturn the call. Instant replay would let the call stand."

6) Could the Steelers of the 1970s in their current condition defeat the Raiders of today? As you can tell, I am a Raiders fan.

LS: "Those were some of the great games of all time, and the toughest guys we played. They would say the same about us. The competition was fierce. If you were to set up a rematch between those Steelers and the Raiders, from the 1970s or whenever ... the guys would throw down their crutches ... and get out of their wheelchairs ... to play that game."

Lynn Swann is an incredibly nice guy, and he pointed out to those around him that he was even nice to Raiders fans. He is a class act all the way, but with all due respect for Mr. Swann, I still believe it was Frenchy Fuqua who touched that football.

eric

Chapter 9: Political Nonsense

Now that the minorities of the world have finally wrested power from the PBWGs (Powerful Bald White Guys), the PBWGs will be striking back. While I still suspect that Ben Bernanke and Henry Paulson are the same person, and that the top guys on *Law and Order* are more generic than American cheese, watching the PBWGs riot in the streets would be fun.

Life is too short. So before the next crisis hits, we can debate the political issue that those on my couch argue about during the game:

Is C3PO gay?

For those in California rioting over Proposition 8, be careful how you answer. Robots are people too, and when robots riot, humanoids tremble. The only thing worse would be a PBWG robot.

Enough about Alan Greenspan. Economic issues were covered three chapters ago.

Fear of the Follically Challenged

There was a shooting in Illinois. People will make pious pronouncements, and then the story will fade.

The Wisconsin primary is in four days. Wake me up in three days, twenty-three hours.

Football season is over, and the Daytona 500 has nothing to do with football.

The writers' strike ended. This is sad, but not news.

President's Day could be an uplifting column about the founding fathers.

I guess what I am saying is that my column, which usually contributes nothing to decent society, will offer even less today.

No, I will not be doing recaps of episodes of the *Celebrity Apprentice*, but it is time to go back to the intellect that springs from my couch.

The guys and I were sitting around discussing the issues, and we had already exhausted the topics of C3PO and *Fraggle Rock*. While Valentine's Day would be a great day to debate whether or not lap dancing is cheating, that can wait until next year.

We are in the thick of a presidential race, and I am deeply concerned that discrimination and bigotry will guide people. Sure, people claim they are open minded, saying all the right things when pollsters call. Yet when nobody is looking, will they truly have the courage to stop the discrimination against follically challenged Americans?

It is time for a bald president.

(In the modern era; Dwight Eisenhower was before television was everything.)

Rudy Giuliani turned around New York City. He was amazing on 9/11. Yet Americans turned away from him. They looked deeper at him and concluded, sadly but accurately, "He's bald."

Fred Thompson was warm and cuddly, but all people talked about was frying an egg on top of that gleaming cue ball. Oh, and his wife was hot as well.

Jim Gilmore ran for president, although most people outside his family do not remember this. He was from Virginia. His platform? I forget. I just took one look at him and said, "He's bald."

This discrimination has to stop.

The Republican Party's best chance for winning the election on pure handsomeness went down the drain when Mitt Romney dropped out.

Unlike the Republican Party big tent, the Democrats are as exclusionary as it gets. Barack Obama? Sure, he has funny ears, but so did Ross Perot. His crop on top is fine.

Hillary Clinton? No evidence exists that her hair is a weave. She is also married to Bill Clinton. He may not do anything with dignity or grace, but in terms of aging, he is a swan.

John Edwards? I will never be as pretty as that man, and I am pretty d@ng pretty.

The Democrats are elitist Hollywood snobs. Unless you are straight out of central casting, you are banned from the stage.

Republicans even allowed a man with a full beard and top hat to lead them. His birthday is this month, although he shares it now with a fellow who wore a white wig. The bottom line is that Republicans are the physical egalitarians.

Is actor Roscoe Lee Browne a Republican? If so, he can be vice president. He is black, bald, and charismatic. He might also be deceased, so this suggestion is pending his currently actually existing.

Telly Savalas can be attorney general, if Fred Thompson is unavailable.

The fear of the follically challenged must stop. They are people, they are among us, and they are demanding their place at the table.

This is just another reason to support John McCain.

I see the tide turning. At least 70–80 percent of the Republican electorate supported follically challenged candidates. This is a mandate.

I am just trying to prevent riots in the streets. When fat, bald, white men in their fifties start storming the American equivalent of whatever a Bastille is, watch out.

No longer should men have to go underground and remain in the closet. David Letterman makes $30 million per year, and society has him wearing a toupee. Despite encouragement from Dr. Phil, Letterman will not join him and ditch the dishrag.

John Kerry claimed his band of brothers, but what is fighting with people in a war when they are jealous of your perfect mane?

John McCain is an American hero. He was tortured at the Hanoi Hilton for five-and-a-half years. They broke his ribs and fractured his arms and legs. They also shaved his head. Perhaps this is why he is against torture. Nobody should have their head shaved. To compound the pain, his captors grew thick beards.

Whether it be Al Qaeda or the Taliban, in between bouts of terrorism, these men are growing excess hair. How dare they mock male pattern baldness! That is un-American. These savages must be stopped.

John McCain gave his hair for his country. His follicles are probably still in that Vietnamese prison.

I am lucky enough as of this column to have a full head of spectacular hair. I am not Mitt Romney or John Edwards, but I am handsomer than the average bear.

Yet some of the people that have provided me with some of the best things in my life were follically challenged. I owe them my support.

Blind people have eye doctors. Deaf people can be given hearing aids. Fat people can diet or have liposuction.

There is no cure for the follically challenged.

Somebody must defend them. Otherwise, if we lose our hair, nobody will be left to speak up for us.

Jim Gilmore, Fred Thompson, and Rudy Giuliani had accomplishments. The American people did not care. The Democrats were busy deciding between three perfectly coiffed individuals that had perfect hair and nothing else.

So I say turn up the radios, let the Cowsills sing, "Flow it there, show it there, long, beautiful, my hair,"[52] and pay homage to those who lack what we still hold dear.

John McCain is tested. He will not fear terrorists, even ones that have excess hair.

So before we go to the polls in November, I shall leave you with the chant that caused my team to lose "Color War" at summer camp back in 1980. We were ahead by two-and-a-half points, and a five-point penalty cost us the championship. The unit head did not find it funny. Instead of penalizing us for our chant, he should have worn it like a badge of honor.

Bald is beautiful.

Let the chrome domes roam. Vote for John McCain.

eric

C3PO, Fraggle Rock, and the Log Cabin Republicans

With all the serious events going on in this world, sometimes it is necessary to just step back and think about all those other things that only people with too much free time on their hands think about.

My friends and I have debated the issue back and forth, and still there is only theory. So I will ask the world what they think, and offer my own opinions. Is C3PO a homosexual?

I maintain that he is gay, but one of my friends insists that he is just British. Even by British standards, C3PO is too British. Another friend posits that robots cannot be gay, but robots everywhere from the Tin Man in the Wizard of Oz to Deep Blue, the machine that defeated Gary Kasparov in chess, have developed human characteristics. Therefore, it is fair to argue that 10 percent of robots are homosexual.

I never found R2D2 to be gay. In fact, I always suspected R2D2 was a Republican. He kept his mouth shut, and minded his own business. C3PO was a liberal busybody. Yet something did not sit right. Republicans usually make sense, and R2D2 was incoherent. On the other hand, boxing promoter Don King makes even less sense, and he is a Republican. So if R2D2 is a liberal speaking in tongues no normal person can understand, then perhaps C3PO is the Republican, since he is always preaching responsibility.

C3PO does not dress well enough to be a metrosexual, so between his prissiness and his preaching responsibility, C3PO is most likely a Log Cabin Republican.

The guys and I are considering this compromise analysis, but we are worlds apart on how to evaluate *Fraggle Rock*. For those who grew up in the 1980s, allow the following theme song to stick in your head.

"Dance your cares away/worries for another day/let the music play/down in *Fraggle Rock*/down in *Fraggle Rock*."[53]

I always thought that the Fraggles were liberals. They frolicked around, lived irresponsible lives, and contributed nothing useful to society. The Doozers were the conservative Republicans. They worked hard, played by the rules, and were often bullied by the Fraggles for having the nerve to be productive.

Yet the reason my friends are so brilliant is because they crystallize things in a way I sometimes fail to see. The Doozers were the Democrats. They worked, but they were always pessimistic. Their work was hard but meaningless. They were the lower class, miserable about their lot in life, forever destined to be Doozers. They had nothing to dream about. The Fraggles were carefree and optimistic. They saw a happy world filled with promise. They just wanted the Doozers to lighten up and chill out, and have fun for once in their depressing lives.

Some would argue that the Doozers were illegal aliens, doing the grunt work that Fraggles refused to do. However, the Doozers never snuck into Fraggle territory. If anything, the Fraggles were the ones that did not respect boundaries.

The one character that forever provides confusion is the green Fraggle, Wembley. Wembley was not gay, despite being named after a British stadium. One episode had the indecisive Wembley meeting a very decisive character known as Convincing John. Some would see the wishy-washy Wembley perhaps as John Kerry, with Convincing John the decider being George W. Bush. However, in the end, Convincing John's inability to see that he might be wrong leads him down the wrong path, and Wembley's careful deliberations make him stronger. Therefore, Wembley is the American people, making the difficult but right decisions. Convincing John is so positive he is right that when proven wrong he cannot admit it. He is the media, most likely the *Jayson Blair Times*.

We live in a world with Islamofacism, where large segments of people are trying to murder others just for existing. There is plenty of time to deal with this sad reality. Meanwhile, there are other issues to deal with. They are less serious, but without discussing them, water coolers will be lonely places during the week.

So as my friends prepare to go hang out, one lingering question still remains. Could C3PO take Wembley in a fistfight? A robot vs. a Fraggle. Like many burning issues, I have no answers.

eric

Rosie, Scooter, Dubya, and Monique—Huh?

Rosie, Scooter, Dubya, and Monique. Some people will ask, "How is he going to tie them together? This I would like to see." The answer is, maybe I will not. I remember in college reading the sports column "Notes on a Scoreboard,"[54] by the late Alan Malamud. Like a *Seinfeld* episode, by the time Malamud was done, all the random comments somehow ended up tied up in a nice little bow. There are so many things going on in the news lately, that rather than give each issue a thoughtful column, I figured a slightly less than half-@ssed stab at each issue may add up to slightly less than a complete quality column.

The first issue concerns Rosie O'Donnell. Rosie is the descendant of a man born in Belfast, Northern Ireland. Rosie frequently mentioned her heritage when she was a VJ on VH1, which for young people is what happens when MTV decides you are no longer cool. There is no evidence that Rosie was ever active in causes involving the Irish Republican Army, their political wing Sinn Fein, or the Northern Ireland Protestants opposing them. Her politics are strictly American leftism.

There is also no evidence that she has ever taken a position on the Israeli vs. Palestinian conflict, until recently. She dressed her child up as a homicide bomber. I thought she was anti-gun. No matter. The dots are now connected. She has Northern Ireland in her blood, her kid dressed as a homicide bomber, and this week, bombs went off in London, England, and Glasgow, Scotland. Somebody needs to get Scotland Yard on the telephone immediately. Rosie should be jailed, tried, and convicted. How dare she try to blow up Scotland!

Flimsy evidence? Evidence, schmevidence. This brings us to Scooter Libby. In a world where Bill Clinton and Sandy Berger run free, Scooter almost went to prison. First of all, the fact that his nickname was a character on the Muppet Show is an old and tired joke. Secondly, the guy got Nifonged, meaning his crimes consisted of being Caucasian, wealthy, and politically incorrect. This is how William "90 thousand in the freezer" Jefferson avoids receiving a jail sentence (as of now), but Scooter Libby does not.

We might as well just jail every Republican for existing. Thankfully, President Bush commuted his sentence. While I generally support Dubya, my one continuing objection to him is his overwhelming graciousness with political enemies that are not fit to lick his boots. Stop being so polite, Mr. President. Hold a press conference, and drop a couple F-bombs like Vice President Cheney did. Here is what I would say.

"I commuted Scooter Libby's sentence. I did so because I can. For those who object, I am the president and you're not. Deal with it. My predecessor pardoned people for sport and for contributions to his stained library. I did it because it was the right thing to do. This may anger the *Jayson Blair Times*, but then again, water is wet. Get over it."

The pardoning of Scooter Libby is also a brilliant political move. The Clintons will not dare make it a campaign issue (Let them try mentioning Rudy Giuliani, John McCain, or Fred Thompson's issues with the ladies). It is not possible to get everyone to like you, but it is possible to make everyone hate you. Bush's critics always hate him, but lately his base has been demoralized. A commutation helps, and will be long forgotten come 2008. Nobody cares about Scooter Libby. They care about Iraq and the War on Terror.

Before I elaborate on that, the politically irrelevant fact of the week is the appearance that Hillary Clinton is putting on weight. This does not bother me. I have as well. Maybe my vision is bad, but it seems she is getting thick in the backside. I believe Dave Chapelle calls that a "badonkadonk."[55] I am not saying Hillary is anywhere near approaching Monique from *Showtime at the Apollo*[56] (who I seem to have an unhealthy fascination with), but Hillary is getting some chunk in the trunk.

This could be an issue, because Americans have a certain image of a president. We do not want them fat or bald (What does this mean for Rudy and Fred?). We do not want them to smoke, the only potential weakness for the otherwise platinum image of Barack Obama. Also, for those who are unaware, Barack Obama is partially black. He is also handsome, and looks good in a swimsuit. Heck, sign me up!

The delicious irony of Obama vs. Hillary is that Hillary runs well among blacks because of Bill Clinton, while Obama runs well among guilty white liberals who want to vote for someone black so they can feel good about themselves. They are the "good" kind of whites, not the bad kind who become Republicans. Why not support Condoleeza Rice or Colin Powell? Because they are not "authentically" black. They are not liberal.

Folks, Barack Obama is barely blacker than I am, and I am pasty white. The only person less black than Obama is Tiger Woods. I couldn't care less if Obama is purple, turquoise, or orange (actually I dislike orange for some reason), but voting for a man because of the color of his skin is … well … racist. I have nothing against Obama. His speech at the 2004 convention was one of the all-time great speeches, at least before we realized there was nothing beyond it.

So with Rosie O'Donnell trying to blow up airports, the president keeping Scooter out of the pokey, and Pokey's friend Gumby having nothing to do with this column, we need to get back to what is really important in life, that being the War on Terror.

On more than one occasion I have said that Iran and Syria need to be turned into 50 thousand hole golf courses. The Damascus Open should star Tiger (Woods, not me), Fuzzy (Zoeller, not Thurston), Hootie (Johnson, not Blowfish), and the rest of the hee-haw crowd that plays that boring game. After the course is built, we need to blow it up again. Why? Because I hate golf.

Mr. Malamud is rolling over in his grave at this attempt. Okay, no more disjointed columns. From now on only one world event is allowed to happen at a time.

Oh, and golf was invented in Scotland. There. A nice little bow.

eric

Chapter 10: The Right to Laugh and Sing

How many Jewish Republicans will publicly admit that they have a bizarre fascination with Monique from *Showtime at the Apollo*?

I just did. I can't help it. She is big and beautiful, and for some reason, it is always her birthday. Every time I watch the show she is singing that it is her birthday. She must be two hundred by now, which makes her one sexy bunny rabbit, assuming that bunny years are the same as dog years.

Around Easter time bunnies come in the form of dark chocolate. Don't even go there, girlfriend. Besides, until she comes on television and states her love for eating Kosher vanilla wafers, I will deny any elaboration.

I do not do weddings, bar mitzvahs, or windows, be it glass panes, 95, or XP.

Conservatives may not find this funny because their friends are in the room. Read this chapter alone.

Liberals may not find this funny because they are liberals.

I may not ever sing the *Body Electric*, but I do sing political songs, for worse or much worse.

My Performance at the Laugh Factory

I had the pleasure of being the opening act for conservative comedian Evan Sayet. The event took place at the famous Laugh Factory in Hollywood. Evan offered me some guidance, but did not censor me in any way.

While I am very relaxed in front of crowds, I am nervous before going on the stage. I just want to get it over with. Nevertheless, once finished, I sit down and relax.

Given a choice between succeeding and sucking, I prefer the former. Thankfully, the crowd gave me enthusiastic applause throughout my performance. I now pretend knowing they would. I told Evan that while I would be honored to do another set, I heard rumors that it needed to be new material. Apparently I cannot say the same stuff each time. I had better get cracking.

One very sad note is that the Laugh Factory did not allow videotaping this performance. On the one hand, I am not on YouTube, so my parents do not need to keep changing their last name and address any more. The downside is I still lack proof that some people out there find me as lovable as all people should.

I started with a bang and never let up. Below is my off-the-cuff routine.

"Guard the rails, because I am about to go off.

As the son of a Holocaust survivor, I don't sing 'Kumbaya' with people who want to kill me.

Being the son of a survivor does not make me a victim because my dad wins every argument. When I would tell him as a teenager that social studies class was too hard, he would ask, 'Did you get shot at this week?' The answer was no, at which point he would have me visit my room and open the books.

My parents live in South Florida and informed me that in 2000, world peace actually broke out. We are now at peace. After all, it was heartwarming to see fellow elderly Jewish Holocaust survivors have the courage to let bygones be bygones, put aside the past, and vote for Pat Buchanan.

My dad gave me strict instructions. 'Son, if your mother and I ever get to the point where we can't figure out a ballot ... or we are too feeble to push the thing through ... euthanize us; the house is yours.' I love my parents, but it is a nice house. That's why I walk around with a clipboard appraising things.

I see some Jews in the audience. Without pointing them out (I pretended to point at specific people), I just want to advise everybody that if you are going to speak to an audience that contains Jews, do not try to get to the event by using a Palestinian GPS tracker. I made a wrong turn, and ended up at a cemetery. I then heard a sinister voice tell me, 'You have reached your final destination!' I got so angry that I threw the GPS tracker out the window, which was good, because five seconds later it exploded.

The world is upside down. We now have a world where the president of France is more pro-American than half the people living in the United States. We live in a world where the leader of France wants to fight, and people wanting to lead America want to surrender. France is laughing at us because they want to act like us, and we are becoming them.

We live in a world where Israel is a mess because Ehud Olmert is a disaster. Things are upside down when Jews are fleeing Israel for a better quality of life for Jews by moving to Germany.

People are carping from the sidelines that we need to withdraw from Iraq. All I hear from Democrats is withdrawal, withdrawal, withdrawal. I wish they would apply that philosophy to their sex lives, then there would be fewer Democrats.

I am also tired of listening to Iranian President Armageddonijad. The solution is not dialogue. The solution is to take Iran and Syria and turn them into 50,000-hole golf courses.

I refuse to negotiate with a third world despot that is probably awake at 2:00 AM watching the Playboy Channel and dialing 976-B Triple A.

Regarding the war, when a war is lost, and there is no hope, we have a moral obligation to pull the troops out and not risk one more death on a senseless lost cause. Therefore, we must remove all police officers and other troops out of Detroit and deploy them to Iraq where they can actually make a difference.

I keep hearing about senseless killings and war zones. I have never been to Fallujah, but I have been to New York City public schools.

Liberals talk about not being able to secure the Anbar Province. They can't even secure Philadelphia.

(A romance with a woman renders her city off limits. This was communicated to me in a manner I understand. I would rather jokes be off limits than ever have her yummy bouncies be off limits.)

Liberals have no idea how to win a war on terror. They don't know Pakistanis from Afghanis. They would just arrest all guys with excessive beards. I could just picture them fighting the War on Terror. 'We've shut down two Chabad houses and arrested the members of ZZ Top. We are winning, everything is under control.'

We need to defeat liberalism, but we keep letting principles get in the way. Liberals can win because they ignore principles. We need to ignore principles, starting with abortion. A woman came up to me and said that she was tired of Republicans being against her right to an abortion. I told her, 'Have a thousand abortions. Join the abortion of the month club for all I care. Preach to your friends to have them as well.' She wondered why I was so tolerant, but folks, again, it goes back to how close the 2000 election was. Every vote counts. It will help us because the liberals will be the ones having most of the abortions. They are killing off their own voters. They are trying to commit legalized eugenics. We need to let them.

Then we can move on to gun control. Liberals favor it, and conservatives are against it. We should take the guns away from the liberals and give them to us. That way if there is ever a controversial election like 2000 that can't be resolved peacefully, we will win, because we will have all the guns.

Then we can move on to taxes. Liberals want higher taxes, and conservatives want lower taxes. Liberals also favor wealth redistribution. We should simply take money from them and give it to us. They can't stop us. After all, as I just said, we will have all the guns.

Then they will try and attack us on gay rights. Folks, I have no problem with gay men. Heck, they are doing me a favor by reducing my competition.

This tolerance does not extend to lesbians. Jesus hates them.

I guess I am just bitter. I don't know what I am doing wrong. Tammy Bruce still won't go out with me. I wish we could just take a page from Al Gore's carbon offsets and trade women. We could donate Roseanne Barr to the gay community in exchange for Tammy Bruce coming back to the straight side so that I can delude myself into thinking I have a shot.

I do have some good news. I have appointed myself the leader for black America today. After all, I am much more qualified than Jesse Jackson. I have done nothing, which is an improvement over Jesse. Zero beats a negative.

Jesse Jackson used the n-word. He should be banned from this club. (The owner of the Laugh Factory, in the wake of the Michael Richards scandal, banned use of the n-word. I totally support this) I never did.

Jesse Jackson threatened to cut off a black man's body parts. The only thing I want to cut from black men is their taxes.

Jesse Jackson is only threatening to do to Obama what Hillary wants to do to Bill every night because of Monica. Jesse Jackson is not an angry black man. He is an angry, jealous woman.

For those who think I can't represent the black leadership, I will offer a meaningless platitude in the great tradition of Barack Obama. 'It is wrong to judge a man's race by the color of his skin.' Therefore, anybody who says I can't represent black America just because of the color of my skin is a racist.

Another woman stirring up controversy is Michelle Obama. Some men see women like Michelle Obama, Hillary Clinton, and Oprah Winfrey, and are threatened. These women are uppity and need to tone it down. Other people see these strong, successful women as a sign of how much progress America has made and how far we have come. I see these women and think, 'Wow ... baby got back.'

Oh, like I am the only guy in this room that has fantasies about Monique from *Showtime at the Apollo*.

As for Barack Obama, I am proud of him. He has proven that a black man in America truly can make it to the top of the heap and contend for the leadership of the free world by being just as full of cr@p as the white man.

Yet I want to give Barack Obama credit. I will always be grateful to him for taking down Hillary Clinton. We couldn't beat the Clintons for eight years, and he did it. No matter what else happens, I thank him for that.

In that spirit, I now present a song I wrote celebrating the destruction of the Hillary Clinton campaign. It was written the night of the Hawaii and Wisconsin primaries. The best part was when the early returns from Hawaii came in, and Hillary had exactly 666 votes. I immediately Tivoed it. As for the song, I shall now present my version of 'Copacabana,' a celebration of Hillary's implosion.

Thank you. I can't tell if the red light is on or not, so I am going to keep talking until I get the signal. (I then got the signal.)

I just want to say that it is an honor to live in a country with great men like John McCain, Rudy Giuliani, Fred Thompson, and Evan Sayet. I hope they all win their lawsuit against Dr. Bosley.

God bless you, and God bless America."

I was greeted warmly by the crowd at the end of the evening, and the praise was overwhelming. Given that virtually everybody I know in real life keeps me humble, getting a swelled head will not be problematic. Then again, adulation is nice.

I thank Evan Sayet for having horrible taste in warm-up acts. May he never learn, since I never will.

eric

YES WE CAN Make Fun of Obama

My friend Evan Sayet has his monthly night of politically conservative comedy at the world famous Laugh Factory in Hollywood.

I anticipated only being a happy spectator for his November show, and performing at his December show.

I decided to publish my comedy routine before actually performing it. I was concerned that Obama might ban conservative comedy before I performed. He will not be sworn in yet, but I do not argue with the Messiah.

I find it ridiculous, and not in a good way, that comedians find it impossible to make fun of Obama. They say it is difficult. It is not. Some say it is because he is black. Others say that he is just so "cool," Like Will Smith, that there is just nothing to lampoon. While he is not a serial hound dog like Bill Clinton, comedians that cannot find any material poking fun at Barack Obama are simply lazy.

I came up with a ton of material. It took me about fifteen minutes to do so. Even if only a portion of this stuff works, fifteen minutes is not much time to create a routine. At the end of the routine, I will sing the revival of the GOP to the tune of Gloria Gaynor's "I will survive."

Unexpectedly, another comedian failed to show up. Evan asked me to do a set. Luckily I had my routine for the following month in my back pocket. I offer my homage to "His Royal Earness."

Obama Jokes

"I wasn't expecting to be here. I'm totally unprepared, disorganized … I have no idea what I'm doing. Oh no, wait a minute, that would be Barack Obama.

People say we cannot make fun of Obama. In the spirit of unity and harmony, let me say, 'YES WE CAN. YES WE CAN. YES WE CAN.'

Okay, that was my entire routine, goodnight. (Pretends to walk off stage)

There is plenty to make fun of. This is a guy who thinks that Fannie Mae starred in commercials for Polident.

This is a guy who thinks that the subprime mess was connected to Bernie Mac.

I am not saying his head is disproportioned, but they renamed the presidential plane 'Ear Force One.'

Some people say he is effeminate. Not true. This guy is a world-class athlete. He can jump twenty feet in the air and reach his nose.

I am not saying he is a snob, but picture John Kerry and Jacques Chirac having a baby.

I apologize for that last joke. It is one thing to say a man is half black. It is another to imply a man is half French.

I'm not saying we have a long way to go before reaching racial harmony, but Senator Robert Byrd did not need to ask Obama to valet his car.

If you really want to prove racial progress in America, Obama should go on the Senate floor and ask Senator Robert Byrd to valet *his* car.

Yes, there still is racism in America, but we have lived long enough to see people bury the hatchet. We will now see a black President put aside racial differences, go to the Senate floor, and shake hands with a Kleagle from West Virginia.

Barack Obama wanted to name Hillary Clinton or John Kerry Secretary of State. Perfect choices. Obama favors 'tough diplomacy.' Kerry can take Armageddonijad and bore him to death. Hillary could nag him to death.

Obama has been given extra Secret Service protection. After all, somebody has to stop people from breaking into the White House since Bill Clinton won't stop his own wife.

People said Obama was too cocky, that before the election he was measuring the drapes. That's not true. Hillary took them back in 2000.

Yes, Obama should reach out to people, but do we really want Ted Kennedy as Secretary of Transportation?

People say that Obama is as cool as Will Smith. Will Smith took care of the alien invaders. At least he secured our borders.

People say Obama has a Jewish problem. Yeah right. I have a Jewish problem. Obama doesn't have to sit across from my relatives at Thanksgiving. My dad looks at Obama and says, 'Son, why can't you get a haircut like that nice young man? You'll never be president without a shave.'

Obama will never know what it's like to experience the pain of being a Jewish man until he goes on twenty JDates.

When asked about the suffering of the Jewish people, Obama reached an understanding when he lamented, 'Yes, I've heard the horrors of JDate.'

I'm not saying the media was biased, but Chris Matthews puts on 'Eau D'Obama Anus' perfume before leaving the house.

I am not saying Obama can be smug, but he puts it on as well.

I am not saying the black community is crossing the line in celebration, but does Snoop Dogg really need to spank Ann Coulter in his new video?

Black America has a new breakfast special. Barack Obama is a cool glass of milk. Michelle Obama eggs people on to support her husband. Charles Rangel brings home the bacon. Al Sharpton provides several pounds of bull. Best of all, Jesse Jackson is toast.

I'm not saying Jesse Jackson is angry and bitter, but Bill Clinton came up to him and said, 'Honey, let's go back to Chappaqua.'

I know some liberals that don't own a TV and get their information from NPR. They say they are proud to vote for a black man. How the heck do they know he's black? All they have is a radio! I thought they were against racial profiling.

Barack Obama was asked if he would send the military to hot spots with black populations where suffering was occurring. While he did not commit to send troops to Darfur, Bill Clinton did say that South America policy should consist of finally invading Donna Brazile.

I am not saying Obama has more to learn about the Jewish community, but I did appreciate the holiday card he sent me wishing me a happy Chaka Khan.

Thanks to Obama's election, I am now an environmentalist. I've reduced my emissions by 30 percent. I no longer have VP dreams about Sarah Palin.

I'm not saying I say 'I'm not saying' too much ... I'm just saying ..."

eric

I Have Finally Snapped

I have finally snapped.

People asked me if I was okay after Barack Obama defeated John McCain. I told them that like Gloria Gaynor, "I Will Survive."[57]

That phrase gave me an idea. Because nobody sane was around to let me know it was a terrible idea, I went with it.

So in the spirit of 1970s disco, I can now express my feelings regarding the 2008 election.

1) "At first I was afraid ... I was petrified

November 4th, 2008, the music died

I stayed at home eating ice cream feeling sorry for myself

We lost the election ... I wanted to lay down and die

But we'll be back ... take it from me

In Twenty-Ten the crowds will all be screaming G-O-P

The people want their taxes cut, and they want their trade free

They do not want big government, they just want liberty

So not so fast ... slow down Barack

You get the office key but you still cannot change the lock

We are a loyal opposition

We will be manning our positions

We are alive ... and we will thrive ... we will survive"

2) "Remember 1992 ... we were so blue

An Arkansas fast talker and his lying crew

His wife was going to take away all that we fought for

And when she tried ... there was Newt in '94

Yes we came back ... the Senate, House, and more

We told the liberals turn around now, you're not welcome anymore

We know that they can't rule

They are like kids destroying schools

Right now they are living large

But the adults will be back in charge

So just stay calm … the left got lucky

We've got Coleman in Minnesota and McConnell in Kentucky

We've got Rudy … and we've got Fred

Dems have platitudes, and maybe a bit more hair on their head

You want handsome … well we have Mitt

He is full of hair and ideas, the left is full of (redacted)

So let's stand up … answer the call

We stand for freedom and liberty, they stand for nothing at all

They have no agenda … they have no plan

Obama has the flash, but that flash is in the pan

The left will crumble … and they will bumble

We are alive … we will thrive … we will survive"

3) "This is only one short painful chapter

In the reign of terror of the Pelosiraptor

Let them drink their Frisco wine, let them eat their brie cheese

In two years they will surrender on their sissy liberal knees

We won Iraq … We'll win Iran

We defeated Germany and Japan

To those who think the best days of America are gone

You are liberal, you are boring, and as usual you're wrong

We are conservatives … and we are right

If we can defeat the terrorists, with all of our might

We can surely defeat liberals, they will mess it up themselves

So get some rest and be ready for GOP in 2012

We will survive … we will thrive

Republicans snap out if it, look alive

We will survive!"

In the spirit of California Proposition 8 and gay marriage, I am prancing around my house singing this song like Kevin Kline in the movie *In and Out*.[58]

No, not really. Yet when nobody is looking, Republicans are allowed to frolic. Frolicking is healthy.

I will not ever imply that anything about this column was remotely healthy.

The loose screws in me cranium are about to hit the floor.

Dang carpet. I wonder where they landed.

eric

Copacabana–From Hawaii to Havana

With apologies to Barry Manilow, who should himself apologize for so many reasons, I bring you the 2008 political version of the "Copacabana,"[59] from Hawaii to Wisconsin to Havana.

1) "Supporters of Hillary

They yelled 'You go, girl!'

Oh she of ever changing hair

and not an ounce of flair

She would meander

and cackle 'ha-ha!'

and while she tried to be a star

Obama came in from afar

He commanded a crowded floor

And Oprah added more

They were young, hip, and attractive

Who could ask for more?

It was pure Oprah

and Obamamania

From Hawaii to Wisconsin to Havana

Obama reached out

Hill hates Republicans

Barack inspired passion

Hill was out of fashion

Obamamania

Hill lost the love"

2) "His name was Fidel

He ruled an island

Decrepit in his chair

He saw Hillary standing there

When she finished

He called her over

Two socialists in love

Until hubby Bill took off the gloves

And then the punches flew

Chairs were smashed in two

One man collapsed from boredom upon the floor

But who bored who?

Not Oprah

Or Obama

They were hot from Honolulu to Havana

Obamamania

had swept Wisconsin

Barack brought more passion

Hill fell further out of fashion

Obamamania

She lost more love"

3) "Her name was Hillary

They once screamed 'You go, girl!'

But that was many years ago

When she and Bill ran the show

There is still dancing

but not for Hillary

Fading like Fidel

Her dreams have gone to hell

She's now even more unkind

She beats Bill till he's blind

She lost her youth

She lost the election

Now she's lost her mind

Because Oprah

and Obama

Are off to Texas and Ohio with momentum

They worry about John McCain

and the general election campaign

Heroism vs. passion

Both gave Hill a smashing

Yet she learned nothing

2012 with love"

I admit it. I have some serious screws loose.

I guess I am just giddy. First the New England Patriots lose the Super Bowl.

Then Fidel Castro leaves not with a bang, but with a whimper, in the form of a note, most likely one spelled badly.

Anything truly is possible. I truly still believe Hillary will somehow find a way at the eleventh hour to steal ... You know what? Never mind. I will declare an optimism-only zone.

Thank you Hawaii, Wisconsin, and Havana. The world is three small steps closer to being a better place today.

Despots do not go gently into that good night. They hang on by their fingernails, dragged from the world stage kicking and screaming.

Lord willing, get dragged away they will. Fidel Castro and Hillary Clinton are not gone.

Yet slowly, ever so slowly, they might just might be on the verge of leaving.

Hillary is right that Obama is an empty suit, but it is a likable suit that looks nice. Unfortunately for her, she is an unlikable empty pantsuit. She will hopefully soon be confined to wherever people keep leisure suits. Perhaps she can wear one while playing shuffleboard at some political retirement home, far away from Washington DC.

The 2008 race for the Democratic nomination and the right to face Republican John McCain continues. He is one tough hombre. It would be fitting if the old war hero outlasts the Cuban cancer that bedeviled ten previous U.S. presidents.

(Quick election update: with 8 percent in Hawaii, Obama led 77 to 23 percent. More importantly, Hillary had exactly 666 votes. I could not make that up if I tried.)

The old warhorse will prosper, while Fidel Castro and Hillary Clinton will get lost once and for all.

At the risk of plagiarizing Barack Obama, or perhaps Deval Patrick, on this issue … I have hope.

eric

Chapter 11: President Ronald Reagan—the Gipper

I love God, my grandparents, and Ronald Reagan … in that order.

I could write a thousand pages about him, which would still not do him justice.

My tribute to him was written before tough economic times hit in 2008. I left my tribute unchanged because one bad year does not invalidate twenty-five mostly good years, including much of the twenty-first century. In the long run, the optimism Mr. Reagan projected will be what gives this tribute timelessness.

My grandparents are in heaven smiling upon their children and grandchildren. President Reagan is smiling upon conservative Republicans everywhere. We are his children and grandchildren. We must respect his legacy always.

President Reagan is even smiling upon liberals right now. He was just that good and decent a man.

God bless you, Mr. Reagan.

Thank You Again, Mr. Reagan

Dear President Reagan,

I wish you were still alive to see the world today that you left behind. It is not flawless, but it is better than you could have possibly imagined.

Twenty years ago you challenged Mr. Gorbachev to "Tear down this wall."[60] As you know, it came crashing down. Millions of Eastern Europeans are now free. You understood that freedom is not an American value. It is not uniquely Western. It is a gift from God, and everyone worldwide is entitled to it.

Today there are a billion Muslims, mostly Arabs, living under captivity. Some people believe that these people hate America and everything we stand for. No, they don't. They want to be free. They want to come here, and live the American Dream. They want to be able to make their government stronger without the fear of being shot on sight. Most of all, they want a sense of hope and optimism. This seems to be in shorter supply since you exited the world stage.

Mr. Reagan, if only you could see the Internet generation. The Russians were once seen as our enemies. People ducked under their desks in fear of nuclear war. Now Americans and Russians chat with each other on instant messenger. We send happy faces and jokes.

While young children worldwide play with each other online, adults are engaging in global commerce like never before. eBay and other Web sites allow people to conduct business globally with the touch of a button. Best of all, despite the efforts of some know-nothing politicians, Internet commerce is currently not taxed.

The economy is strong. No, we have not defeated the business cycle, but President Bush brought back Reaganomics. You faced a recession and a bear market in stocks, but your supply side tax cuts helped fuel an economic expansion and a bull market that defied expectations. President Bush also started out with a recession and a vicious bear market, but thanks to aggressive tax cuts, the stock market is higher than ever, and the economy is clicking on all cylinders.

Things are not perfect Mr. Reagan. Although we made peace with the Russians, Islamofacism is spiraling out of control. However, there is hope on the horizon. You bombed Libya in 1986 when Khadafi Duck was going crazy. This briefly kept him in check. Would you believe that our current president has brought democracy to Afghanistan, and toppled Saddam Hussein in Iraq?

On top of that, Khadafi Duck decided to move Libya toward normalcy. He did not decide to act normal due to twenty years of negotiations. He saw the handwriting on the wall and realized that he enjoyed being alive.

Mr. Reagan, our current president, George W. Bush, is under siege. He is a good man, but he is not a good communicator. He is plainspoken, but not articulate. He has an opposition that hates him in ways that make your presidency seem a love-fest. Yet he remains undaunted, not because of so called stubbornness, but because he understands that visions do not get implemented overnight.

In 1987, there was talk of "Reagan fatigue." People said you were losing your luster. The 1988 Republican candidates were said to be part of a losing ticket. You were mired in a scandal about nothing, and some said your presidency was exhausted. One year later, your vice president won a decisive victory. Gracious to the end, you refused to criticize those who came after you, preferring to let them write their own histories. If only one of the men you defeated had your class and graciousness.

It's amazing what twenty years can do. You are ranked among the all-time greats, and every Republican nominee wants to carry your mantle. I hope they understand this as some of them run in terror from President George W. Bush. It amazes me how they can claim your mantle, yet run from the man who has embraced it not just in words, but in deeds.

America is still that shining city on a hill. My grandparents came here with nothing, escaping the Nazis. They saved up enough to survive. Their children made it to the American middle class and owned a home in a nice suburban neighborhood. I managed to get an MBA and have advanced even further. The American Dream is not a cliché for the privileged few. It is the norm.

The two things that do seem to be missing today are civility ... and humor. Not humor at the expense of other people, but self-deprecating humor, a willingness to realize that while we are creatures of God, we are quite flawed. Your many quips are legendary, but the one that stays in my mind is how you reacted after you were shot. Looking up at the doctors, you said "I hope you're all Republicans."[61] Many people who wanted to dislike you simply were unable to do so.

The media were polite with you, but were not your friends. You simply talked over and around them to those who mattered ... the American people. You treated people with dignity, and were as beloved by Wall Street bankers as Iowa corn farmers. Would you believe that another movie star actor is now the governor of California? In addition, yet another movie and television star became a senator from Tennessee and is a legitimate presidential contender. The reason people like him is because he is simply ... well ... likable.

As I said, Mr. Reagan, there are plenty of problems in this world. Yet the one thing you brought to the table was optimism. This was not pie in the sky Pollyanna thinking. It was a true and unwavering belief in the human spirit and the beauty of America. Would you believe that France, Germany, and Canada all elected leaders that like America? Pro-American sentiment is spreading, despite attempts to prove otherwise.

People in Iraq voted in three separate democratic elections. It has been a bumpy ride, but isn't all democracy fragile in the beginning? People are less patient than they used to be.

You were there to guide the nation when the Space Shuttle Challenger took seven lives from us. Your words that day healed the nation. I do not care who wrote them. Only you could have said them. Our current president had to deal with a space tragedy where more astronauts died. It never gets easier. Yet after taking time to heal, space exploration has soldiered on.

Speaking of soldiers, our military might is strong. Sometimes we fight, and sometimes we negotiate. Sometimes we have political opponents who want to fight battles that can be solved with conversations and talk to people that need to be removed by force. You understood right from wrong, standing squarely with a small democracy called Israel against dictatorships that wanted to destroy it. That conflict still exists, but like you, our current president has allowed Israel to fiercely defend itself, consistent with his support for the nobility of democracy.

I remember being a teenager when you and Mr. Gorbachev shook hands. It was one of the greatest days in world history. Mr. Bush and Mr. Putin sometimes have an uneasy relationship that is complex, but they are certainly not at war. They often hold joint press conferences and air their differences in a healthy manner.

Mr. Reagan, I hope you are resting comfortably in heaven. Just know that your vision of the world, slowly but surely, is being implemented, and the world is consistently better off for it. Anyone who thinks that they are destined to a life of misery and hopelessness should talk to people who lived through the Iron Curtain in Eastern Europe.

One other front we are grappling with is that of world pestilences and diseases. Africa is suffering from AIDS, as is the rest of the world. However, by freeing pharmaceutical companies from endless regulations, they have created drugs that have plunged their profits into research and development, saving many lives and curing many diseases. Perhaps if they had a little more time, they could have cured Alzheimer's disease and saved you the ignominy of your final years. Then again, perhaps your work was done, and you exited the world stage having completed everything you needed to do. Nevertheless, a lot of people still miss you, sir.

Yes, Mr. Reagan, the Berlin Wall came crashing down. It tumbled and crumbled. If only you could see that what you started was only the beginning.

Godspeed, Mr. Reagan. For free people everywhere, I thank you very much.

eric

Chapter 12: President George W. Bush– The Dub

The cartoon television character on *American Dad* says that President George W. Bush "Does not base his decisions on polls, opinions, or even facts ... for almighty God is his copilot."

Lighthearted mocking is fine, but make no mistake about it, George W. Bush is a great man. I will always be proud to have had him as my president.

On September 14, 2001, he picked up that bullhorn and rallied a nation. On September 20, 2001, he grieved with us, and strengthened us.

Despite critics that are not fit to lick his boots, he has maintained his dignity, his calm, and his decency. For those who want to know fabulous first ladies, his mother and his wife more than qualify. Anybody with women like that in his life has to have a strong measure of goodness.

History will vindicate this man, because as Winston Churchill said, "I will be writing it."

Liberty, freedom, and the nobility of human dignity are gifts from God. God had a fine servant in George W. Bush, who spent much of his eight years delivering the best of the human spirit to those that hungered and thirsted for it.

May God bless George W. Bush. He acted out of goodness, and was successful because he was ... and is ... right.

eric

Batman—The Dark Knight After 9/11

Like many, I had the pleasure of seeing *Batman: The Dark Knight*.[62] The movie was exceptional, and I believe it should earn multiple Oscar nominations.

As a movie itself, it is a brilliant entertainment vehicle. Yet watching this movie twice is necessary to appreciate its equally brilliant political commentary.

The Joker, played by the late Heath Ledger, is more than a criminal. He is a terrorist.

Like any other terrorist, negotiation does not work with the Joker. He cannot be reasoned with, because he has nothing to lose. He is not afraid of dying. Also, the Joker, like true terrorists, does not even want anything. He cannot be bribed. He craves neither money nor power. The destruction and carnage he inflicts is not the means to any end. The pain and suffering he causes is the end itself. Michael Caine, as Alfred the butler, sums up the Joker perfectly. "Some people just like to watch the world burn."

The movie does not bother to explain why he acts the way he does. He is simply a homicidal sadist. He kills people because he can, because they are there, and for sport. He also enjoys torturing them before murdering them. He prefers the slow twisting knife to a quick gun kill.

Nevertheless, he is perfectly comfortable with guns and other munitions.

He also does not mind using mentally and physically handicapped people as unwilling suicide bombers. As for his willing accomplices, he murders them the moment they cease being useful.

Driving home after the movie, my friend was trying to figure out who would be the evil terrorist most comparable to the Joker.

My opinion is that neither Osama Bin Laden, Ayman Al-Zawahiri, nor Saddam Hussein fit the analogy. These men were bloodthirsty killers, but they were also pragmatic. None of them were willing to die or kill indiscriminately. They killed for specific reasons. Osama and Zawahiri wanted to spread Islam and create a caliphate. Saddam killed for the most basic of reasons, to enhance his own power.

So who best fits the role of completely psychotic, and willing to kill anything and everything?

Abu-Musab Al-Zarqawi.

Zarqawi enjoyed violence for the sake of violence. He even murdered his fellow Sunni Muslims.

My friend proffered a theory worth considering. What if Bin Laden and Zawahiri gave up Zarqawi? Was he too bloodthirsty for even them? By killing too brutally, victimizing anyone and everyone, local tribal leaders switched sides and joined the Americans against Al Qaeda.

The Joker was too evil for the other criminals. The mobsters wanted him dead, regretting that they ever did business with him. Harvey Two-Face wanted him dead as well. The Joker did not have loyal followers. He had victims that he brutalized into helping him.

The Joker also showed no interest in money. Without spoiling the movie, what he does with his share of the money he steals defies any reasonable behavior. Given that money is unimportant to him, he cannot be negotiated with.

In a world of terrorists, there are those that fight them. They come in the form of police officers, district attorneys and their fellow prosecutors, politicians, military personnel, and various special forces such as SWAT teams.

In any war, the bad guys are usually united. The good guys get bogged down arguing over procedures. The bad guys do not have to worry about warrants, Miranda rights, or writs of habeas corpus.

The delicate balance that the good guys face in the Batman movie and in real life is how to catch the bad guys without becoming them.

Harvey Two-Face sees the ruin that is his life as one of the good guys, and descends into becoming what he hates. He becomes one of the bad guys.

Harvey Two-Face could be represented by the American people. We struggle on a daily basis with the choice between doing what is morally and legally right, and doing what is effective. These two roads often diverge, and moral hazards and how we respond to them make us human. Harvey Dent, brilliantly played by Aaron Eckhart, lets his despair consume him. The good way does not work. He slides into badness.

Others in the movie refuse to succumb. Batman and Commissioner Gordon refuse to give in. Commissioner Gordon is a law and order policeman through and through. He will not cross the line.

This is why so many people are uncomfortable with Batman. He operates outside the law. He is a vigilante. The debate among the people of Gotham City about Batman is a debate about vigilantism itself, especially in a post 9/11 world.

Those favoring the rule of law at all costs see Batman as a threat. Yet those who support Batman do so because they see civic institutions failing to protect and defend them.

This argument goes all the way back to ordinary people like Bernard Goetz. He shot several people who approached him with screwdrivers. They were going to rob him (For those who dispute this, grow up. They were going to rob him). His choices were shoot or be victimized.

This is at the heart of the gun control debate. Some feel that only police officers and judges should have guns. Others feel this would embolden criminals. We now know according to every credible study that increased citizen gun ownership leads to dramatic reductions in crime. Deterrence works.

Batman is a deterrent. His methods scrape dangerously against the law. In fact, Batman takes steps in this movie that would make the ACLU cringe. A debate between Christian Bale's Batman and his henchman, played by Morgan Freeman, about how far is too far is a fabulous metaphor for how far we can go in attempting to catch terrorists.

Issues such as warrantless wiretaps, Foreign Intelligence Surveillance Act (FISA) courts, and military tribunals bubble beneath the surface of this movie.

Also, Gotham City does not have the equivalent of Guantanamo Bay. They merely have the county jail. The Joker knows this. In fact, he wants to go to jail. That way he can use the jail itself to further his ambitions. Criminals in jail meet other criminals. Had the Joker been given solitary confinement, perhaps he could have been stopped.

One quality of Batman is that he will not murder. If he catches a criminal alive, he will preserve that life. He is willing to capture the Joker and kill him if he has to do so. Yet he will not murder him. The Joker has no such constraints.

So who is Batman?

Batman is controversial. He has his supporters and detractors. He is loved in good times and hated in tough times. He is even blamed for exacerbating problems, when the audience knows that deep down he is the good guy willing to do what they will not. People criticize Batman, but they simply do not understand that he protects people. Most importantly, Batman himself is willing to be reviled and let others take the credit. He is not worried about popular opinion. He is busy saving lives.

Batman is President George W. Bush.

President Bush wants to kill terrorists. The argument is not whether to do it. Except for the most extreme left-wingers, consensus exists in America to get the bad guys. The argument among the good guys is over methods.

President Bush, like Batman, gets raked over the coals. Yet when all is said and done, Batman's critics have no viable alternative solutions. If they did, Batman would be unnecessary.

Some Americans have a deep dislike for President Bush, often crossing the line into hatred. Yet when asked what they would do to keep America safe, crickets chirp loudly.

Diplomacy can work with those wanting to live. With bloodthirsty madmen like Zarqawi, there is no room for dialogue. We killed him in a targeted air strike, and the world is forever better off for his death.

The question regarding Batman is whether he is a net positive or net negative. For those focusing on methods, he is a negative. For those caring about results, he is an overwhelming positive. Leftists, prepare to be frustrated by the new Batman movie. With regards to the War on Terror, the message is very politically conservative.

Gotham City is at war, and terrorists are using Gotham's civil institutions against it. Batman dangerously approaches the line. Some would argue that he crosses it. Yet when all is said and done, he gets the job done. He delivers results, which is more than anyone else is doing.

Yes, this is a movie. However, entertainment has always been about social commentary. It is refreshing that in an industry dominated by left-wing nonsense, the biggest blockbuster of the summer, and perhaps of all time, is offering an anti-hero that prefers a hard-@ssed approach to crime and terror.

Actually, crime and terror should not be lumped together. Crime can be defeated with jails and courtrooms. Terrorism requires much more aggressive methods.

Gotham City is like any city in America. It is actually the metaphor for New York City.

New York City was decaying. Then the Rudy Giuliani crackdown took place. Yet even Mayor Giuliani could not have been prepared for the horror and pure evil that was 9/11.

One reassuring aspect of the movie is that despite some despairing that the Joker has won, when all is said and done, he does not win.

The arguments over the methods used to capture the Joker can and should be argued. Those debates are part of a healthy democracy. Having said that, I maintain that Batman did the right thing. He saved the city, and took the backlash. Saving lives trumped dithering and dawdling.

In the same way Batman leaves, George W. Bush will be leaving office in several months. His detractors will never give him his due. His supporters are just glad that Zarqawi is gone. Now we need to get the rest of the Zarqawis.

All hail the Dark Knight. He got the job done.

eric

Puppies and Kittens are Crying ... Blame the President!

The MSNBC debate between the children that make up the Democratic Party was laughable and insignificant for two reasons. First of all, it was on MSNBC. Secondly, it was a debate among Democrats. Rather than recap nonsense, I decided to paraphrase what these Democratic debates are actually about.

Question 1: My kitty cat ran up a tree. I called 911, but the fire department was too slow in arriving because there was an actual fire somewhere else. George W. Bush does not care about me. What would you do to make me feel relevant and significant?

Hillary: My daughter Chelsea has a cat. It is an outrage that the president does not care about puppies and kittens. Our dog, Buddy, helped save my marriage during tough times. I will not let other families be the victim of such cold Republican uncaring. Dogfighting is wrong, and even though Michael Vick has nothing to do with this, I as a feminist will not allow George W. Bush to continue his alpha male frat boy anti-feminist animal policies.

Obama: Unlike my opponents, I have been against animal cruelty from the very beginning. While others were focusing on Al Qaeda, I was in the Illinois State Senate, where we spent our time worrying about issues such as this. We must have the audacity to hope for a more caring world where cats and dogs are treated equally to humans.

Edwards: Ma'am, I bet you were cold shivering outside waiting for those that never came. I bet you caught a cold, and nobody was able to take you to the doctor, and that you do not have decent health care because George W. Bush does not care about you. George W. Bush cut the funding for first responders, and I think it is an outrage that our firefighters are fighting a fire while you are lost in the cold. Not in my America.

Question 2: We want to form a union so we can go on strike, bring work to a halt, and be guaranteed pay regardless of the quality and quantity of our work. Management opposes this, and is firing people that refuse to work. What will you do to ensure that we can be as glorious as Europe, where we are not treated like removable parts simply because we want to get more and do less?

Hillary: George W. Bush and Dick Cheney represent Halliburton and Enron. We need to take their profits so that the money can be used to form more unions. We will not rest until every business has either moved overseas, gone bankrupt, or fired all their workers. We will force them to unionize so that you can get your fair share from all those greedy businessmen. The fact that they will have no money to give you is okay, because at least then there will be equality. We cannot have a Republican economy where business thrives and some people have more than others. France has a heavy union presence, and their economy is doing fine and will be even better when Bush and Sarkozy are replaced with Segolene Royale and myself.

Obama: I believe in unions, and unlike my opponents, I have never been against any union of any kind, even if it is a union between two men, provided the polls are not against that. George W. Bush is against gay marriage in the workplace, and people have the right to unionize with whoever they see fit. How dare George W. Bush try to crush unions between two loving and consenting adults just because they work together? I will always stand for the civil unions against the Halliburton-Enron radical right Christian management of Bush and Cheney.

Edwards: Ma'am, I'm a mill worker's son. It breaks my heart that managers line their pockets while workers barely have time to take their paid vacation, sick days, smoke breaks, coffee breaks, and other God-given rights. George W. Bush gets paid sick days, and so should you. If you get fired from your job for refusing to work, I will make sure as president that the company is shut down until you are rehired and made a member of management. Unfortunately, since you will be management, I will have to take away everything from you and give it to the next worker who complains about you so that everybody can be the boss. The American people are the boss.

Question 3: I am unhappy. I want. Gimme gimme gimme. I deserve. I am entitled. George W. Bush makes me cry. What can you do for me?

Hillary: It is an outrage that we are spending billions in Iraq when we have Americans suffering at home. You were happy when my husband and I ran this country. Your suffering began in 2001. I know you did not tell me what the exact problem is, but you don't have to. I know what is best for you. You need somebody who cares about you, whatever you said your name was. It takes a village to raise a child, and adults are overgrown children. Mommy is here for you, sweetie. I will be handing out candy and lollipops to all good little kids like you. George W. Bush never gave you candy, did he? He wants you to buy your own. I may not feel your pain, or any pain for that matter, but I am not George W. Bush. That is why you should vote for me.

Obama: George W. Bush will never make you happy because he does not understand what is important. He grew up rich. Rich people cannot ever understand poor people. Just because rich people hire poor people and give them the income they need to feed their families, that does not make them good people. Poor people are dying in the streets every single day. I tried to stop this when I was in Illinois, but relocating them to Indiana so the problems were not in my backyard was thwarted when cold Indiana Republicans refused to show compassion. George W. Bush ran as a compassionate conservative. The fact that you are crying right now does not mean you are a crybaby who would complain about everything anyway. It means you have been the victim of an uncaring president.

Edwards: How dare George W. Bush not include psychology benefits in a universal health care package? He does not understand that until Americans spend their life savings on psychologists, psychiatrists, psychotherapists, and psychoanalysts, they will never know what is wrong with them. People cannot rely on themselves. We need educated people with PhDs to tell us what is wrong with us. I wanted to buy a 60 thousand square foot house, but I settled for half of that so that I can spend the rest of my riches on making myself feel better. Look at my hair. It's perfect. I'm incredibly handsome. I feel good about myself. If you vote for me, I can make you feel good about yourself as well.

Moderator: The rest of you onstage are insignificant, but as the audience is leaving, please simultaneously shout out reasons why you dislike George W. Bush. This concludes our panhandling session. Next month we will prod actual homeless people to ask questions about why they think the war in Iraq is wrong. They will be rambling drug addicts in real life, but we will dress them up to make them look like down on their luck factory workers. For those of you who are concerned that we did not deal with the War on Terror, Al Qaeda, Osama Bin Laden, or other trivial matters, I remind you that this network will not deal with cold heartless issues by a cold heartless administration that does not care about lost puppies and kittens.

George W. Bush is bad, and Republicans are being selfish for not debating on our unbiased network, instead debating on animal and tree hating Fox News. Thank you and goodnight.

eric

President Bush Simply Gets It

I have said it before, and I will say it again. I love "the Dub."

I am an unabashed, unashamed supporter of the president.

I love the guy. I voted for him in 2000. I grieved with him on September 11, 2001. On September 14, I cheered when he grabbed that bullhorn and hugged that fireman and let the people who murdered my fellow New Yorkers know that they "soon would be hearing from all of us."[63] On September 20, he and I both fought back tears during one of the greatest speeches in world history. I looked in his eyes and saw potential greatness.

He has met that potential. Forget today. Forget the next twenty months. It is about the next twenty years. In a world full of confusion, this man simply "gets it." He gets it.

Very few people in life get it. Colonel Ralph Peters in the *New York Post* gets it. The *Wall Street Journal* gets it. Rudy Giuliani, John McCain, Mitt Romney, and Fred Thompson all get it. Ronald Reagan, Margaret Thatcher, and Ariel Sharon certainly got it. John Howard and Nicolas Sarkozy get it. Columnists John Podhoretz and Charles Krauthammer get it. Dick Cheney definitely gets it, more than most people ever realize. Sean Hannity gets it. Colonel David Hunt gets it.

"It" is the defining issue of human existence. It is about forcefully, aggressively, and proactively making the world a better and more peaceful place by rooting out evil wherever it exists. Not just proactively, but preemptively. That is the Bush Doctrine. It should be mandatory American foreign policy forever.

Make no mistake about it. This is not a morally relative world. There is good and evil. Good does not win just because we pray to God. God helps those who help themselves. Blood, sweat, and tears are shed so that good people everywhere can enjoy peace and liberty. Without liberty, there is no life.

President Bush's entire remarks should be mandatory reading, but I will try to do this great man a modicum of justice by offering a moderately effective summation.

"I want to open today's speech with a story that begins on a sunny morning, when thousands of Americans were murdered in a surprise attack—and our nation was propelled into a conflict that would take us to every corner of the globe.

The enemy who attacked us despises freedom, and harbors resentment at the slights he believes America and Western nations have inflicted on his people. He fights to establish his rule over an entire region. And over time, he turns to a strategy of suicide attacks destined to create so much carnage that the American people will tire of the violence and give up the fight.

If this story sounds familiar, it is—except for one thing. The enemy I have just described is not al Qaeda, and the attack is not 9/11, and the empire is not the radical caliphate envisioned by Osama bin Laden. Instead, what I've described is the war machine of Imperial Japan in the 1940s, its surprise attack on Pearl Harbor, and its attempt to impose its empire throughout East Asia."

I have absolutely nothing to add to that. I was genuinely surprised by the intro.

"The lesson from Asia's development is that the heart's desire for liberty will not be denied. Once people even get a small taste of liberty, they're not going to rest until they're free. Today's dynamic and hopeful Asia—a region that brings us countless benefits—would not have been possible without America's presence and perseverance."

Everybody wants to be free. Freedom is not American. It is human. Kunta Kinte from the book *Roots* refused to call himself Toby. Why should Arab women be beaten if they choose to take off their burkas and demand equality to their husbands? Why should children be taught that suicide vests are the way to glory? Human beings should never be forced into such pain.

"The militarists of Japan and the communists in Korea and Vietnam were driven by a merciless vision for the proper ordering of humanity. They killed Americans because we stood in the way of their attempt to force their ideology on others. Today, the names and places have changed, but the fundamental character of the struggle has not changed. Like our enemies in the past, the terrorists who wage war in Iraq and Afghanistan and other places seek to spread a political vision of their own—a harsh plan for life that crushes freedom, tolerance, and dissent. Like our enemies in the past, they kill Americans because we stand in their way of imposing this ideology across a vital region of the world. This enemy is dangerous; this enemy is determined; and this enemy will be defeated."

There is nothing "hokey" about wearing a t-shirt of an American flag that says, "These colors don't run." This country was founded on noble ideals, and

I will be d@mned if those ideals will be crushed in my lifetime because I did not do everything I could to support them.

"Some said Japanese culture was inherently incompatible with democracy. A lot of Americans believed that—and so did the Japanese—a lot of Japanese believed the same thing: democracy simply wouldn't work."

Are people saying Arabs are not human beings? That they can't do it? Nonsense. They can, they should, and with God's help, and America's, one day they will. Otherwise, barbarism has won and civilization has lost. That is not an acceptable outcome. God gave us this world, and man will not destroy it.

"Whatever your position is on that debate, one unmistakable legacy of Vietnam is that the price of America's withdrawal was paid by millions of innocent citizens whose agonies would add to our vocabulary new terms like 'boat people,' 're-education camps,' and 'killing fields.'"

Being right is subjective. Doing right is imperative. To quote Bob Dole, who knows more than a little about protecting freedoms, "Everything in this world flows from doing what is right."

"There was another price to our withdrawal from Vietnam, and we can hear it in the words of the enemy we face in today's struggle—those who came to our soil and killed thousands of citizens on September the eleventh, 2001 ... after the 9/11 attacks, Osama bin Laden declared that 'the American people had risen against their government's war in Vietnam. And they must do the same today.'"

The entire world is watching. Will we embolden our enemies? Will we betray our friends? Or will we keep our word? Treasury bills are the safest investment worldwide because the United States of America has never defaulted on an economic obligation. The entire world trusts the United States Treasury. Shouldn't our political covenants be just as, if not more, sacred?

"In Iraq, our moral obligations and our strategic interests are one. So we pursue the extremists wherever we find them and we stand with the Iraqis at this difficult hour—because the shadow of terror will never be lifted from our world and the American people will never be safe until the people of the Middle East know the freedom that our Creator meant for all."

Amen! Somebody buy this man a soda now!

"Across the Middle East, millions of ordinary citizens are tired of war, they're tired of dictatorship and corruption, they're tired of despair. They want societies where they're treated with dignity and respect, where their children have the hope for a better life. They want nations where their faiths are honored and they can worship in freedom. And that is why millions of Iraqis and Afghans turned out to the polls—millions turned out to the polls. And that's why their leaders have stepped forward at the risk of assassination. And that's why tens of thousands are joining the security forces of their nations. These men and women are taking great risks to build a free and peaceful Middle East—and for the sake of our own security, we must not abandon them."

If they can lift their purple-stained fingers with bullets flying around them, we can lift a finger to show our thanks. These people want to live freely! They have hope! They have a taste of what we have, and they demand the Iraqi version of the American dream!

"The greatest weapon in the arsenal of democracy is the desire for liberty written into the human heart by our Creator. So long as we remain true to our ideals, we will defeat the extremists in Iraq and Afghanistan. We will help those countries' peoples stand up functioning democracies in the heart of the broader Middle East. And when that hard work is done and the critics of today recede from memory, the cause of freedom will be stronger, a vital region will be brighter, and the American people will be safer.

Thank you, and God bless."[64]

God bless President Bush. He will be the first man to tell you that he is far from perfect. He is a simple, plainspoken, sincere man. I used to think he was a good man. I was wrong. He is a great man.

The world will be a better place if we do our part. I don't care if I am the last man standing next to the president. He is right, and the history books will be very kind to him. I know this, because to paraphrase the great Winston Churchill, "I intend to write it."[65]

I get what you are trying to do, Mr. President.

I get it, sir. I thank God that you get it as well.

May God bless America, our soldiers, their missions, and freedom-loving human beings worldwide.

Luv ya, Dubya!

eric

Ms. Pelosi, Meet Mr. Gingrich

Nancy Pelosi, aka the Pelosiraptor, finished her budget battle with President Bush. Ms. Pelosi, with all due respect ... you got your hide kicked.

Dubya slapped you around, lifted your skirt up, and branded a big old "W" on your hide. He let you know who was boss, and it wasn't you.

It is one thing to be the first person to do a job. It is quite another to look at history and ignore it. Nancy Pelosi must not be a student of history, because she only had to go back twelve years to see the seeds of her own demise.

In 1994, Newt Gingrich was a hero. He led the Republicans to power after forty years of Democratic control. He then helped pass several planks in the Contract With America. He tried to reform Medicare, which was a noble endeavor. Then the government shutdown happened. Newt Gingrich squared off against Bill Clinton. Clinton mopped the floor with Gingrich. How did this happen? Gingrich was rising, Clinton was sinking. What did Gingrich overlook?

Gingrich missed the key determinant in the battle. There is only one president of the United States.

Trying to take down a president is akin to the analogy of trying to kill a king or a bear. If you shoot the king and only wound him, he is coming at you with his entire army. The bear does not give a second shot. The president has an army, ranging from hundreds of staffers, a media that, while hostile, must cover him, and a leadership role that is unmatched. The president is the commander in chief and the chief diplomat.

Gingrich was a very strong speaker. Clinton was a weak president. It did not matter, because it was not a fair fight. The playing field was not level. I could play chess against Gary Kasparov, and even if he forfeited his queen before the game started, his skill level is so deep that he would win anyway.

Gingrich overreached. The public was disgusted with Clinton and the Democrats. This did not mean the entire country loved Republicans.

Flashing forward to 2006, Nancy Pelosi never grasped that the public was angry toward Republicans and George W. Bush. They were not embracing liberalism. The public was upset at the way the war was progressing, but they were totally open to staying, provided that they saw evidence it could be won.

Disagreement with the president did not mean people hated his guts. The public was exasperated with Republican sex scandals. Many conservatives were frustrated not that the president had swung too far to the right, but that he did not go far enough.

The Pelosiraptor had one other disadvantage compared to Mr. Gingrich. Gingrich had a plan many people disagreed with. Pelosi had no plan at all. Disgust with Republicans made Pelosi speaker, but governing is difficult when the majority has no uniting philosophy. Does anybody remember Pelosi advocating any policies during the campaign?

Pelosi should have learned from Gingrich that America does not have a parliamentary system of government. There is no prime minister. The speaker of the house is not a head of state. They are the head of 535 Lilliputians that each answer to maybe a few thousand people.

Nancy Pelosi put on a burka and sipped tea with Bashar Assad. She looked like an imbecile, making statements about foreign policy that she had to disavow several minutes after uttering the words.

When President Bush meets with a world leader, it matters. He speaks for America. Nobody else has that power. Senators and house members do not. Not even ex-presidents wield such influence. Presidential spouses certainly do not have as much gravitas. The vice president and secretary of defense can only convey so much.

Newt Gingrich overreached, and within four years of being speaker, became a private citizen. The Pelosiraptor is well on her way to being a private citizen, which would be the best thing she could do for America.

Could she recover? Absolutely. Anything is possible. Unfortunately, political parties eat their own, and Democrats are cannibals. Pelosi tried to break the president, and she instead got broken. The temptation upon achieving power is to seek vengeance and punish the new minority, but this strategy backfires. Americans are not Democrats or Republicans. They just want solutions and accomplishments. Pelosi did not deliver results.

Ms. Pelosi, you got too big for your britches. You may wish to step out of San Francisco and Washington DC and observe Middle America. They eat red meat, watch football, like country music, and want to win the war. You might want to learn about Toby Keith. There are angry Americans out there, but they are angry at terrorists, not the president.

Ms. Pelosi, George W. Bush is the president. You are not. If you keep your job, show some respect next time. You went after the Dub. He took your best shot, and stayed alive and kicking. That is why a year later, you ended up with a Texas-sized boot in your @ss.

eric

Chapter 13: Adult leaders, aka Republicans

Liberals remind me of children that wreck the house when the parents are out of town. When George W. Bush came into office, it was the adults returning home after eight years of baby boomer temper tantrums. Gone were the hippies and the Age of Aquarius, along with the "w" keys from the office computers. Liberals called that a childish prank. Conservatives called it vandalism. The "o" keys will not be missing because obeying the law does matter.

The children are already rioting in the streets, demanding their nature-given right to contribute less and receive more. How dare conservatives criticize dregs of society for detracting from society?

I remain optimistic. Soon enough the adults will be back home. The place will get cleaned of all the filth that the kiddies leave behind.

There are past and present Republicans that decent people everywhere should be proud of admiring.

Dick Cheney and the Wyoming Jewish Cabal

When Dick Cheney was asked about his unwavering (and appreciated by everyone except Jewish liberals) support for Israel, he offered one of his finest deadpanned responses. He stated, "You cannot become president without winning Wyoming, and you cannot win Wyoming without the Jewish vote."[66]

The stereotype of the Bush-Cheney leadership is that President Bush is controlled by a cabal of "Neocons," which is code word for "Jews" (the bad kind, not the Barbra Streisand kind). Let's see how this conspiracy works. George W. Bush, who got elected governor of Texas, is not Jewish, and has never needed Jewish support. This is reconciled with the fact that he supposedly takes his marching orders from Dick Cheney, the Rasputin in hiding. Dick Cheney is not Jewish, and while Wyoming does have a larger concentration of Jews than say … Libya perhaps … it is not going to be mistaken for little Israel. This is then explained by Dick Cheney taking orders from his subordinate, former Secretary of Defense Donald Rumsfeld. Rumsfeld is not Jewish, nor was his former boss, Gerald Ford. Rumsfeld gets his influence from Deputy Defense Secretary Paul Wolfowitz! Further down the line is Douglas Feith! Shazamm! There truly are six degrees of Kevin Bacon. So when Ronald Reagan spoke about the domino theory, this is what liberals thought he meant. Beware a wolf in Feith's clothing! The Jewish Neocons are infecting the president through Vice President Cheney.

Bill Clinton can be considered the first black president, but … and let me say this slowly … he … is … Caucasian. It is not racist to judge a man's race by the color of his skin. Race is about pigmentation. However, despite being white, Bill Clinton can identify with blacks based on his experiences and beliefs. Therefore, George W. Bush and Dick Cheney can be pro-Israel and supportive of Jewish causes without being slaves to a Jewish cabal. Experiences and beliefs make these views understandable.

One explanation for conservative support of the Jews and Israel is the nonsensical notion that all Christians want to convert all Jews. Jesus will be resurrected. We will all worship him, and live happily ever after. This theory reduces all Christians to unenlightened, intolerant bigots (as opposed to enlightened, tolerant bigots on the left). If President Bush and Vice President Cheney truly had the power of Jesus, couldn't they just get Jesus to stop anti-Semites? Heck, Sean Hannity can't even get Jesus to make Alan Colmes straighten up and fly right, or at least fly less left. (I am not claiming

Alan Colmes is anti-Semitic or a self-hating Jew. He is just awful on Jewish issues.)

President Bush is an evangelical, which is not equivalent to zealotry. Evangelicals believe in Jesus, who teaches his disciples to do good deeds and choose right over wrong. Wow ... sinister stuff, that evangelical movement. Next thing you know they might preach blasphemy such as helping the poor, quitting drugs, and loving thy neighbor.

Why do men with nothing to gain electorally support Israel? For the one reason that the left will never be able to accept: because it would obliterate their view of the veep and the Dub ... Dick Cheney and George W. Bush "get it."

That's it, plain and simple. They get it. Starting at the top, George W. Bush visited Israel while governor of Texas. He went to the Wailing Wall with Ariel Sharon. When he saw the stretch of land, and how small Israel is, he replied to Ari Fleischer (who is Jewish, which is why he led the Neocon cabal by having Bush speak for him) "They've got driveways bigger than this in Texas."[67]

Israel is small, but not as small as the argument for an evenhanded approach to the Arab-Israeli conflict, especially where Palestinians are considered. The two sides are unequal. Many Christians and Jews (even some liberal Jews) grasp that Israel is a democracy that wants peace, while the Arabs want to destroy Israel, with Palestinians being a society of homicidal lunatics. There are Palestinian moderates, defined as those who support homicidal lunacy wholeheartedly, but are too poor to pay for ammunition and have given up all their children already. They do not actively destroy Israel, but polls insist they wish they could.

Forgetting momentarily that Palestinians are a fictional, invented people with a deep history running almost sixty years (only a few thousand behind the Israelites), what they really are is the worst of the Arabs. The reason that twenty-three Arab states refuse to help them is because they know what most rational people know ... Palestinians are troublemakers, agitators, and bloodthirsty criminals, even worse than Berkeley students. How many countries do they have to get thrown out of before people see they are troublemakers? When Robin Williams joked about Michael Jackson, he stated, "You know the guy is far gone when Al Sharpton is standing there going, 'Hey man, I don't want any part of this guy.'"[68] This is how Arabs view Palestinians. Think about it. How crazy do you have to be to have Arabs not want to deal with you? How wacked-out, out-of-your-mind nuts do you have to be as a people to be too crazy for Arabs? Too crazy for Arabs to deal with means any rational person finds them over the cliff of sanity. Some claim that if Palestinians were given hope, they would stop committing murder. How about they stop committing murder first? They have yet to try this approach.

So Palestinian lunatics funded by Arab terrorists kill innocent Israelis/Jews. The Jews are the good guys. Their enemies are the bad guys. It is that black and white. Rational people get this. President Bush does. While this ruins the image of Bush as a dolt, it is perfectly logical to conclude that the president grasps a concept that almost everyone against genocide grasps.

All-powerful conservatives must be seen as either stupid or evil (President Bush is seen as both, proving the logical flow that only enlightened liberals fresh from their 1960s style drug-induced hazes could reconcile). Since even the most hateful leftists cannot claim Dick Cheney is unintelligent, he gets the evil card. He is not even an evangelical, but perhaps President Bush does rule over Cheney and give him marching orders to secretly be one. Cheney is evil for other reasons that liberals are still inventing. There must be sinister motives for his supporting Israel, because if he were to support the good guys, as most do, then he might be good himself. This realization could lead to mass suicides on Ivy League campuses (I do not endorse suicide, but perhaps they might disable their own jaws for a few days, forcing them to listen to opposing viewpoints).

What scares leftists even more is that there might be other issues where the president and vice president are right. Come to think of it, on most issues they are right. This means that their critics are wrong on issue after issue.

Jews are good people. We pray for peace. We want to make the world a better place. Israel is a peaceful nation that wants peace. So let me explain it to Israel's enemies and anti-Semites everywhere. I get it. You don't like us. Guess what? Deal with it. We are here to stay. You start wars; we finish them. We win; you lose. We pray for peace, but too many people confuse kindness for weakness. You don't get it, but you will … one way or another. Either way is fine with me.

Most people get it. President Bush gets it. Israel's fight for survival is a perfect corollary to America's War on Terror. The enemies are the same. The fight is equally just for America and Israel. Presidents choose people based on their values. The president's goal of a better world was enhanced by the fabulous vice presidential choice of Dick Cheney.

Besides, if Dick Cheney was truly under the spell of a Jewish cabal, he would overanalyze the problem, dither in an attempt to be liked by his enemies, and like most Jews, wring his hands and blame himself, at least partially. His refusal to try and understand his critics and give them legitimacy while singing "Kumbaya" proves that he is influenced not by (liberal) Jews, but the best friends Jews have ... conservative Christians.

Somehow, Dick Cheney overcame the powerful Jewish lobby and got elected in Wyoming, which as we all know is essential to traveling on Air Force 2. Or maybe Dick Cheney supports Israel because he just gets it.

eric

Alaska Governor Sarah Palin—Shock and Awe

Shock and awe entered the 2008 presidential campaign. Arizona Senator John McCain chose Alaska Governor Sarah Palin as his vice presidential nominee.

The coldest state has brought America the hottest governor.

The Tygrrrr Express arrived in Minneapolis, Minnesota, aka "Repub Hub," for the 2008 Republican Convention. It is already a fabulous experience thanks to John McCain choosing the phenomenal Sarah Palin.

First, I would like to give credit to the news organizations that put out the headline that is bound to spawn a million jokes by the adolescent male population, of which I am often accused of being a part of. "McCain taps Alaska Governor Sarah Palin."[69] My desire not to have the Secret Service shut down my blog prevents me from commenting further, although she did make my list of the "Top 120 Political Yummy Bouncies."

As hot as she is, make no mistake about it. She is tough, smart, and a solid choice for vice president based on her ability to govern effectively. Before offering some thoughts on Governor Palin, kudos should be given to John McCain. I have repeatedly stated that I am "often wrong, but never in doubt."[70] My advice to John McCain, which was never solicited or accepted, was that he opt for the ultra-safe choice.

My dream choice was Rudy Giuliani, but my realistic choice was Minnesota Governor Tim Pawlenty. Tall, good hair, and inoffensive ... safe, boring, and not harmful. Safe is not John McCain. He took all of his poker chips and pushed them to the center of the table. He went "all in." Perhaps a guy that spent five-and-a-half years as a POW is just not going to be afraid to take risks. Sarah Palin is the epitome of a riverboat gambler choice. It also might very well work.

The minus side includes that her beauty might work against her. Women say they want to support other women, but they hate beauty queens. Sarah Palin is a former pageant girl. This is not her fault, but women are a jealous bunch. Another minus is that she does not have foreign policy experience. Then again, she has more experience than Barack Obama. Governors, unlike senators, actually do things. That is why senators rarely make it to the White House. She is an executive, and has actually balanced a budget. Obama is a talker. She is a doer.

Her pluses are numerous. For one, the base loves her. The base changed from dispirited to elated. This woman is so pro-NRA that her youngest child is named "Trig." (as in Trigger, perhaps?) Another plus is that in a year when the Republican brand is toxic due to perceptions of incompetence and corruption, Sarah Palin is a very competent executive who has rooted out corruption in her home state. She even took on Republicans, filing indictments and decimating the old boy network. She has popularity levels in the stratosphere at home. Obama is a rock star for his image. Palin is a rock star for her actual accomplishments.

Sarah Palin brings me one worry. When one makes their name as a corruption fighting crusader, they had better be squeaky clean. Bill Clinton was able to escape his corruption intact because people had such low expectations for him from an ethical standpoint. He could crawl over the bar. People do not mind those that engage in bad deeds. They mind sanctimoniousness and hypocrisy. Eliot Spitzer was the epitome of self-righteousness, and his corruption brought him down. Sarah Palin had better have her ethical house in spotless order, because the spotlight is about to shine brightly and intensely upon her.

Sarah Palin is about shock and awe because the shock value comes in the form of her being chosen. In the age of twenty-four hour to the millisecond news cycles, keeping secrets is not easy. In the morning, I hit my Internet button, saw the headlines, and picked my jaw off of the floor. The awe part is that she is as inspiring from a success standpoint as she is physically beautiful. I track what words people type in to search blogs when I look at my own blog. The words "Sarah Palin" in the same sentence as some "suggestive terms" were typed in abundance. I suspect that the young male college vote is now in play. People will claim sexism, but admiring a woman for her beauty in addition to her intelligence is not sexism. Ignoring all other factors and relying solely on beauty is where the slippery erotic slope comes in. Does Sarah Palin look like the naughty librarian in those videos that every guy pretends to know nothing about? Do we want her to pull the ribbon out of her bun and let her hair flow? Of course.

Yet this is not about modeling lingerie, or about being impersonated on *Saturday Night Live* by the similarly sexy looking Tina Fey. It is about leading the free world. She is solidly and unapologetically conservative. She could be the next Margaret Thatcher, only (with all due respect to the deeply beloved Iron Lady) sexier. Yet this is not about her bottom, which some reporters tactlessly commented on. It is about the bottom line, which is cutting taxes, cutting burdensome regulations, enhancing liberty and freedom, and killing terrorists. She is a hockey mom, target shoots, and eats moose stew. She also is a devoted mother to her five children, including her youngest child that is afflicted with Down Syndrome.

At her introductory press conference, the song *Right Now*[71] by Van Halen played in the background. It was a jolt of fresh air to see how in only twelve hours, the news can switch from an empty speech about nothing to a call for actual leadership and service. This woman will not be afraid of dealing with Iran, Iraq, or Afghanistan. She will not be afraid of taking on Republicans when they stray from conservative principles. She certainly will not fear anything as weak as a twenty-first century post-modern liberal.

John McCain hit a home run out of the ballpark. Alaska Governor Sarah Palin is our rock star, and she is solid as a rock.

A hero and an executive vs. a zero and a legislative gasbag. Republicans are set.

eric

My Interview With Lt. Governor Michael Steele

At the 2008 Republican Convention, I had the pleasure of meeting former Maryland Lieutenant Governor Michael Steele.[72]

Despite his lighthearted manner, Michael Steele is no Pollyanna. As a Republican who happens to be black, he has seen the ugliness of ideological bigotry. He has had Oreo cookies tossed at his feet. This was not done by conservatives.

Nevertheless, he keeps his head level and his disposition ultra-sunny. His comments had the convention crowd rollicking.

I did a "walk and talk" interview with Michael Steele.

1) What are the most important issues of 2008?

MS: "The economy and energy. We have to get off of foreign oil. That means doing everything, including drilling right here, right now."

2) Who are your three favorite political heroes?

MS: "Frederick Douglas, Abraham Lincoln, and Ronald Reagan."

3) How would you like to be remembered one hundred years from now? What would you want people to say about Michael Steele the person?

MS: "I was someone who gave a d@mn."

4) The Democrats play identity politics. Given that the Republicans are the party of John McCain, Rudy Giuliani, Fred Thompson, and Michael Steele, and the Democrats are represented by Barack Obama and John Edwards, are the Democrats bigoted against the follically challenged? Can John McCain finally crack the glass ceiling in the modern era? Is America ready for a bald president?

(Governor Steele cracked up, and was fabulous about answering the question.)

MS: "Absolutely! The Democrats absolutely are prejudiced against the follically challenged! The Republican Party represents everybody. Yes, we can elect a bald guy president. Yes we can, yes we should, and yes we will elect bald John McCain the next president. That question was the question of all questions. Excellent question. I love it."

Mr. Steele then turned to his handler, whose job is to get the governor through the throngs without being slowed down, and said, "Get that guy's information. Get his business card!"

He shook my hand vigorously, gave me a healthy pat on the back, and laughed on his way to the elevator. I ran into him a couple more times throughout the convention, and he waved to me and smiled a wide grin.

As I said, his manner was affable, sincere, and fun. It was a pleasure meeting and interviewing Michael Steele because of his incredibly likable personality.

Also, for those who claim that America is racist unless we elect a black president right now, I say that they should put up or shut up, and get to work helping Michael Steele reach the White House after John McCain and Sarah Palin finish their terms.

I will drill this message into the heads of people. If others request I take an easier approach, I will just respond as only Michael Steele can.

Drill, baby, Drill!

eric

My Interview With Governor Linda Lingle

At the 2008 Republican Convention, I had the pleasure of meeting and interviewing Hawaii Governor Linda Lingle.[73]

I have always been a fan of hers. Governor Lingle is a Jewish Republican. It still astounds me that a place with few Jews and few Republicans would elect her. Maybe I should not be astounded. Thrilled is a better word.

I visited Hawaii in 2006 and 2007, attending the Pro Bowl both years. I wanted to meet her, but that is the busy time of year for the legislature. The closest I got was front row, fifty-yard line, at the Pro Bowl. She flipped the coin on the field to start the game.

Governor Lingle has a deep commitment to her Jewish faith. Local Chabad Rabbi Krasnjanski sometimes prays with her. The hotel I stay in when I visit Hawaii is the Ala Moana. The Chabad House is located in that hotel, so I pray with Rabbi Krasnjanski as well.

Governor Lingle is a rock star in Hawaii, and definitely a rising star in the Republican Party. Out of thirty-three bills that came before her in the last legislative session, she vetoed twenty-seven of them, signing only six. As a conservative, I admire her. As I said, as a Jewish conservative, her being in office is a thrill.

While the outpouring of affection for Alaska Governor Sarah Palin is well deserved, I am shocked that Linda Lingle does not get equal attention. She would have also made a fabulous vice presidential nominee. Hopefully a future ticket will include her.

Even as I was ending my last evening at the convention, I had lamented that despite doing over fifty interviews with many senators and governors, I had not interviewed her.

For those who wonder why her in particular, the reason is cultural. I am deeply committed to my religious faith and my political beliefs. I take great pride in seeing Jewish Republicans succeed. Arlen Specter and Norm Coleman are fine senators, and Eric Cantor is one of the top members of the House.

Yet Linda Lingle is a Jewish Republican governor. I want to see a Jewish president in my lifetime. I want that Jewish president to be Republican. Governors get elected far more often than senators.

As a member of the Republican Jewish Coalition Leadership, I can tell you that it is about more than just getting Republicans elected. It is about bonding with other Jews. That is why it is not the Republican Catholic Coalition.

My friend Larry Greenfield, the California executive director of the RJC, was the one that persuaded me to attend the convention. On the third night of the convention, I told him that I was having a wonderful time, but still wish I had interviewed Governor Lingle.

Later that night, after Sarah Palin gave a speech that electrified the entire planet to the right of Leon Trotsky, the crowd spilled out into the halls. I was a fish swimming upstream. As I tried to get past the herds and reach the convention floor, I wondered who my next interview would be.

Among the throngs, I ran into Larry Greenfield. He said, "Hey buddy, have you met Governor Linda Lingle?"

Larry knew I would be wide-eyed. He had a genuine look of happiness on his face, as if to let me know that when he is standing before God and wants testimony, I would be happy to vouch. He then turned to the governor and said, "This is Eric. He is a Jewish Republican blogger. He gets a ton of traffic."

I was surprised she did not have a bunch of security around her. Then again, they may have gotten swallowed up by the crowd. I told her that I was a big fan of hers, and mentioned praying with Rabbi Krasnjanski. She was very receptive, and expressed her admiration for him as well.

I also let her know that my mother is active in her local Chabad in Florida, and that my mom cried when reading about the governor. My mom was just very inspired. The governor was touched by this.

As for doing a "walk and talk" interview, it was more like a "try to stand up and not get crushed and repeat the questions over the yelling throngs" type of interview. Nevertheless, the governor was quite gracious. Even though I was not appointed by anybody, I tried to protect her to make sure that the crowd did not crush her. I was walking ahead of her up the stairs, and backwards. That way I could ensure her safety.

Despite chaos, the interview was completed, and we both reached our destinations safely.

1) How does a nice Jewish Republican woman become governor of Hawaii, a state not known for Jews or Republicans? How did you get elected?

LL: "The key is to work hard. I have a good team around me. People know that I care. Also, I ran at the right time. There was a corruption scandal in Hawaii at the time. Hawaii is a Democratic state, so the Democrats were the ones linked to the corruption. I am a reformer and a fiscal conservative."

2) Does Judaism in any way apply to your job?

LL: "My upbringing gives me empathy for others."

3) Who are your three favorite political heroes?

LL: "I have heroes, but my main heroes are personal. My grandmother is my hero."

4) What are the most important issues of 2008?

LL: "Security. This involves national security and the economy. Economic health is economic security."

5) How would you like to be remembered one hundred years from now? What would you want people to say about Linda Lingle the person?

LL: "As somebody who tried to do the right thing for America. Again, as somebody that worked hard with a good team around her. As somebody who cared."

As we were finishing, I saw a crevice near the railing that provided daylight from the throngs. I moved out of the way so her staff person could usher her to a quieter area. I wished the governor good-bye and then completely reversed gears, walking back toward the convention floor, where I was initially headed.

I skipped Hawaii in 2008, but will go back in 2009. It will again be for the Pro Bowl, meaning that the legislature will be in session. Nevertheless, I will send regards through Rabbi Krasnjanski, and very warm regards they will be.

eric

Chapter 14: Election 2008

America does not need twenty-four month elections. Some feel this gives Americans the chance to thoroughly vet their leaders. The 2008 election is proof that this is a fallacy. The man still has been feted, but never vetted.

Perhaps I could yell, "Vet him, don't fete him," but then I would be mistaken for an enraged Dr. Seuss speaking racial charlatan. I am amazed how Jesse Jackson could criticize gangsta rap and then give most of his speeches in rhyme.

Nevertheless, the election is over, and nobody had their blankety-blanks cut off.

With that I offer some remnants of the 2008 campaign.

Iowa—Praying For Ice Storms

Folks, the Tygrrrr Express is reporting live from the Iowa Caucus ... well, actually I am in Los Angeles, so this is completely fictional, but only an imbecile would trek thousands of miles in January ice storms for a non-story.

Tygrrrr Express: Anderson Cooper, what do you see?

AC: Well Eric, as you know, the Hillary Clinton campaign has been handing out shovels and providing sea salt to make the roads safer. Unfortunately, two elderly ladies slipped and fell, breaking their hips. The Clinton campaign was first on the scene, making sure both women were okay. One of them appears to be a Hillary supporter, and while she wants to be taken to a hospital, they are trying to drag her into a caucus van. The campaign insists that they will look for a hospital adjacent to a caucus precinct, and that they understand her willingness to stand in line for hours with a broken hip. They came prepared with wheelchairs.

The other woman seems to be an Obama supporter, and it appears the Clinton campaign is just leaving her there. A Clinton spokesperson stated that if they took the woman to the hospital, the Obama campaign would accuse them of stealing votes, and that the only ethical thing to do is to leave her there so the Obama people can get her. When asked what could happen to her if the Obama campaign does not get her, the spokeswoman for Hillary replied that, "Barack Obama should be faulted in that case for not having a strong enough organization. He is obviously not ready for the rigors of the presidency."

John Edwards is now on the scene, and he has promised to sue whoever is responsible for this woman falling and hurting herself. The woman stated that she was not angry, but that she really did need medical attention. Edwards stated that he would start by suing God, and if that failed, he would sue the city. In fact, he stated that he would sue in Sioux City, because it sounded like Sue City. Realizing this would anger other caucus voters, he decided to sue South Dakota instead, since that is where the woman was born. Back to you, Eric.

Tygrrrr Express: Thank you, Anderson, you over-glorified pretty boy. Okay, now that the Clinton News Network has reported on the Democrats, let's see what Fox News has to say about their lovers on Republican lane. Bill O'Reilly, what are you seeing?

BO: Well, Eric, first of all, I could kick Anderson Cooper's @ss in a heartbeat. He thinks having perfect hair will get him viewers. He's wrong.

On the subject of perfect hair, as you know, Mitt Romney is incredibly handsome. Some undecided elderly ladies were walking to caucus. When they told him they were undecided, one of the ladies mentioned she had a granddaughter. Springing into action, Romney promised the woman his eldest son, who is also incredibly handsome. Another woman also has a granddaughter, and Romney has offered her his second eldest son, who is also incredibly handsome.

Fred Thompson is bald and destined for success. He is in his hotel room with his feet on the coffee table and a lit cigar. He has made it clear that "only an idiot would go outside in this weather," and that the room service is spectacular.

Rudy Giuliani is in Florida. From what his campaign has reported, the weather is gorgeous, and while there is no snow on the ground, most of the elderly voters still complain about the cold and the quality of the local buffet. He feels ready to take on Al Qaeda based on his experiences cleaning up New York City, steering the city through 9/11, and driving on Highway 95 to Okeechobee at the same time as senior citizens. He is tested, and they are testy.

John McCain has just been offered the use of a wheelchair by one of the other campaigns mistaking him for a grumpy old Iowa voter. Apparently this was a prank by the Huckabee campaign, who insisted that he was against the prank from the beginning while doing it.

Wait, we are getting word that Mitt Romney's fifth son is only 80 percent as handsome as his other sons, rendering him the black sheep of the family, or by normal standards, the eggshell white sheep rather than lily white. Luckily, the fifth woman's granddaughter is significantly more hideous than the other girls, so the fifth Romney son will be acceptable compensation for her vote. Rumors are flying that Romney has ordered his wife to start procreating again now because he is out of sons to pawn off.

Tygrrrr Express: Bill, that is fascinating, and your toupee is better than Letterman's. Who is going to win on the Republican side?

BO: Weren't you paying attention? This whole state is one gigantic church. Even the Jews and Muslims here are Christians. Huckabee will win, because as you know, Jesus just had his birthday. While this has nothing to do with Pakistan, Iowa is not about serious issues.

Tygrrrr Express: Fascinating, Bill. Chris Matthews, you shill for left-wing wackos, what is going on with the candidates that only you care about?

CM: Eric, I am going to scream at you like my caricature on *Saturday Night Live,* because that is what I do. This place is colder than Zell Miller after forgetting his meds and challenging me to a duel. Yet the action is so hot that it's hotter here than Zell Miller forgetting his meds and challenging me to a duel.

Tygrrrr Express: Chris, let's play softball like you and Larry King do every night. Has the cold weather affected your softballs?

CM: Yes, they are freezing and quite salty. Speaking of salty, Dennis Kucinich is very upset that his one campaign staffer forgot to bring the t-shirts that read, "I'm Dennis Kucinich." The original idea was to have Eddie Murphy campaign for him, but that plan was aborted when Eddie stood next to Kucinich and yelled, "I'm Gumby, d@mnit!"

Mike Gravel is yelling louder than I am, but he is actually gaining support here. Apparently, when the Hillary campaign ordered tons of sea salt with instruction to use it to "support the gravel," that confused the voters. Some giant trucks with "gravel" written on them were seen as an endorsement of the Alaska governor. His support has doubled, and he could pull down four votes, or 80 percent of his family.

Tygrrrr Express: Anything else, Chris?

CM: Yes, this vote is closer than a welldigger's @ss.

Tygrrrr Express: That does not make any sense, Chris. Do you mean it is colder than a welldigger's @ss?

CM: Yes, this vote is witch-teat cold. The situation is more tense than a Dan Rather-Katie Couric smackdown. I wouldn't mind giving Katie a smackdown on her shapely ...

Tygrrrr Express: Hold that thought, Chris. We are getting a report in from Florida. Despite the fact that he will be out of office in a year, President Bush's opponents are still counting ballots from seven years ago. Apparently a box of lost votes for Al Gore was found in the swamps of the Everglades. How ironic is that? If only Gore had searched the pristine nature he loves, he would have won. Actually, wait, scratch that. They found ten votes. At this rate, they will have enough votes to reverse the 2000 election by 2010.

We now go to Larry King in Florida. Larry, is the action intense?

LK: No, Eric, in fact, nobody is here except Mr. Giuliani. I know the action is in Iowa, but with my phlebitis, the warm Florida sun works better. As for the voters, they definitely prefer Tony Bennett to Frank Sinatra. Say, did you know of my love for Angie Harmon?

Tygrrrr Express: You mean Angie Dickinson? Angie Harmon is married to Jason Sehorn, the athlete.

LK: The baseball player?

Tygrrrr Express: No, that is Jason Giambi. Anyway, it seems that the governor of Florida is having a beef with the governor of Arkansas?

LK: You mean Jeb Bush and Hillary Clinton?

Tygrrrr Express: Larry, despite George W. Bush being all powerful, he could not keep his brother in office. Hillary Clinton was never governor of Arkansas. She married that guy, the only reason we know who she is. I was referring to the Huckabee-Crist conflict.

LK: Oh yes, that issue. Well, Governor Huckabee keeps referring to the governor of Florida as Charlie Christ. It is Crist, as in wrist. There seems to be confusion because Crist is supporting Giuliani, but Christ is supporting Huckabee. Also, given that Rudy is married to a lovely Hebrew woman who is the heir to the Nathan's hot dog empire, there are rumors that he is changing his name to Rudy Jewliani. Christ was Jewish, and now Crist is supporting Jewliani.

Tygrrrr Express: Larry, his wife is a different Nathan, and that report was even more worthless than your normal show. Given that most of the voters there died a couple years ago and nobody told them, do you feel at home? Wait, hold that thought, we have returns coming in from Iowa.

It seems ten people voted for the Democrats. Hillary Clinton received four votes, with Obama and Edwards each receiving three votes. The Hillary Clinton campaign is calling it a landslide and proof that George W. Bush is evil.

The Republicans had eight people vote. Mike Huckabee received three votes, with Mitt Romney, Fred Thompson, Rudy Giuliani, John McCain, and Ron Paul each receiving one vote. Huckabee was prepared to take the oath of office, but Justice John Roberts explained to him that the Iowa Caucus does not directly elect the president. Upon realizing this, Huckabee promptly quit the race.

The Republican side is a mess, as the other five candidates scramble for Huckabee's three votes. Ron Paul is claiming an avalanche of support, and his second place tie is impressive. Duncan Hunter was expected to drop out, in keeping with his promise to quit if he did not finish in the top six or get at least one vote.

Apparently, Tom Tancredo is demanding that the other candidates address why all the illegal immigrants are being hidden, and why the Iowa police have not acted. Mitt Romney explained that there simply were only white people in Iowa, and that as an ultra-white person himself, he was qualified to state with certainty as to the state's homogeneity. Barack Obama absolutely agreed, and stated that he will not discuss his black heritage until he reaches South Carolina. Eager to jump on that bandwagon, Hillary Clinton will not go public with the news that she is actually a woman until she gets to California, a more progressive state. She will then ditch the pantsuits and go back to the girly girl hair she had in 1992.

Okay, for final thoughts … Pat Buchanan, go first.

PB: The problem with the Jews is—

Tygrrrr Express: Never mind; how about you, Charles Krauthammer?

CK: This process is a complete joke.

Tygrrrr Express: Sir Charles of Krauthammer, right as always. Alan Colmes, your eyebrow creeps me out. Final thoughts?

AC: I have the same initials as Anderson Cooper.

Tygrrrr Express: Yes, but your nickname should be shared with Rob Reiner. Speaking of all in the family, Larry King, you have twenty families, any thoughts?

LK: Mitt Romney has handsome sons. I can't wait to celebrate Hanukkah with them.

Tygrrrr Express: Umm, Larry ... never mind. Susan Estrich ... your thoughts?

SE: (High pitched inaudible screech that only dogs and Howard Dean can here)

Tygrrrr Express: Never mind. Bob Beckel, you like hookers. Why do you think George W. Bush is a moral failure?

BB: Eric, that was a cheap shot, and if there is anything I know, it's cheap shots. I ran Walter Mondale's campaign, so I think—

Tygrrrr Express: No, you don't. Greta Van Susteren, you do a fabulous imitation of Beaker[74] from the *Muppets*. Final thoughts?

GVS: Well, in talking to Scott Peterson on what Natalee Holloway's mother thinks about Anna Nicole and Britney—

Tygrrrr Express: Greta, I wish you and Geraldo would be deported to Aruba permanently. I heard you did a cavity search of him and found some of the treasure in Al Capone's vaults. Enough.

We have further news that private citizen and Yassir Arafat's award-winning compadre, Al Gore, claimed that there was a groundswell for him to enter the race, and that he had the support of Iowa football coach Hayden Fox. Apparently, he got confused. Hayden Fry was a former football coach, now deceased. Hayden Fox was a fictional football coach on the TV show *Coach*, played by Craig T. Nelson. Senator John Kerry claimed that he had the support of football coach Bo Schembechler, until it was pointed out that Mr. Schembechler is also deceased and was the coach of Michigan, not Iowa.

This concludes the waste of time that is the Iowa Caucus. For the eighteen people who voted, eighteen is a lucky number in Jewish culture, but since none of you are Jewish, I hope you get hypothermia for forcing eighteen thousand journalists to cover your every movement from your morning shower to your evening bedtime tuck in. Mr. Clinton, stop pretending to be a journalist.

On a side note, several terrorist attacks on American soil were foiled today. The media was busy covering Iowa, given that there are no Pakistan or Iraq caucuses today.

Dear God, I pray for ice storms to blanket them all until their lips are too frozen to speak.

eric

Fred Thompson—From the King of the Hill to the White House

Politicians aiming to reach the White House often engage in a courtship with all things connected to television. Less talked about is how much television mimics the White House. While shows like *The West Wing* do this directly, it is often more fascinating to watch the indirect parallels. Television reflects the world we live in, and the president of the United States leads this world.

The 1980s brought Ronald Reagan. There was glitz and glamour. Nancy Reagan wore stunning dresses, Frank Sinatra crooned, and the top television shows were *Dallas* and *Dynasty*. Wall Street boomed. J.R Ewing was not a criminal to most Americans. "It was just business darlin'"[75] as only Larry Hagman could say with that grit-eating grin. Rock bands like Poison and Warrant had big smiles, bigger hair, and happy sounds.

George Herbert Walker Bush wanted a kindler, gentler nation. *The Cosby Show* and *Family Ties* reached their zenith. It was during this administration that television shows provided analogies by the leaders themselves. George H. W. Bush "wanted an America that looked more like *The Waltons* than *The Simpsons*."[76] Dan Quayle made controversial statements about *Murphy Brown*.[77] While Quayle's remark was the more criticized of the two, his flaw was being ahead of his time. Bush's *Waltons* comment showed he was behind the times. It was a *Simpsons* world. The glitz was gone. The Huxtables were wealthy, but quiet about it.

The Bill Clinton presidency was best reflected by the top show of the 1990s …*Seinfeld*, a show about nothing. This is not to say Bill Clinton was good or bad. He was peripheral. Conversations about nonsense took place. He was part of those conversations. The world went by, and we all mused. The 1990s truly was a decade about nothing. We had the Internet revolution, but most of us just watched it happen. Even if Al Gore was there at the beginning, he did not create eBay, JDate, cybersluts.com, Yahoo Finance, or anything else that truly made the world a better place online. Glam Rockers faded away, as did their hair.

George W. Bush intervened, but 9/11 accelerated the next intervention. *Seinfeld* was fantasy. Reality television boomed. (In keeping with the Larry David-*Seinfeld* link, the John Kerry campaign should be called the *Curb Your Enthusiasm* campaign. It certainly curbed mine.) In the real world, people were trying to kill us. Compared to that, eating live bugs on TV did not seem so bad.

Could *Seinfeld* have succeeded post 9/11? Or was it a perfect show for the fat, dumb, happy decade of the 1990s? Would people have cared about Monica Lewinsky in a post-Bin Laden world? Would Clinton have even had the time or the energy? It is difficult trying to get laid when you spend every waking minute worrying about the world blowing up.

These questions become paramount because as the lines get blurrier, the fictional characters we watch on TV could determine our next leader.

One of them is Fred Thompson. Even Ronald Reagan did not transition as easily as Fred Thompson. With his "aw shucks" country boy demeanor, his easy smile, and his pickup truck, Fred Thompson could be your neighbor. He was also a lawyer during the Watergate Hearings. His acting roles have always shown him as the cool, calm, steady hand of a leader. As the top man at the airport in *Die Harder*, as everyone else is freaking out, he calmly gives orders regarding the airplanes to "back 'em, stack 'em, and rack 'em."[78] In *Wiseguy*, as Knox Pooley, one minute he is leading a white racist mob, the next minute he is selling condominiums in Florida. He sold racism to young whites and property to old ones (even as the fake racist, somehow he was still likable).

As D.A. Arthur Branch, he has made *Law and Order* watchable again. When Sam Waterston goes on one of his bombastic liberal speeches, which seem to be more common than Al Pacino ranting in a movie, Arthur Branch has the quietest ... and last ... word. While I yell at my TV set for Jack McCoy (Waterston) to shut up, Big Arthur slowly calms him down, all the while giving orders. When his character fired a liberal prosecutor for being an activist, the stunned liberal activist asked him if her colleague agreed. Big Arthur replied, "No. But it's my office ... and my decision. You're fired."[79] He said it in a whisper, because big dogs don't have to bark loud.

While Arthur Branch is a fictional TV character, Fred Thompson is very similar on the surface ... an easygoing, likable guy that simply wants to get things done. He is a rock-solid conservative, but is appealing in the way Ronald Reagan was. Fred Thompson won't scare little children. He did get rolled by the Democrats during the Whitewater hearings, but he conceded this, and vowed not to get fooled again under the guise of being genial. Smart men learn. Thompson seems smart.

The last thing about Fred Thompson is he can talk to Hank Hill. Again, while *King of the Hill* is a fictional show, and a cartoon at that, it does what most shows fail to do...show red-state America in a positive light.

Yes, Boomhauer is incomprehensible, and Dale Gribble is the stereotypical government conspiracy nut. However, they are not treated as the norm. Hank is friends with them, but he (and the rest of the town) sees them (especially Dale) as wingnuts. Hank Hill likes football, red meat, and while he believes in Jesus, does not preach to others. His primary concerns are feeding his family and helping his son grow up right. He is uncomfortable talking about things people don't talk about.

Hank Hill might not be totally comfortable talking about gays, but he is not hostile toward them. He goes hunting, but does not have bloodlust. He drinks beer, not Evian water. He votes Republican, but is more interested in talking about the Dallas Cowboys. He is a "guy's guy." A touchy-feely liberal asked him, "How about you just bond with me? How about you just understand me?" He replied, "How about I just kick your @ss?"[80] He was not looking for a fight. He just wanted to be left alone from all the touchy-feely garbage that in his (and many) mind is bringing down America. When a Massachusetts client wanted to call him J.R. and have him wear a cowboy hat, he replied, "You know Texas has changed a lot in the last 150 years."

King of the Hill works because it treats Red State America with dignity. It does poke fun at "Bubbas," but it pokes more fun at elitists that misunderstand them. In the end, Hank is a Bubba, but what is a Bubba anyway? A Bubba is a hardworking family man who just wants to watch football, drink a beer, and eat a steak without being attacked by liberal, vegetarian tofu nuts while doing it. It was Bubbas at Iwo Jima, not New England liberals on college deferments.

Liberals look down upon Bubbas at their own peril. It is difficult to lead fifty states when you only condescend to talk to people in eighteen of them. The last ten presidential elections have been won by people you could drink a beer and watch a ballgame with it. Al Gore, John Kerry, Michael Dukakis, and even Bush Sr. were people you could drink Chardonnay with and go to the opera. That does not make them bad people, but it is not what most Americans enjoy. Bill Clinton cheered on his Razorbacks. "Dubya" used to own the Texas Rangers. You can't get more "beer-ballgame" than that.

The one mistake people make is underestimating Bubbas. If they are so dumb, how do they keep winning elections? It takes brains. Lots of brains.

Fred Thompson is smart, likable, and easy on the ears. While it would be a shame to have *Law and Order* become wretched again, it would be worth losing a TV show to have a good leader in the White House. He is a legitimate candidate.

Hank Hill would vote for Arthur Branch. Hank Hill decides elections.

"Back 'em, stack 'em and rack 'em." Go get 'em Fred.

eric

Mitt Romney—More Than Just Dilbert's Mormon Manager

In the brilliant comic strip *Dilbert*, the main worker bee is confronted with the dysfunctional goings on in his office. Fat and balding, his destiny is a cubicle as others leapfrog past him on the corporate ladder. One final straw comes when the boss tells Dilbert, "This is Bob. He has no experience in this industry, but he is tall with perfect hair. He is your new manager."[81]

It is ironic that at a time in history where substance is desired more than ever, a promising candidate for president is bogged down for the shallowest of stylistic reasons.

Mitt Romney is tall, and, yes, he does have perfect hair. Not good hair. Perfect hair. As a heterosexual male, I confess, the guy is handsome. His square jaw is a cross between Dick Tracy and the overexaggerated cartoon patriarch on *American Dad.*[82] Unfortunately, focusing on Mitt Romney's style obscures a substantive and successful career.

Mitt Romney saved the Olympics at Salt Lake City, Utah. A corrupt endeavor besotted by financial mismanagement needed a business leader … someone who could get through bureaucracy and get things done. Despite his right to chest-thump at a job well done, he instead chose to engage in a self-deprecating manner. At the Century Plaza Hotel for the annual California Republican Party Convention, Mitt Romney joked about his Olympic triumph. He stated, "My sons told me that as long as they lived, they never thought they would see their dad on the front page of the sports section." In another one-liner that had the crowd in hysterical laughter he spoke about his confrontational approach to the Massachusetts legislature. "People in Massachusetts say that Arnold Schwarzenegger gets along better with Democrats in the legislature than I do in Massachusetts. He should get along better with Democrats. He's sleeping with one."[83]

This leads to another irony concerning Romney. The biggest criticism of Romney by some conservatives is not his confrontational manner, but his comity. He gets along well with the Democratic Massachusetts legislature. In a time of polarization, sleeping with the enemy is not to be tolerated. Then again, just because many Democrats agreed with Ronald Reagan did not mean he agreed with them. Being genial is not akin to compromising. Occasionally reaching an agreement with political opponents is not necessarily an abdication of beliefs. Outsiders and backbenchers can speak about ideological purity. Leaders have to get things done.

Romney helped pass a health care bill. Those criticizing the bill have not given enough time to see if their criticisms have panned out. It's too soon. Additionally, this bill is not Hillarycare or Ted Kennedy's plan. Yes, Ted Kennedy's name is on it, but Ted Kennedy would block any popular bill not giving him partial credit. His name does not automatically invalidate the law.

As for other issues, Mitt Romney is being portrayed as the one thing that no square-jawed man should ever be seen as … a flip-flopper … especially on abortion. He was pro-choice when running for governor of Massachusetts. Now he is pro-life when running for president. This is in contrast to principled leaders such as Bill Clinton, Al Gore, and Jesse Jackson, who were all pro-life before running for the Democratic nomination for president. George H. W. Bush in 1980 ran as the pro-choice Republican candidate, yet in 1988 he was ardently pro-life. Steve Forbes went rightward between 1996 and 2000. So why should Mitt Romney be given a pass? Because he governed Massachusetts.

It is one thing to have an ideology. It is another to be an ideologue. Ideologues make bombastic speeches. Pragmatists win elections and get to govern. They get things done. Conservatives are not welcome in Massachusetts. Republicans yes, but not conservatives. Richard Nixon won forty-nine states in 1972. He lost Massachusetts. A Democrat would have to kill someone before being defeated. In some cases, even that is not enough. Massachusetts will elect libertarian Republicans such as William Weld and Mitt Romney. The state has allowed Michael Dukakis, Ted Kennedy, and John Kerry to lead them. Short of praying that global warming causes melting polar ice caps to flood the state until it breaks off, floats away, and joins Antarctica, Massachusetts Republicans have to field candidates who will support cutting taxes and killing terrorists. Period.

Another criticism of Romney is that he is a Mormon. This should be of deep concern to anyone who is bigoted. For those concerned that I just declared that anyone opposing Romney solely because of his Mormonism is bigoted, well stop being bigoted and then this concern will dissipate. JFK was a Catholic. Joseph Lieberman is an Orthodox Jew. Even those in America who are white Christians are subdivided between Methodists, Baptists, Lutherans, Mormons, Presbyterians, Episcopalians, and other multi-syllabic derivatives of Christianity. As a Jewish person, I have no idea how they differ. That does not mean they are less than noble religions. It means I am as uneducated as every other kid who went to public schools. (Maybe Mitt Romney can fix that. Even if he can't, neither can anyone else. He's not Superman)

The current struggle with Islam is not that Islamists want to practice Islam. It is that they want everyone else to submit to Islam. When I met and spoke to Mitt Romney, he did not seem to have any interest in converting me to Mormonism. He seemed more interested in speaking about tax cuts. Having religious faith does not mean forcing others to share this faith. Belief in God does not mean the person is God. Freedom of religion does not mean freedom from religion. These are all old clichés, but the hostility toward many who express pride in their religion is even more tiresome. Whatever the Mormon equivalent of Sharia law, Mitt Romney seems more interested in the U.S. Constitution as a governing body. As long as he supports Supreme Court justices that agree with this philosophy, he is a conservative in the truest sense.

As for Sharia law, Mitt Romney does not want U.S. citizens to be subjected to it. His aggressive speeches concerning the War on Terror show a man who understands that the struggle for our livelihood as free citizens goes beyond anything we have faced in our lifetimes. Mitt Romney is pro-America, pro-Israel, and anti-enemies of free people. We know this because he emphatically says so in his speeches. He does not complain about how quickly to surrender. He understands that leadership is not about carping. It is about rolling up sleeves and getting to work.

I am not saying Mitt Romney can do anything. However, cutting taxes in Massachusetts is impressive. He is likable, genial, and successful. He is not an artificial candidate or a "pretty boy." Think of him as being as handsome as John Edwards, only with realistic solutions to important problems.

The last thing to think about is something that is applied to all candidates. Ronald Reagan raised taxes in 1982. Therefore, every candidate deserves one get out of jail free card, or a mulligan for those who dress badly and wear checkered trousers.

If the worst we can say about Mitt Romney is that his religion is not understood by most, then his detractors should throw in the towel. Mitt Romney is a good decent man who deserves to be considered a serious presidential contender. No he is not perfect. Nothing in life is perfect. Even his hair is not completely perfect. Well, yeah…it is.

eric

Ron Paul, Sean Paul, John Paul, and RuPaul—Which One is the Least Coherent?

In listening to Ron Paul, which I can do only for a few moments before bursting out laughing, it occurred to me that I do not have the special Marvin the Martian rabbit ears required to understand his strange dialect. Like other Pauls in history, his message is incomprehensible to those who do not speak gibberish. I compared him with other incomprehensible historical Pauls to see which one made the least sense.

I started with the late (rest his soul) Pope John Paul. I personally liked Pope John Paul II. He was a religious @sskicker. Unlike in Judaism, where there is anarchy to the point of *Lord of the Flies*, Catholicism has structure. Like them or not, the rules are crystal clear. When asking the pope to change standards so people can feel better about being sinners, the pope reminded people that the church IS the standard. People must change. Stop being a screwup, or stop being Catholic. I love this guy. I have guidelines on how to behave.

One reason I never grasped the pope's message is because he spoke in Latin. For those in public school, Latin is not where the first letter becomes the last letter followed by "ay." Latin is a romance language. This makes the pope speaking Latin ironic, because he was forbidden from having romances. My inability to understand his sermons in Latin was no more difficult than understanding them in Croatian. His sermons had cool titles like "Ecclesia de Eucharistia" and "Centecimus Annus." Not since rock group the Police put out the albums *Zenyatta Mondatta* and *Outlandos D'amour*[84] has popular culture been so cool while requiring so much translation.

To show solidarity with the Jews, the pope wore a yarmulke, and he was a good sport by going on the 1980s comedy *Night Court* with Harry Anderson. I must say that once his words were put into English, he was understandable, and a pretty cool dude as far as popes go.

This brings me to Sean Paul. Unlike the late John Paul, Rastafarian singer Sean Paul insists that he already is singing in English. His song "Temperature"[85] is a great dance song, and despite what I originally posed, does not overtly mention Barack Obama. Here are some of the lyrics.

"The gal dem Schillaci/Sean da Paul
So me give it to/so me give to/so me give it to/to all girls
Five million and forty naughty shorty
Baby girl/all my girls/all my girls/Sean da Paul sey

[Chorus:]

Well woman the way the time cold I wanna be keepin' you warm
I got the right temperature for shelter you from the storm
Oh lord, gal I got the right tactics to turn you on, and girl I
Wanna be the papa/You can be the mom/oh oh!

[Verse 1:]

Make I see the gal them bruk out pon the floor from you don't want no
worthless performer
From you don't want no man wey can't turn you on gal make I see your hand
them up on ya.
Can't tan pon it long/naw eat no yam/no steam fish/nor no green banana
But down in Jamaica we give it to you hot like a sauna"

Contrary to those who follow the pope, "The Gal Dem Shellaci" is not one
of his liturgical musings. I think it is a pasta dish that either goes well with
red wine or Diet Coke, or translation for "The girlie dems get shellacked."
As someone that does not smoke marijuana, it is not 100 percent English to
me. Then again, a message about having fun without harming others should
not be discouraged, even if subtitles are required. So Sean Paul for now gets
a pass.

This brings us to political gadfly Ron Paul, who on the surface appears to be
tire executive Morrie Taylor without logical reasoning. Below is a transcription
of his fiery exchange with Rudy Giuliani, with Paul's comments translated
from the original democrat/liberal gibberish.

Rep. Ron Paul, R-Texas, GOP presidential candidate: "They attack us
because we've been over there, we've been bombing Iraq for ten years. We've
been in the Middle East. I think Reagan was right. We don't understand the
irrationality of Middle Eastern politics."

Rudy Giuliani, GOP presidential candidate: "That's an extraordinary
statement of someone who lived through the attack of September 11, that we
invited the attack because we were attacking Iraq. I don't think I've ever heard
that before, and I've heard some pretty absurd explanations for September 11.
I would ask the congressman to withdraw that comment and tell us that he
didn't really mean that."[86]

Blaming the United States of America for 9/11. There are three explanations for this. (1) Ron Paul is a liberal Democrat. (2) Ron Paul works for Al Jazeera. (3) Ron Paul is a crackpot. I suspect all of the above.

Based on his uselessness to anything resembling intelligent discourse, I therefore declare Ron Paul to be the least comprehensible of the Paul brothers.

As for black drag queen RuPaul, whatever he/she/it actually is, RuPaul's problem is one that is disturbing to the visual senses, not the auditory. Apparently RuPaul has crossover appeal to blacks, women, and the transgendered. My lack of understanding of this Paul renders me unqualified to analyze what went wrong and where. Ron Paul therefore still disturbs me most.

eric

Why Rudy Giuliani is Right

I have never been happier to be a Republican. This is because I understand that the 2006 election was not a repudiation of conservatism, nor was it by any means an embrace of liberalism, which has been in retreat for over a quarter of a century. I am optimistic because the Republican class of 2008 is the strongest group of individuals to seek the office since Ronald Reagan. (George W. Bush, while a phenomenal president, was not a strong candidate.) One of the strongest candidates to ever seek the Republican nomination is Rudy Giuliani.

At this point some conservatives are suffering from frozen mandibles, or lockjaw for short. How can a pro-choice, pro-gay rights, and pro-gun control Republican win the Republican nomination? Simple. The religious right are not the troglodytes they are often made out to be. They are clear thinking individuals that realize that several factors make Rudy a fantastic candidate for them.

First of all, New York Republicans have to be moderate. George Pataki is pro-choice. Even Al D'Amato played the moderate card to perfection. He voted down the line for pro-life issues, but never talked about it. He was a stealth conservative. He worked on breast cancer issues, endearing him to moderate women. Rudy Giuliani had to be liberal in New York. Yes, he was wrong to have endorsed Mario Cuomo. Ronald Reagan raised taxes in 1982, and outside of my family, no one commands as much respect from me as the Gipper (rest his soul). Rudy Giuliani is not Nancy Pelosi. He is conservative where it counts.

Secondly, Rudy cleaned up New York City. Gotham City is now a world-class city. Under David Dinkins, a good, decent man not tough enough for the job, New York City was dying. The problems existed long before Mr. Dinkins, but the Dinkins reign of error exacerbated them. Rudy Giuliani took on everyone who stood in his way.

The Mob? Fugheddaboutit. Yassir Arafat? Out of my city! The Anti-Semitic Saudi prince? Take your $10 million of blood money and shove it where the Manhattan sun doesn't shine. Unions? Go to work or be fired. Virgin Mary defilers? He lost in court, but cleaned their clocks in the court of public opinion.

Those who like Giuliani say he is a bully, but gets things done. Those who dislike him say he gets things done, but is a bully. As someone who takes being called "heavy handed" or "high handed" as a compliment, I don't want someone warm and fuzzy. I want someone effective. I don't need eloquence, class, grace or an endearing smile with a fake lower lip quiver feeling my pain. I want someone who will take terrorists and b*tchslap them.

Yes, I said b*tchslap them. I do not just want them defeated. I want them humiliated. I want them wiped off the face of the earth quicker than you can say the name of the Iranian president (in all fairness, it is hard to pronounce).

This is the third issue concerning Giuliani, where Rudy can appeal to the religious right. We are not at war with an indescribable enemy. We are at war with Islamofacist monsters. They want to kill all Jews and all Christians, as well as Muslims who have the nerve to not be genocidal lunatics. This is a religious struggle. It is Judeo-Christian civilization vs. Islamofacist barbarism. Conservatives can overlook a few abortions provided Rudy really is pro-life in the form of preventing good Christians from being murdered. That is being pro-life.

All politicians talk about winning the War on Terror (Republican ones anyway), but Rudy has helped lead the fight to actually win it. Others have words. He has deeds. With steely-eyed determination, he told Bin Laden, "Not in my city." While others thought the War on Terror started in 2001, Giuliani at the 2004 Republican Convention traced terrorism all the way back to the 1972 Munich Olympics. He spoke of the 1985 Leon Klinghoffer atrocity. He spoke of the *USS Cole*, Oklahoma City, and Mogadishu.

Fourth, Rudy Giuliani is a conservative where it counts. He cut taxes. He promised to appoint strict constructionist judges. He cracked down on the squeegee men, because cracking down on small crime does reduce big crime. He unequivocally supports Israel, which is music to the eardrums of evangelicals. Even liberal Jews, who go out of their way to support policies and candidates that are bad for Jewish people, support Israel (most of the time).

Yes, Rudy has been divorced. He has committed adultery. His loyal right hand, Bernie Kerik, was tainted by scandal, although if I was given the opportunity to date Judith Regan, I would throw my career in the toilet as well. I mean the whole point of getting power for men is to date women like Judith Regan. Money won't do it. She already has it (Several minute digression while I fantasize about Judith Regan in ways that the Bible would not condone ... those pouty lips, that perfect flowing hair gently caressing her ... okay, I need a few more minutes).

Back to Rudy. He was wrong on gun control, although again New York City is not Middle America. He had no choice. He can be abrasive, but somebody has to stand up to Al "Strom" Sharpton. More importantly, somebody has to stop Hillary Clinton.

New York Post columnist John Podhoretz understands that Hillary Clinton should never be underestimated. She is smart, calculating, tough, and ruthless. She will deck you in the face and then smile, and then play the delicate girly crying routine when a less aggressive pol dares to fight back (R.I.P. Rick Lazio).

Rudy Giuliani does not back down from Mafia kingpins, drug lords, or even teachers unions, and everybody including mobsters fear teachers unions. He will not be afraid of Hillary or her thuggish band of character assassin Clintonistas. He will match her blow for blow. Hillary Clinton is not the devil, but her agenda would be anathema to conservatives. Rudy is pro-choice. Hillary would bring the abortion of the month club to town and have her be fawned over in a way only rivaled by Oprah's minions. Her views on the economy, gun control, and most issues are toxic. Bill Clinton won in 1992 partly because the religious right abandoned George H. W. Bush even though he catered to them enough to drive away moderates and collapse the Reagan coalition, until Newt Gingrich unified it, with help from Bill Clinton. Republicans will not make the same mistake. If Hillary wins, they get nothing. If Giuliani wins, they have some voice, even if less than they desire.

Rudy Giuliani appeals to moderates, but his election would be a dream for social conservatives, if they could just get out of their own way. Perhaps they will have no choice. Rudy Giuliani will not fear them.

Nobody is perfect. Leaders do not get everything right. They get the big things right. The big thing in the twenty-first century is the War on Terror. Everyone from liberal Jews to moderate Muslims to conservative Christians must understand this.

Mr. Giuliani has my vote. He earned it. Now he needs to roll up his sleeves and get to work. We all do. Taxes do not lower themselves, red tape does not cut itself, and terrorists do not surrender themselves. It takes leadership.

If liberal Jews, moderate Muslims, and conservative Christians all have concerns, then Rudy Giuliani is on the right track.

Good luck, Mayor Giuliani. You are the right man at the right time. The religious right will understand. Do what you have to do. Then lead us well.

eric

John McCain—It's the Man Himself

Abraham Lincoln is credited with saying that you can't fool all of the people all of the time. For presidential candidates, it is only necessary to fool a plurality twice, and occasionally thrice if your spouse runs as well.

Rarely has a politician been so misunderstood by the entire electorate as John McCain.

Those who should embrace him are his biggest detractors. Those who would normally heap ill-informed scorn on him shower him instead with ill-informed praise.

John McCain is a media darling. This alone leaves the left drooling and the right suspicious. He favors campaign finance reform, which only enhances his love affair with the media. The media loves campaign finance reform because they love restrictions on free speech with themselves exempted. That gives them more power. McCain was also a rival to President Bush, which again scores points with liberals and the media (redundant, I know), and grates conservatives, who in general like the president.

So why is everybody wrong? Because McCain is a down the line conservative. He is ultra-conservative. He is an arch-conservative. Every word applied to conservatives in pejorative terms fits McCain like a glove. He is pro-life, anti-gun control, and a staunch supporter of the Iraq war and the surge. The media adores him for criticizing the way the war is being run, but the irony is he wants an even bigger escalation, which would make liberals apoplectic if President Bush suggested this.

Conservatives distrust McCain even though he is one of them because anyone adored by liberals and the media in conservative minds should be distrusted. Yet if conservatives believe that liberals are always wrong (I do not, because blinking VCRs are still right twice daily), wouldn't liberals being right about McCain defy logic? Everything about the liberal view of McCain defies logic.

So why do so many who know nothing about John McCain support him? More importantly, why do many who know everything about McCain and vehemently disagree with him support him? Because of John McCain the man Himself.

Many people know that John McCain was a war hero, but little more. Others know he was a prisoner of war. What people do not know is the depths of John McCain's heroism. A famous admiral's son, the North Vietnamese offered him early release and an end to his miserable experience as a prisoner of war. He was chained, beaten, and tortured. When I say tortured, I mean real torture, not the summer camp games of Abu Gharaib and Guantanamo Bay that liberals love to carp about. Not the torture of working a thirty-five-hour week that French people complain about. Not the $200 an hour pleasure beating from Mistress Evil (man she was hot ... dressed like Catwoman, could use a cattle prod like no woman ... what a lovely woman ... gimme a few minutes).

Okay, back. He was T-O-R-T-U-R-E-D. Given that most rational people would surrender after listening to ten minutes of a Barbra Streisand album, having bones broken for sport would break most people. McCain was given the right to go home. He said no. He made a commitment to his military brethren that he would not leave them behind. Either everyone would be released or none would. The North Vietnamese released nobody. McCain was beaten day after day. He did not yield. Several years later, he was released with the rest of his men.

This is why liberals and the media love McCain. They are in awe of him. They are sheepish around him, and honored to be in his presence. In keeping with the blinking VCR theory, on this issue, the liberals are right. I have met the man. I have shaken his hand, looked into his eyes, and briefly conversed with him. I had on an Arizona Diamondbacks t-shirt, and as the line was approaching, I felt compelled to quickly put on a collared shirt and an appropriate necktie. I felt it was the respectful thing to do. He was the potential presidential candidate, and yet it seemed more important that I had his approval.

I totally disagree with McCain on campaign finance reform. It is a violation of free speech. As predicted, liberals broke the rules anyway by creating 527s. Then again, Ronald Reagan raised taxes in 1982, which will forever be my answer to a politician who needs one get-out-of-jail-free card to avoid a black mark on an otherwise spotless career. McCain was part of the Keating Five, but he took the blame. He leveled with the American people. He took responsibility for his actions, which saved the taxpayers a multi-year investigation. (Are you listening Bill and Hillary Clinton? If you confess what you did, there is no scandal. The short-attention-spanned media gets bored, and the story dies quickly.)

Conservatives are angry because McCain is admired by liberals and the media. Ronald Reagan, with regards to the fringes, noted that they agreed with him, not vice versa. McCain is not a liberal posing as a conservative. He is a conservative that liberals like. Conservatives should get out of the way and let liberals figure it out themselves (or as in most cases, not). This poses no ethical dilemmas because McCain has always stated he was a conservative. Nobody is listening.

So why do I admire John McCain, despite disagreeing with him on his signature issue and other issues? Because the world needs leadership. It needs real heroes. John McCain is a hero. I do not agree with his persona or all of his policy positions. I agree with who he is. I admire the man himself.

It was an honor to shake your hand, Senator McCain. Thank you, and a hearty hero's welcome home.

eric

The People Have Spoken

The American people have spoken. Barack Obama is the forty-fourth president of the United States of America. John McCain conceded. There are no hanging chads or recounts. The election is over. There will be many days ahead for everything from analysis to criticism to self-reflection. Today, disappointed as I am, I offer only congratulations.

Senator Barack Obama won this race fair and square. We can argue about merit and policy, and in the coming months we absolutely will. However, getting elected in politics is a game. Barack Obama played it well enough within the established rules to win.

Was he lucky? Absolutely. Yet winners capitalize on lucky breaks. Barack Obama cannot have predicted the financial crisis, but enough Americans felt that they could trust him with the nation's highest office.

Am I worried? Absolutely. However, I am willing to wait and see. Barack Obama is a complete mystery to me. There is still much about him that we do not know.

Is he a stark raving leftist ideologue or a ruthless cold pragmatist? Will he govern from the left or the center? I want to see his cabinet and what they do.

For now, I want Senator Obama to know that I love my nation more than I ever disagreed with him. I saw how the left treated George W. Bush. I will not become part of an angry mob. I do not hate this man. I genuinely want to work with him.

If he truly wants to govern in a bipartisan manner, I will hear him out. If he decides that those disagreeing with him are enemies, I will work full throttle to protect and defend what I believe in.

For now, I offer some disjointed thoughts.

For one, it is a genuine shame that his grandmother did not live to see his achievement. I lost my grandmother six months ago. Given that my grandmother was a Democrat, I am sure both of these women are in heaven smiling right now.

For another thing, I pray to God for Obama's safety. God forbid...I do not even say the unthinkable...it would rip this country apart for half of a century. Get this man double or triple the Secret Service protection, whatever it takes to keep him and his family safe. Our very survival as a nation could depend on this.

I am also thinking how much I love America. I am not bitter today. I am a Republican, and Republicans have won seven of ten presidential elections prior to this one. We cannot win every single one of them.

I am grateful that we live in a land where the transition of power is peaceful.

I hope that Barack Obama has the decency and class to now recede into the background until January 20, 2009. George W. Bush is still our president, and he deserves to finish his term with dignity.

The tone in Washington has been poisonous for the last twenty years. The way George W. Bush is treated in the next ten weeks could impact how Barack Obama is treated over the next several years. For those who think that George W. Bush does not deserve an ounce of good will, just remember that Obama has promised unity.

I believe that Barack Obama is more interested in accomplishing things than in exacting revenge. After all, he has not been part of the acrimony. Bill Clinton and George W. Bush were not part of it, yet the hatred that has been going back and forth since Robert Bork was "Borked" by Ted Kennedy has not subsided.

Barack Obama keeps speaking of wanting to unite people. A few kind words about our current president would be a well received olive branch.

Beyond that, I can only say that we live in a nation where a black man can become president. We will one day have a female president, a Jewish president, and perhaps even a black female Jewish president. Farfetched? Not in America.

Some will criticize the voters for making the wrong choice. I refuse to do this. As Karl Rove has said many times, "The masses are not @sses."[87]

The American people are the ones that won liberty from England, invented television, put a man on the moon, invented the Internet, defeated Nazism and Communism, and found a way to balance deep religious convictions with a functioning secular democracy.

The American people chose Barack Obama. I disagree with the verdict, but respect the American people too much to question it. I have spent years castigating the left for never giving George W. Bush a fair shot. I will extend the courtesy to Barack Obama.

Most importantly, I will not despair over this election. I determine my own fate. As Rush Limbaugh has remarked, my success is not defined by who wins elections. Even those who disagree with Rush should agree with this view. I will go to work, love my family, be good to my friends, and continue to build a life with the love of my life. On Sundays I will watch football.

This campaign has been draining for me, and I am only a blogger. Like everybody else involved on any level with the campaign, I could use a break. There are other topics.

I will do what we should all do. I will live my life as best as I can.

Good luck, Senator Obama. Excuse me. Make that President-elect Obama. You earned this, as well as the upgraded title you will receive again in ten weeks. Use your future title wisely. America and the rest of the world depend on this.

eric

Hillary Said … Oh, Who Cares!

Let's enjoy a quiet Saturday where nothing of consequence is occurring politically.

Hillary Clinton gave one of the most inspiring speeches in the history of America. With a grace, class, and flair that only she could radiate, Hillary helped us reach our better selves. As I remain glued to her speech, hanging on every word, I was moved to tears. This is why I woke up early on a Saturday morning to … wait … never mind. Nobody cares.

Who the heck am I kidding? I was sound asleep, and wrote this the night before.

The last time I checked, losers endorsing winners is not news. Also, Hillary took a surrender lap longer than most candidates take victory laps.

For those wondering why it took Hillary so long to admit defeat, one need look no further than the sports schedule.

She could not surrender Wednesday evening. The Detroit Red Wings and Pittsburgh Penguins were playing game six of the National Hockey League Finals. The game was a thriller. In game five, Detroit was one minute away from winning it all at home. Pittsburgh pulled their goalie, and pulled out a miracle. They tied the game with thirty seconds left, and won in triple overtime. In game six, Pittsburgh trailed by two goals, and scored one with ninety seconds left. Yet a furious finish fell short this time, and the Red Wings were once again champions.

Hillary could not surrender Thursday evening. The Los Angeles Lakers and Boston Celtics were playing game one of the National Basketball Association Finals. In the 1980s, these teams played in some of the great championships of all time. The Celtics had Larry Bird, Kevin McHale, Danny Ainge, and Robert "Chief" Parish. The Lakers had Magic Johnson, Kareem Abdul Jabbar, and the rest of the "Showtime" cast. Today the Lakers have Kobe Bryant and Pau Gasol. The Celtics have Kevin Garnett and Paul Pierce. The Celtics won the opener 98-88.

Hillary could not surrender Friday evening. Discounting the twelve people forced to work Friday nights on Fox News, CNN, and MSNBC, most people have lives. We are not at home watching television. Hillary could not concede Saturday night for the same reason.

Saturday afternoon was out of the question. The Belmont Stakes were in the running, and Big Brown was aiming for the Triple Crown. For those unaware, the Democratic primary ended after the Kentucky Derby when Obama's horse won and Hillary's horse collapsed and needed to be euthanized.

While the race itself is only two to three minutes, two hours of coverage was enough to force Hillary to alter her speech time. She tried 10 AM, but *Hannah Montana* had either a new episode or a very good rerun. Those who claim to care about villages and children should not hate on Miley Cyrus, despite her descending into soft-core porn photo shoots.

Therefore, Hillary had the choice of 8 AM or 8 AM. Sunday morning was not an option since that is when five political talk shows that only the hosts care about are on TV. I have never seen "Face the Depressed," or "Meet the Nation," but apparently they bore themselves to sleep when nobody is watching. Therefore, Hillary could not compete with such fanfare.

Sunday afternoon is game two of the Lakers and the Celtics in the NBA Finals.

Little did Hillary know that her attempt to talk about how it means so much to her to be such an accomplished woman in a sexist world would face such stiff competition from other women that actually have real accomplishments. Her speech will fall during the French Open Women's Final live from Paris. Women's tennis gave us Billie Jean King, who defeated Bobby Riggs and advanced the cause of women everywhere. Hillary is giving a speech about advancement as a woman that lost to a man. If anything, she has set the women's movement back at least six months.

Hillary was able to capture the votes of men in Democratic primaries only because compared to people like John Edwards and Barack Obama, she was the man in the race. In keeping with the tennis analogy, Martina Navratilova was genetically female, but she was often described as playing tennis "like a man." She aggressively rushed the net rather than sit back. Hillary aggressively rushed the net, but it did not change the fact that men only watch women's tennis when the players are hot. Navratilova, Chris Evert, and Hillary were around in the '90s or earlier, but this is the twenty-first century.

In the general election, men would not support Hillary. John McCain is a man and a war hero. Hillary is the woman who tries to talk to a guy when he is trying to watch sports.

Thankfully, American men this week told Hillary what they have been trying to communicate to her for the last sixteen years. The message was simple.

Hillary, shut up. I am trying to watch the hockey/basketball/horse racing/tennis game.

Now that the NFL Network exists, Hillary can be less relevant than sports television programming 100 percent of the time.

So yes, Hillary gave her speech. I turned the ringer off, just in case she or one of her supporters tried to call and sell me sleeping pills or some other product.

I could have Tivoed it, but again, the French Open, Belmont Stakes, and *Hannah Montana* took priority.

Hillary, despite the badonkadonk, will not be on the list. The door will hit it on the way out, because her backside, her pantsuits that cover it, and her presidential campaign are all yesterday's news. I have to admit it. I cannot even think about giving Hilldawg a good paddle. I am so giddy that she is gone.

Now the drama will be whether a woman still is elected president in 2008, or if Obama actually does have a pair. Hillary's hags, or harpies, or whatever they call themselves, will not vote for John McCain. They can cry, scream, cajole, and threaten in the great tradition of hostile women. The bottom line is that female Democrats care about only one issue ... abortion. Barack Obama could sell crack on the street, but the pro-choice movement would explain that Obama was selling crack to pregnant women to help them miscarry. John McCain could save a man having a heart attack on the street, and the media would find a way to show that the man he saved is connected to a pro-life movement and is therefore an oppressor.

Since the only thing that matters to the women in the Democratic Party is abortion, the symbolic figurehead running the party does not matter. They have no other issues.

Anyway, Hillary's speech was most likely one minute for every year of her experience. She wanted thirty-five minutes, but if the records are reviewed carefully, she will just wave to the crowd like the Queen of England. Her loyal subjects can howl with delight, knowing that the woman almost said something about almost doing something.

All I know is I slept well knowing she was not going to be president. Perhaps I slept well because I do that on weekends.

I just hope I am up by noon. Unlike Hillary, I was born and raised in New York, and am excited about the Belmont Stakes. John Kerry is running in the fifth position. As for Hillary, I will not be the one to bet on the bobtail nag.

The media will anoint Obama president if Big Brown wins and claim McCain and the horse are too old if Big Brown loses.

Did somebody bet on the bay? I will ask Bay Buchanan.

eric

Chapter 15:
War—Good for Virtually Everything

Singing "Kumbaya" did not free slaves, defeat Hitler, keep Israel free, or defeat the British in 1776. This was done by violence. The greatest civilizations from Greece to Rome to the British Empire to America today got to where they were by war.

Somebody needs to tell the truth. As a practical joke, the liberals had their peace pipes replaced with crack pipes. It seemed funny at the time, but the danger is still being felt by angry liberals that yell about peace while burning Republicans in effigy. For people that scream about being docile, they sure love force when it suits them.

Force works. Force allows leftists to sit outside and protest for their right to be human defects. The right to be counter to anything worthwhile and productive may be a gift from God, but that gift is protected by soldiers.

I hate war, but enjoy being alive. If leftists had their way, we would all be dead. Some may see Mao Tse Tung and Pol Pot as adorable fuzzy little dudes. They were bad. Stalin and Saddam had endearing Inspector Clouseau-type mustaches, yet were still much worse than most of the *Pink Panther* cast, even Herbert Lom.

Sometimes war is the answer. When dealing with Iran and Syria, just picture a 50,000-hole golf course. The Damascus Open could be like Pebble Beach. If I had a hammer, I would hammer terrorists all over this land.

Turn Iran and Syria into 50,000-Hole Golf Courses

When the late gangsta rapper Ol' Dirty Bast@rd was accused of violently beating up his girlfriend (as opposed to the non-violent method),[88] David Letterman poked fun at those who were surprised by this act by posing the question, "Isn't that what Ol' Dirty Bast@rds do?"[89]

Some things, like the truths our forefathers spoke, are self evident. It is what it is. A = A. You are what you are. This brings us to those wondering why Iran would kidnap fifteen British soldiers. For those who do need to be hit upside the head with a bar towel to know they are in a bar, the answer is simple. Iran did this because they are Iran. That is what they do. Do we really need to interview Armageddonijad and look at his resume to see that he went to Mullah University where he studied kidnapping 101?

There are times in life for negotiation. As a teenager in the 1980s, I believed that peace between America and the Russians could be achieved through diplomacy. This is because the people who gave us such beauty and culture, from ice skating, to chess grand masters, to poetry, did not want to blow up the world. Once they found out we did not want to blow up the world, we were able to talk to them. Ronald Reagan was tough, but he was also the Great Communicator. He was liked and trusted, and the world benefited.

North Korea requires negotiations. The North Korean people do not want to die. Heck, all they want to do is eat. It is going to require patience and discipline, but the North Korean leaders know we have no desire to destroy them. If they would just tell us what the heck they want, be it cable TV or complimentary call girls when you supersize your meal, we can work with them. America will defend itself, but at some point they will realize we have no desire to fight them. They have nothing we want.

Having said that, when dealing with Iran and Syria, there is no diplomatic solution. There has never been a time in history where negotiating with either of these two pimples on the world's rumpus has ever worked. The only thing that works is force. Arab Muslim governments discover the beauty of negotiation when they are getting destroyed on the battlefield.

For those people misguided enough to believe that Khadafi Duck in Libya dropped his weapons program due to twenty years of negotiations, think again. For all his bluster, Khadafi was a pragmatist. He enjoyed being among the living. He saw what happened to Saddam Hussein. Like a man being hassled by his wife after a long work day, Khadafi declared, "I just want to put my feet on the coffee table. Who needs this aggravation?" In 1986, it is safe to say that when Reagan bombed his home, it took out Khadafi's coffee table, and probably his comfortable air mattress.

President Bush declared that anyone who helps or harbors terrorists is a terrorist. Iran and Syria foment terrorism. To list the examples would be tedious. Just go purchase an Iranian thesaurus and see if it contains anything besides "jihad," "infidel," "Allah Akbar," and "Zionist donkey aggressor." To these people I say, "I get it. You dislike us. Too d@mn bad."

Given that negotiation with these scoundrels has never worked, and that force is the only solution, it is time we put Iran and Syria on notice that they can also be wiped off the map. By turning those nations into 50,000-hole golf courses with plenty of sand traps, we can also perform an American public service. Given how colossally boring golf is, sending golfers overseas means less golf on American soil. That is a bonus. 2010 Iran and Syria could become 1950s Cuba.

Yes, I am advocating imperialism. They think we are imperialists anyway, so we might as well act like it, at least for a few weeks. We should set up Coca-Cola, McDonald's, and brothels, and ensure they are inundated with *Baywatch* episodes and Anna Nicole Smith news reports.

I hate killing and war but hate being murdered more. While it is possible that somewhere in the backlog of history somebody in charge of Iran or Syria might have accidentally contributed something to the world that could loosely be considered positive, more than likely this did not occur. Waiting for another such aberration of humanity from these miscreants is not an option. Every day that Iran and Syria exist in their current form is a day closer to world extinction. We need to strike while we can. Iran's army reminds me of Marvin the Martian trying to blow up the earth with the Uranium 238 Space Modulator. Syria's army consists of an Ali Baba character in a Bugs Bunny cartoon yelling "Hassan, Chop!" when Bugs and Daffy try to steal his treasure.

So rather than light scented candles and sing "Kumbaya" as soldiers get kidnapped, we might want to do what we did in Iraq: find the bad guys, and b*tchslap them.

Iran and Syria want to kill us, because that is what killers do. We need to defend ourselves and the world, because that is what the world, despite its fake and irrelevant criticism, needs us to do ... defend free people everywhere from evil.

Let the bidding begin from contractors worldwide. It is time to start leveling their infrastructure and building that 50,000-hole golf course. If we don't, we will continue to be attacked by Ol' Dirty B@stards. Like water being wet, that is what Iran and Syria do.

eric

The Iraq War—Legally and Morally Right Then and Now

I received an e-mail recommending that congress censure President Bush. Rather than delete the e-mail, I decided to offer an alternative viewpoint.

War critics are guilty of one mistake that many writers and politicos make: a lack of full disclosure. Many against the war are on the left politically and are committed to defeating President Bush. If this Iraq war had never happened, these people would have found another cause. This is not meant to minimize passions on this issue, but most of these critics are not centrists. They are partisans. So let me engage in full disclosure by saying I am a partisan as well, a staunch supporter of the president. I would probably be voting for him no matter what. Having said that, here is my rebuttal to this woman's e-mail, devoid of any emotion, filled with only logical reasoning.

1) David Kay did say the statements that appear on the surface to support the anti-war crowd. However, those statements were not taken in their complete context. Mr. Kay has also said that Saddam Hussein was *actively trying* to get weapons of mass destruction. The fact that he may not have succeeded was not for lack of effort. Mr. Kay believed Saddam Hussein was a threat to world stability, which is why he joined President Bush's commission concerning this issue. We do know that Saddam Hussein *did use* these weapons in the past. If he had the chance to use them again, it is logical to think he would. He used poison gas on the Kurds and lobbed scud missiles at Israel. He invaded a sovereign nation of Kuwait and set it on fire. He also murdered a million of his own people. Based on these facts alone, a preemptive strike is justified. Other nations have used preemptive strikes (Israel in 1967). On some occasions that is appropriate. It would have been dangerous to wait for Hussein to acquire the weapons again, at which point America would be subject to blackmail.

2) President Bush has been called a liar. We are told that he lied so we could go to war. That is a very serious charge, and I am a firm believer that if someone is going to bring a charge on another human being's integrity, that charge must be substantiated. There is *no evidence* that Bush deliberately lied. Bill Clinton lied about Monica Lewinsky. While that is not as serious as an issue involving war, that is the definition of a lie. George Bush Senior lied when he broke his "Read my lips: no new taxes" pledge. Again, not as serious, but a lie nonetheless. If ... and I stress the word if ... President Bush was given faulty intelligence information, it is vital to find out why the information was flawed. It is also important to understand that this was the same information Bill Clinton and Democrats on the Intelligence Committee relied on. (Tommy Franks was appointed by Clinton.) John Kerry had this

information, and he voted for the war. It is possible that President Bush, Bill Clinton, and John Kerry were all lied to, but that does not make them liars on this issue. It is also possible that nobody lied to anyone, but that the flawed intelligence was an honest mistake. A colossal mistake, but again that does not mean anyone lied.

3) I keep using the word "possible" because we do not even know that a mistake even occurred. We have not found weapons of mass destruction (WMD) yet. That does not mean WMD do not exist, but that we have not found them *yet*. We may never find them, but that does not mean they did not exist. It is possible the information the president had was correct, and that Hussein effectively hid the weapons. It is not easy to find something in a whole country that could fit in the size of the spiderhole Hussein was found in.

3-1/2) A theological argument ... I cannot prove God exists. I take it on faith. The atheists cannot prove God does not exist. I am not implying that the president be taken on blind faith, but it is impossible to say he lied just because we have not seen the evidence *yet*. Again, no evidence disputing the existence of weapons has surfaced.

4) If Hussein had no WMD, why did he keep kicking inspectors out? Perhaps he wanted the world to think he was more powerful than he really was. This is a justification for removing him. If we act based on a perception he gives us, we should not feel bad when we act. If this scenario is true, *Hussein lied, not President Bush.* A good parallel to this involves suicide bombers. If a group takes responsibility for a terrorist act such as a suicide bombing that they actually did not commit, should they be punished for merely saying they did? Absolutely. Confessing to a violent crime is an attempt at intimidation. That can only be countered with force that removes such behavior.

5) Saddam violated Rule 1441. Rule 1441 was not about inspections, as Colin Powell pointed out. It was about the disarmament of Iraq. When sanctions were eased under the "oil for food" program, Saddam did not use the oil revenues for food. This has been proven. That violated Rule 1441, which again justifies invasion.

6) Now I will offer an argument that most politicians will not have the guts to argue, not even Republican politicians. WMD as an issue is *irrelevant*. Did Saddam have WMD? Who cares? I don't. He was a ruthless madman who murdered millions. He invaded sovereign nations. He was a threat to world stability based on his actions during the Gulf War. He repeatedly declared war

on America, promising the "mother of all battles." For those believing he was bluffing, do we have to wait to be attacked?

7) The world is better off without Hussein. The Iraqi people are free. News reports showing how upset the Iraqis are with America are one-sided misrepresentations. The Iraqis do not want Hussein back. Most Iraqis worship at the altar of American freedom fighters, and they should. Libya's Khadafi decided to try and become "normal" after the war. This was not because of years of negotiation. Khadafi saw the handwriting on the wall. Iran and Syria are getting nervous. When backed by actions, words have meaning. President Bush's words and actions have our enemies terrified. That is a fabulous aftereffect in terms of a deterrent.

8) The president has an obligation to protect America. Anyone who succeeds in attacking America (Bin Laden) or even talks about it (Hussein) is a target.

9) Move-on.org—Whenever reading an article, always look at the source. I disclosed my partisan affiliation. Moveon.org is a left-wing organization that has compared Bush to Adolf Hitler. As a holocaust survivor's son, I find that beyond offensive. While it may seem unfair to link everyone supporting an organization to that organization's beliefs, most Moveon.org's supporters have a personal hatred for President Bush that goes beyond rational debate. (Read the Web site for evidence.)

10) My heart goes out to the families who have lost loved ones. I cannot begin to imagine their pain. I have a cousin who was separated from his family for over a year due to his honorable service in the National Guard. He is now home. The men and women in our military are heroes, and deserve to be treated as such. However, service in the military is voluntary. As awful as it is that anti-war critics' friends and family (and my cousin) are/were in harm's way, they chose to serve. I choose not to serve in the military out of selfishness, but am at least decent enough to thank people who serve voluntarily so I can live my self-indulgent American kick-back life.

There are three reasons why people might oppose this war:

1) Some people oppose all war. Singing "Kumbaya" does not work when people want to kill you. As Tommy Franks recently said, "War is bad ... but sometimes not going to war is worse."

2) Some people simply oppose anything Bush supports. When winning an election becomes more important than supporting a just cause, we have lost our soul as a nation.

3) Some people simply opposed this war on principle. I respect that. Some were against it. I was in favor of it. I will not question their integrity. They should never question mine. However, many have questioned President Bush's integrity. I think it is very reasonable to state that President Bush acted on principle. To suggest otherwise without evidence attacks him as a human being. I supported the war based on my conscience. I believe President Bush did as well, just as many opposed the war on conscience.

When the history books are written, long after we are all gone, I will go to my grave knowing President Bush did the right thing. The war was just, decent and morally right on every level of humanity. I am against a censure of President Bush. I am also against the censure of Moveon.org, because as disgusting as their comments are, free speech requires I accept their right to spew venom. Voltaire once said, "I do not approve of what you say, but I will defend to the death your right to say it."[90] I am diametrically opposed to most anti-war critics politically, but their right to free speech was exercised appropriately, and my response was appropriate in kind. For those who believe the war was right, do not recommend censure. Send President Bush a simple, short thank-you note over the Internet for helping keep America free and safe in the tradition of George Washington, James Madison, Abraham Lincoln, FDR, JFK, and Ronald Reagan.

Thank you, Mr. President. Thank you for making the world a better place to live. May God bless you, your family, the men and women in our military, their families, and free people everywhere. May God bless the USA.

Respectfully,

eric

General Petraeus, Please Tell the Entire Truth

One of the most dishonest acts of blogging is creating sensationalistic headlines offering provocative themes that are completely misleading. I plead guilty. Deal with it.

General David Petraeus is very diplomatic, but he will not tell the complete truth when he testifies. He will discuss the surge. He will give his assessment of how the War in Iraq is progressing. He will most likely state that he needs more time. We are making progress, we have a long way to go, but there is cause for cautious optimism. Yet there is one thing he will refuse to say, so I will say it for him.

The senators with the most hostile questioning of him are not fit to lick his boots.

What clearly makes America work is that the military is under civilian control. That should never change. At the same time, it would be nice if the civilians questioning others actually knew something, anything, about what they were talking about.

It is one thing for senators to rail against Alan Greenspan or Ben Bernanke. The blowhards had no power to actually do anything about anything the Federal Reserve Chairman said that they found objectionable. With the military, there is a budget involved, and Congress controls it. It would be helpful if those determining whether General Petraeus gets the time he needs actually had life above the neck. Here is how the testimony would go in my fantasy world.

"Senator Clinton, the fact that you are questioning me about how I do my job strains all credulity. It defies belief. At 3 AM, my men are asleep after a twenty-hour day, and the four hours we sleep would be easier if you were no longer near that phone. Please take your stories about sniper fire in Bosnia and disappear. I know about sniper fire, and your trips around the globe are safe because of my men."

I would pray that the general would pause long enough to allow me to get some soda and chips and enjoy the show.

"Senator Obama, you say you stand for change. Change comes through blood, sweat, and tears, not platitudes. You don't spend time in Iraq. As corrupt and dangerous as Chicago may be, it's a civilized first-world city compared to what Iraq was under Saddam Hussein. You may say I have no right to denigrate Chicago. I will be happy to stop doing so when you stop denigrating Iraq.

Either get on a plane and shake the hands of the men who keep you free enough to mouth vacuous campaign slogans, or sit there and smile so people do not figure out that you know nothing about the issue."

In my fantasy conference, he would go through liberals like the decorated trooper he is.

"Senator Boxer, if you are truly against torture, then be quiet, because your shrill voice is torture to me. Stop pretending you care about women's rights. I am fighting for the right of women in the Middle East to avoid having to wear burkas against their will. I am freeing women from the bonds of slavery and female circumcision. You know what female circumcision is about. It's why you never smile. Now take your 'I am woman, hear me roar' attitude and go fix my dinner. I've been in the field all day, that being the battlefield. If dinner isn't ready by the time I'm done speaking, I'll remind the audience about all the women worldwide who are dying while you prattle on about nonsense."

He would spare none of these miscreants.

"Senator Kennedy, I felt safer in Iraq then I would as a passenger in your car. Senator Byrd, you are the reason many Americans support euthanasia. I would say more but you can't hear me, and if you could, you wouldn't understand me. Senator Mikulski, just because you are tough enough to play defense for the Baltimore Ravens doesn't mean you are qualified to take on Al Sadr."

He would then knock over the table like an angry coach at halftime.

"Senator Boxer, get a mop and clean this mess up. I clean up messes around the globe for you. It's time you start pulling your weight. Senator Kennedy, pull half your weight and make a difference."

An angry, flustered Boxer would then start babbling about the search for truth. At that point General Petraeus would do his best Colonel Nathan R. Jessup impersonation, yelling, "You can't handle the truth!"[91]

Once the senators were done crying and insisting that they were not the least relevant people on earth, General Petraeus would agree with them.

"Of course you're not the most worthless. The House of Representatives makes you clowns look knowledgeable. I plan to kick their @ss tomorrow with more ferocity than we are kicking Al Qaeda's @ss."

Republicans in the Senate would give him a standing ovation, and ask if he had any closing remarks.

"Senator Boxer, you are not fit to lick my boots. Try and prove me wrong. Here they are. Take your tongue and get to work. I want them spit-shined by 0600 hours. Don't worry if your mouth gets tired. You don't use it for anything valuable anyway. You might learn more if you are too tired to talk."

I eagerly await the real press conference, although it will contain fewer fireworks. In terms of the war, General Petraeus will be the most honest man in the room. In terms of what he should say to the liberals sitting in judgment of him, he will be too polite to be completely truthful.

eric

Unless Your Name is General David Petraeus, Your Opinion on the War is Irrelevant

Unless your name is General David Petraeus, your opinion on the war is irrelevant.

Period. Exclamation point. Done.

Leadership is not about what feels good ten days from now, or ten months from now. It is about history. It is about doing what is right, even when 70 percent of the public gets their news from long since discredited institutions that came of age and gained fame by being against war to begin with.

What I care about is winning World War III. Nobody is better equipped to do that now.

I trust Ted Kennedy's opinion on clam chowder, Harry Reid's opinion on gaming, and Nancy Pelosi's opinion on ... well, she must be good at something. Actually, if we lose World War III and are forced to convert to Islam, she could teach my future daughters how to wear burkas.

General Petraeus was confirmed 95-0. In the grand tradition of supporting the troops while undermining them, the Lilliputian left in Congress voted for a man but then decided his report was irrelevant.

The Democrats that voted for the war when it was popular, and then voted against it as soon as it became unpopular ... these are the most contemptible of people. President Bush never asked to be a war president. He never wanted three thousand New Yorkers to be murdered. He did not want Saddam Hussein to obtain the tools to blow up the world. He took steps to prevent this. Reconstruction after the U.S. Civil War took longer than we have been in Iraq. Patience is a virtue. Apparently the Democrats in Congress simply have none.

If I need advice on how to hold peace rallies while simultaneously practicing hate speech, I will consult Moveon.org and the *Daily Kos*. Yes, they have freedom of speech. I have the right to express that they are talking out of their hides.

We can support General Petraeus and contribute to saving the world, or we can undermine him. When the history books are written, those who chose to undermine him will be seen as uglier than the souls of those currently at anti-war rallies.

eric

Vets For Freedom—Back To Iraq

I had the honor and privilege recently of interviewing three men from the group Vets For Freedom.

Jason Meszaros heads the Minnesota chapter. Nathan Martin runs the Ohio Chapter. Pete Hegseth heads up the entire organization at the national level. I had the pleasure of meeting Jason and Pete at a Republican Jewish Coalition event in San Francisco several months ago. I have emailed with Nathan and Jason, and visited their blogs.

The link to the entire radio interview is on BlogTalkRadio.

Jason had his article recently published in the Minneapolis news site Twincities.com.

What he emphasizes is that partisan politics must take a back seat to reality and facts on the ground.

Here are some of the exchanges.

Eric: This is not *Hardball,* and I am not Chris Matthews. Pete, as long as you promise not to come to my day job and tell me how to do it, I have no interest in telling you about the facts on the ground in Iraq.

Pete: Eric, I like that deal. I'll take it.

Eric: Pete, what is going on in Iraq? Give us the facts. Arianna Huffington says we're losing.

Pete: The surge, and more importantly, the new counterinsurgency strategy in 2007, is the driver behind the progress. Iraqis are prepared to maintain security gains because Americans fought so dearly. It is important that we get the word out. Jason is a particularly effective advocate. We have to get the word out that we are succeeding, and why we are succeeding.

Eric: I am proud of you guys. Welcome home. I believe what you say, that the surge is working. However, Americans want tangible metrics. What statistics do you have?

Pete: Since June of 2007, attacks down 85 percent, sectarian violence down 98 percent. Talking point of Iraqi civil war does not exist. In addition to our surge of 30,000 troops, the Iraqi Army surged, and added 133,000 members, plus 98,000 Sons of Iraq. Over 200,000 Iraqis have stood up to fight. Caches are being found at a rate of over 70 percent higher than last year.

That is on the military side. On the political side, Iraqis have passed fifteen of the eighteen benchmarks. The Maliki government has taken the fight to Basra and Sadr City. There is also reconciliation and elections coming up.

This July America lost five service members. Last year we lost seventy. Violence continues to drop.

Jason: The Iraqi Sunni bloc rejoined the government. They are working with the Shiites and Kurds. The country is healing politically.

Eric: We ask so much of you guys. What do you want from us? Maybe I could use basic training. I am fat and out of shape from sitting on my couch. However, I don't want to do basic training. What can I and other ordinary Americans do to help you guys win?

Nathan: Americans need to do what our forefathers did. We need to look past ourselves. We need to make America better for future generations. Support our troops by allowing them to do the job. America is not a strong America if we lose.

Eric: I think we are a dead America if we lose.

Pete: Jason had an outstanding op-ed today, which I urge listeners to check out. Partisan politics must be taken out of this war. This is much more than an election cycle. It is about winning the wars we start. Also, arm yourself with the facts. I see signs in Iraq saying, "Marines and army are at war, and the rest of the country is at the mall." Folks at home need to stay informed. Read military blogs like *Blackfive.net*.

Jason: We soldiers know how to win this war. We need people to put aside their political biases and just support us. Get informed. Talk to soldiers. Ask us. We will give you the good and the bad. We give it straight up. Talk to people who were there in 2006 and 2007. Find out how the surge has succeeded.

Eric: What do you say to those that point out that 9/11 had nothing to do with Iraq? How do we react to the idea that Afghanistan is the good war, Iraq is the bad war, and that Saddam had nothing to do with Bin Laden? How do you argue the point that it was wrong from the beginning?

Jason: The events of 9/11 had nothing to do with Iraq. That is true. However, it is not true to say Iraq had nothing to do with terrorism. That is the distinction. Replace 9/11 with terrorism. Saddam's connection to terrorism was incredible.

Arguments such as WMD are not worth bothering with. The connections to terrorism were there.

Pete: We try to bring the debate to 2006, 2007, and 2008. Regardless of whether you thought it was right to go in, we are there, and must have the right strategy. Historians can debate 2003. I supported it; others did not. It is irrelevant. We are there, and must insure we are successful. What we do now is more indicative of who we are as a country.

As for good and bad wars, leaders of Al Qaeda repeatedly declare that Iraq is the central front. They came close. In 2006, Anbar was almost lost. It is also about what our members have seen. We were fighting jihadists from around the world, Syrians, Chechens, etc. We are beating them there. This is why they are forced to go to Afghanistan. It is their last haven.

Eric: Some members of Congress say that they support the troops by bringing them home. I personally feel we should support Congress by sending them home. Can good patriotic Americans support the troops, but be against the mission?

Nathan: It's difficult. Somebody can say that they hate football, it's a violent sport, but that they root for the Pittsburgh Steelers. It's difficult to do that. In any other line of work that would be called silly. People don't love plumbers but hate what they do. To lambaste a soldier and then say you love them does not make sense. Those who sacrificed over the past five years ... the way to ensure their legacy is to emphasize the importance of the mission, and allow them to come home with honor and dignity.

Pete: There is an intellectual disconnect to separate the two. I understand why people want to. They want freedom, but don't like this president. Therefore, they hate the mission. That undercuts the mission. Honor our service by honoring what we are fighting for. I support you, but don't want you to do the dirty work to defend the freedoms I have.

Eric: How do you feel when people such as Max Cleland, John Kerry, John Murtha, and Jim Webb try to speak for the military? Are they military opinion or aberrations?

Pete: They are a product of a particular time. They came out with an ax to grind based on their experiences. Fighting in Vietnam does not mean they understand the current conflict. We started Vets For Freedom to provide a counter voice. Soldiers are not monolithic. The opinion we espouse does represent the vast majority of soldiers on this mission. We believe in it and want to finish it.

When Murtha called our marines cold-blooded killers, it hurt. He was not informed because he was not there. We honor the military service of him and the others, but they are not as informed on this issue as the soldiers fighting now.

Nathan: You will never hear Pete talk about himself. He talks about the mission. It is not about us. It is about every other American that deserves to have their freedoms protected. We want people to be free from a black cloud over America. Some say, "Look at me." That is not us.

Eric: Donald Rumsfeld had a quarter of a century experience. He was the secretary of defense for Gerald Ford. Yet despite his resume, it seemed in 2006 that we were in a state of stagnation. Rumsfeld then lost his job. What is it that General David Petraeus did that nobody else could have done, or nobody else did?

Pete: General Petraeus studied counterinsurgency. He wrote his dissertation on it based on the lessons of Vietnam. He wrote the counterinsurgency manual. He was the right man at the right time. We can armchair quarterback why it took so long. Rumsfeld had his vision, but it took a fresh set of eyes to change everything from the top down. He has the skill set and the intelligence to make it happen. He is an outside-the-box thinker. We were fortunate, and are fortunate to have him at CENTCOM. Some lessons can be exported to Afghanistan, but some new tactics will be needed as well.

Nathan: When victory became a partisan cause, any kind of change would be a media defeat. This pigeonholed the administration. The 2006 elections freed them from this.

Eric: Given that political analysts try to be military generals, I will ask you for some political analysis. Did Barack Obama do the right thing regarding his trip and the flap over the troops?

Pete: Vets For Freedom called on him to go to Iraq. This was not to score political points. It was because he might be the next president, and he needed to benefit from hearing Petraeus. I was dismayed he laid out his plans five days before going. He should have gone first.

All in all, it was good that he made the trip, but his observations may have been predetermined. As for Germany, I don't buy his explanation. If he wants it to be private and apolitical, leave behind the cameras and visit them. I think they realize it was a mistake, and they should admit that.

Nathan: Senators visit places such as Walter Reed all the time. Cameras do not need to be there. If you go for the troops, you can go anytime.

Eric: Over the next one to two years ... do you have any projections? What can be done to make this situation in Iraq what we want it to be, dare I say it, a shining city on a hill?

Pete: Our timeline should be based on conditions on the ground. Jason is right about the significance of the Sunnis rejoining the government.

I and seven others are going back to Iraq to where we served previously to get that assessment on the ground. We need to make sure the gains do not slip away. We will put together policy observations when we come back.

Eric: You guys are the definition of heroes. One of you gave the hypothetical example of hating football. That could get me to take up arms. Sometimes it takes a 9/11 or a canceling of the NFL season to get people off of their couches.

Guys like you are the reason Chris Matthews is able to berate and attack you. The more you do, the more it allows me and others to enjoy the future.

I want to get a commitment from you guys. I don't need it now. I have met two of you in real life. The only thing I would ask is this. You guys secured Fallujah and Anbar. Is the situation hopeless, or can David Petraeus turn around and secure Detroit?

(laughter) Jason: It's not hopeless.

Eric: I won't ask for a battle plan now. We don't want the enemy to get our tactics. If anybody can secure it, you guys can.

Nathan: Americans like you help.

Eric: I am a chimpanzee typing on a keyboard. You are out saving lives. I will be in Israel next week partying on the beach. You will be in Iraq saving all of our lives. So I will say to you guys in advance ... Thank you, and welcome home. I speak for a majority of Americans.

Pete: We'll do this again.

Eric: Thank you, and welcome home. God bless.

(Several weeks later, I interviewed Pete Hegseth in person.)

1) Pete, what did you see?

PH: "It was an incredible experience. I went back to Samarrah, where I was in 2006. In 2006 it was a different situation. Not a single shot was fired while I was there in 2008. I did not even wear a helmet. I walked around in a baseball cap.

I stood above the Golden Mosque and watched them rebuild. A couple of years ago that would not have been a place to stand. If I was a sniper, that would be an area I would target people. Now I am able to stand on top and watch the rebuilding.

For thirty minutes I was completely exposed. My only security was the people who had turned on Al Qaeda. They are now empowered, not intimidated.

There was a classic counterinsurgency in this city.

I actually sat across from and had drinks with a guy that had previously been on a high value target list. He is now on the Samarrah Rescue Council. He told me that in 2006 he was probably shooting at me and trying to kill me. I told him that in 2006 I was probably shooting at him trying to kill him. We laughed. He is now part of the government."

2) Are the gains sustainable?

PH: "The gains made could be lost. We are winning, but it would be premature to declare total victory. Those that want to declare victory and bring troops home now could reverse the gains. A premature withdrawal followed by a dismantling of the Sons of Iraq would be a major mistake."

3) How would you like to be remembered one hundred years from now? What would you want people to say about Pete Hegseth the person?

PH: "I would like to be remembered as someone who played a small role in making the United States of America safe. I was one small part of generations of Americans, military and civilian, to help make America great."

One of the things that Pete Hegseth and other military leaders have stressed to me is that looking forward is what matters. I have met many soldiers. In general they do not deal with politics. They do not tell me who they are voting for. I do not ask. All they ask is that they be given the support of the American people. They define support as supporting their missions.

eric

My Interview With Colonel Bill Cowan

I had the pleasure recently of attending a weekend retreat. Despite the fact that the weekend was a retreat, it was a serious policy conference, with one military leader that does not know the meaning of the word retreat. I had the pleasure of meeting and interviewing a man with "gravitas," Lieutenant Colonel and Fox News military analyst Bill Cowan.

Colonel Cowan is an absolutely funny man. I could have stayed for hours just listening to his stories.

Before interviewing him, I took great joy in hearing him speak on one of the panels. He does not mince words. To say he began with a bang would be an understatement.

"I hope all of this is on the record. I don't like waterboarding. Let me say again, I don't like waterboarding. I prefer electricity.

If Mexican illegal immigrants bombed San Diego, Americans would not stand for it. Yet when Donald Rumsfeld spoke to me, he said the White House would not allow for a bombing of Iran.

A blockade is an act of war. All we do is bullhorn. We need covert operations that are untraceable to the United States."[92]

Later on in the day, Colonel Cowan agreed to do an interview with me by email. However, since it was such a lovely day outside, and there was a lengthy afternoon break in the conference, we decided to just do the interview right there. It was just a couple of guys relaxing by the palm trees.

1) What have we gotten right, and what have we gotten wrong, in the last eight years?

BC: "As for what we have gotten right, the CIA and FBI have done a good job working with foreign intelligence sources. This used to be beautiful. With information sharing and collaborative efforts, the relationships have been effective. The CIA used to just go to cocktail parties. They are not military people. On the military side, we have General David Petraeus. Some of the more stock, conventional leaders considered this a loss. What Petraeus understands is that insurgencies are about people. It is not about killing Iraqis. That only prolongs war.

As for what we have gotten wrong, the Department of Homeland Security is one thing. It does nothing and is a complete waste of tax dollars.

Another success involves Donald Rumsfeld. For all of his failures, and I have been a critic of his, he reshaped military intelligence. He was more proactive than his predecessors with regard to employing special units. Rumsfeld unleashed them. This helps with the rest of the war, which includes Africa, Asia, and the Middle East.

The CIA has been a failure even according to former CIA workers. They are good with intelligence sharing, but not with anything military. When CIA workers were in danger zones, they were afraid to leave the compound. Newt Gingrich and Bill O'Reilly have addressed the CIA's failures in Iran. There are still no clandestine operations in Iran. The CIA is still not hiring for tough positions. Not many people are willing to go to Africa and work in small dusty Africa towns.

We have failed to bring first generation foreign nationals into the CIA or FBI. These are people who were born here, but their families were from places such as Afghanistan. We refuse to hire American Afghanis for fears they will be disloyal. We hire white guys from Yale instead.

We have failed to develop a strategic communication plan to the rest of the world. We have no policy on Iran or Hezbollah."

2) What is your military background?

BC: "I was in Vietnam for three-and-a-half years. I was then with the CIA. I spent two years undercover in the Middle East. I was involved in activities in Lebanon until 1991."

3) Should the United States bomb Iran?

BC: "We have to develop Iraqi special ops to get to Iran. We should have already done this. It should have been covert. We didn't do it. We are still not doing it. I met General Petraeus in November, and he wants us to do it. He is frustrated that we are not doing it.

Decisions have been made at the White House by people that are intellectually challenged. I am referring to Condoleeza Rice and Stephen Hadley. There is no effective long-term strategy. Condi went to Beirut for photo ops.

Rumsfeld should have gone to Syria and put his finger in Bashar Assad's chest. He should have told Assad that if there is one more bombing attack, we will take Syria and blow it up. Vice President Cheney should have let Armageddonijad (sic) and the Mullahs know that we will not hesitate to wipe them off the map. That would certainly give these countries some pause, and the financing to Hamas and Hezbollah would drop sharply."

4) If you had five minutes with President Bush or Vice President Cheney, what would you say to them or ask them?

BC: "I would tell them that we have an overbloated bureaucracy, and that most things don't get to the president's desk. Important things don't reach him. People know this, but they can't make decisions. The president needs a planning and advisory group. We have great intel on where the bad guys are doing things. We just don't go get them. This is a failure of leadership. The problem is not the president. The failure of leadership is in the bureaucracy."

5): If you are president, what does President Cowan do in the first one hundred days?

BC: "Iran is a looming threat. We get our meanest guys, and go to Iran. We let Armageddonijad (sic) know that any nuclear explosions against the United States, Israel, or any of our allies, and Tehran will no longer exist in six hours.

I am not worried about North Korea. Their struggle is financial, not ideological. They want foreign aid to feed their starving people. Iran wants to wipe us off the face of the earth.

I would reorganize the Pentagon. It is bloated. People get paid to write reports that nobody ever reads. I would rebuild our special forces.

I would make radical changes at State. It would tick off a lot of people, but if they don't like it, they can quit. The State Department is not our friend.

I would carefully review resumes. This is not about hiring friends. There are smart people in DC, but the White House does not talk to them.

I would revamp the CIA. I would bring back old CIA guys to talk to the new ones, not 'esteemed senators.'

I would reorganize the army. In doing so I would solicit the opinions of sergeant majors, not retired generals."

6) President Bush gets much blame for 9/11. What amount of blame should President Clinton get? Who else is at fault?

BC: "I am apolitical. I fault all of them. Most Jimmy Carter bashing is appropriate, but Ronald Reagan didn't act regarding Beirut. This was mainly because of Caspar Weinberger and the State Department. Bill Clinton didn't take any decisive action. On September 12, 2001, President Bush said that others were either 'for us or against us,' yet we have done nothing on Iran or Hezbollah."

7) Who are your top three military or political heroes?

BC: "Jerry Boykin, former Delta Force commander, is a hero of mine. Boykin ran the operation against Noriega. Most people don't know this, but the blaring rock music had nothing to do with Noriega. We turned the music up to drown out the media. They had long-range listening devices, and Boykin had the music turned up, and it kept the media out. Then we realized it was affecting Noriega, so we left it on.

Ronald Reagan was a good man. If things got to Reagan, if they got to his desk, he would act right.

David Petraeus is another one. Conventional military guys don't always like him, but he gets the insurgency.

My son is on his third tour, his second in Afghanistan. My son is my hero."

Colonel Cowan then offered me some final thoughts.

"We only lose in Iraq if the Democrats pull the plug. We didn't lose Vietnam in Vietnam. We lost it right here.

Also, make sure you put in your blog my earlier comments about electricity."

Colonel Cowan is simply one of the nicest guys I have ever come across. He was a joy to meet. I look forward to his next television appearance.

The only thing left for me to say to Colonel Cowan is what I tell every soldier upon seeing them.

"Thank you ... and welcome home."

eric

Happy Chaka Khan!

Happy Chaka Khan!

What can I say? For those who do not celebrate this lovely holiday, "I feel for you".[93] For those who truly want good things in life, the world truly does need "Higher love."[94]

As Hebrews get ready to celebrate the festival of lights, I shall use the eight days to either expand or drive away my audience, depending on any number of factors.

Both spellings of the holiday have eight letters. Adding a "C" requires subtracting a "K." It is Chanukah or Hanukkah.

First, let's dispel some myths. People like to pass on beautiful stories of miracles. People hear that Jewish fighters only had enough oil for one day, and miracle of miracles, the oil magically lasted for eight days. For those of you with small children, have them leave the room so some hard truths can be discussed.

Santa Claus is not real, Palestinians are an invented fictional people, the secret formula for Coca-Cola is (redacted), and the person who shot JFK was (redacted). Oh, and this oil lasting for eight days is a bunch of malarkey.

So what is Hanukkah? Hanukkah is my favorite holiday because it is the Jewish version of the Fourth of July. It is a Neocon's fantasy. As a Neocon, I never tire of the true story of Hanukkah. We fought some Greeks in battle and b*tchslapped them. That's it. People think of Jewish people as constantly suffering and weak. Actually, our history has been our military strength. I have nothing against the Greek people of today, but back then they were the bad guys. They destroyed the first Holy Temple, but we took care of them. Gorgias? Get out of here! Nicanor? Knock it off!

We royally smacked them around, and they have not been a power since. We are still here. For those troubled by this ... deal with it.

The actual celebration of Hanukkah is a tad bittersweet for those educated about this holiday. We as Jews won the battle but lost the war.

What I mean by this is that there was a major difference between how Jews and Greeks celebrated holidays. Greeks celebrated holidays created in the wake of their many military victories. Jewish tradition was to eschew naming holidays after military successes. We did not glorify blood triumphs.

The Greeks wanted Jews to assimilate or be killed. Thankfully we never had to face that threat again. Just kidding. Jews were fighting for the right to remain independently Jewish, without forced assimilation into Greek culture. After Judah Maccabee and his brothers helped the people of Israel crush the Greeks in battle, the first thing they did was hoist a victory flag and declare this military victory a Jewish holiday. After fighting for the right to prevent assimilation, we adopted a Greek tradition we were against. To this day, some argue that what Hitler failed to do to the Jews, we do to ourselves through a 52 percent intermarriage rate.

Cynical people would say that we broke the war rule because we were so used to losing that even we were shocked to have won, and we were concerned we may never win anything again. These people can (X-rated, redacted) themselves. Others say that we needed to adopt different traditions to give us flexibility in the future so that we would face less internal conflict when Jewish teenage boys need a historical justification for skirt-hiking and balling Roman Catholic teenage girls. Actually, only I say that, but I am right.

The bottom line is that Hanukkah is the least important holiday in the Jewish calendar. It is an excuse to party for eight days, or fourteen days if you count pre- and post-Hanukkah parties. The only reason Hanukkah gets any attention is because it occurs around the same time as Christmas.

Briefly returning to the Neocon aspect of this holiday, the true lesson of Hanukkah is a political one that the 70–80 percent of Jews that like to sing "Kumbaya" with those that hate our guts would do well to heed. The lesson of Hanukkah is simple. Force works. There is no dialogue or negotiation with those that refuse to recognize your right to exist. Survival is not pretty. It often involves spilling large amounts of blood. When the enemy is on their knees with their face bleeding, negotiation is possible.

The other lesson that comes from Jews during this time is the idea of mercy. We did not rape Greek women, chop heads and limbs off, enslave their people, or indiscriminately engage in deliberate cruelty. We defended ourselves. In keeping with the values that unite Jews and Americans to this day, both remain a people that use their power for noble and good purposes. America through its economic and military power, and American Jews through their sense of justice, help feed, clothe, protect, and defend others worldwide, including many who are neither Jewish nor American.

Hanukkah is a celebration of serious lifesaving accomplishments, but it is also a lighthearted holiday filled with food, alcohol, and worldwide candlelighting ceremonies. Life for the Hebrews has involved much darkness, but for eight nights there is only light.

So as I light candles and hope that a certain young Hebrew brunette will show up at my door wearing a blue and white Hanukkah bow ... and only a Hanukkah bow (negotiations are ongoing) ... I look forward to the next eight nights.

Happy Hanukkah everybody! Shalom!

eric

Chapter 16: 9/11 Forever

Some say 9/11 gets discussed too much. Talk to those that lost victims and then tell me about understanding. If by "understand," they mean "shove the American flag up their hide until they go to the toilet red, white, and blue," then I agree.

Liberals claim that Iraq was a distraction from Afghanistan. If we never invaded Iraq, Afghanistan would have been a distraction from Bolivia, Mozambique, Paris Hilton, and every other hot spot. Liberals sit there and play on their bongo drums while planes get crashed into towers. This is just another reason why the Nancy Reagan "Just say no" campaign should have been heeded more by the left.

What happened on 9/11 was an ongoing salvo in a thirty-year war against America. Now, despite the existence of liberals, we are winning. We will have won when every terrorist is dead and the left is complaining that the Chateau Briand we serve the few surviving zealots at Guantanamo Bay is not chilled to the correct San Francisco temperature.

Perhaps we can make the left uncomfortable by forcing the male prisoners at Gitmo to marry each other. After all, wouldn't it be bigoted to deny these people gay marriage rights? Then again, these terrorists might defy modern science and reproduce. The children would learn the letters A, C, L, and U before crying.

The events of 9/11 are not discredited theory. It happened. Some of the victims were bunny rabbits, trees, and zygotes. If that does not get liberals on our side, then conservatives will do what we have always done: accomplish things without their hindrances.

9/11/8—My Interview With a 9/11 Survivor

Rather than talk about 9/11 from my own perspective, I interviewed somebody who was in the building.

On September 11, 2001, one of the worst days in American history occurred. I thank God that my friend Kevin survived.

Kevin had recently graduated from the University of Southern California and worked as a trainee at my firm. I was a twenty-nine-year-old manager that was attending USC's MBA program at night. In my spare time I was a DJ on the campus radio station.

On Saturday, September 11, 2004, Kevin and his fiancée were on campus for a football game. The USC Trojans were back-to-back national champions, and looking to win it three straight years. Kevin stopped by the campus radio station, where I interviewed him about that day three years earlier.

Eric: Three years ago I was working at a company in Burbank. We had a rookie trainee, twenty-two years old, with stars in his eyes. The company ships him out to New York for some training. He was in the second tower, and got out with very little time to spare. His story is a harrowing one, but also life affirming. So, Kevin, I am just going to turn it over to you. Tell us your story. What was that day like? How did the day start? Take us through that day.

Kevin: Thank you, Eric. Taking me back three years ago from today it's amazing that we were at a training class of three hundred people that were starting at the World Trade Center on Monday, September 10. You couldn't believe the view from the sixty-first floor as we met as a group, and we were so excited about our two-month stay at the World Trade Center for our training program. September 11 started out as beautiful as the day before. We got to the building, went up to our floor, and went to the training program.

About an hour into the program, we were dismissed for a twenty minute break. It was during that break that the North Tower was struck by the first plane. We were actually able to see the fire. Still on break, I went over to this conference room and saw that the North Tower was on fire. Here I was, standing there, like I had concrete shoes, because I couldn't move. Yet I had to move, because I had to warn the other people in my training class. So I ran over to the lobby area on my floor sixty-one and everybody was already evacuating. So I did like everybody else and joined the crowd and started down the stairs. We got down to about floor fifty-five when somebody came on the loudspeaker and said that an unidentified plane had struck the North Tower but that the South Tower was secure.

There was a discrepancy with the news media because reports came out that we were told everything was fine and we should go back to our office, but the speaker over the loudspeaker never said that. All he said was that we should, "remain calm, do not panic," and people took that as "go back to our office."

Well I stayed right there and felt like I was safer in the stairwell, and within thirty seconds the second plane hit the South Tower as we all saw on TV, and all I could remember was that it was a huge jolt, a violent collision. The stairwells cracked, and we knew that something terrible had happened. We continued our descent down fifty-five more flights of stairs and got to the bottom, and as we got outside, we looked up at the towers, and both of them were on fire, in flames. For me, it was just a sense that this was probably not the best area to be around, so I tried to get as far away as I could. I got about ten blocks away, and that's when my tower, tower two, collapsed, about twenty minutes after I had gotten out of the building.

It was such an eerie thing, hearing the people screaming on the bottom of the streets, and you could hear the rumble of the tower's collapse, and I thought, how many people had died? Soon after, the North Tower fell. It wasn't until I was able to connect with my family that I felt some sense of strength. Especially with me being from California, I had no direction, nowhere to go. Looking back, it's hard to believe that three years ago, three hundred people from all over, our second day of training, that all of us were able to get out alive.

Eric: Twenty minutes must seem to you like a lifetime now, but it was that soon after you had gotten out that the building collapsed.

Kevin: Absolutely. Everybody was wondering what had happened. We didn't know if it was a bomb or a plane. Soon after, the buildings were crumbling down. To think that as I was going down the stairs I watched thirty firemen go into the building. I thought afterwards that I don't think they made it out. Those faces will always be etched in my mind.

Eric: I remember being in a cushy office in Burbank, thinking it was going to be like any other day. When the towers got hit, the first thing I thought of was my family. I was born and raised in New York. Everybody was there. The second thing that occurred to me was that our firm had offices in that building, and I knew that you were in that building.

Now my job usually consisted of bureaucratic tasks like helping people figure out their paycheck, dealing with certain complaints. I'll never forget the phone call I got from your father asking me, "Where's my son?" There's no amount of managerial training that's going to prepare you for a situation like that. The one thing your father told me on the phone was that he was not that close to you at the time.

Kevin: Right.

Eric: He was worried that he would never get a chance to tell you so many things that fathers tell their sons.

Kevin: Right.

Eric: He must have stayed on hold for three hours. I must have dialed a million numbers. I'd like you to just talk about your father, what that phone call was like, and how that relationship has been since.

Kevin: Well, you're right, Eric, at the firm in Burbank, when you took that call, my dad and I had kind of lost touch for a few years for whatever reason. He had this sense on 9/11, I had mentioned in passing that I would be going out to New York for training, never told him when, never told him what day, never told him it was going to be at the World Trade Center, and he had this feeling as he saw it on TV, he had this feeling that I was there, and he made this call to the Burbank office.

It was then that he had called me in New York soon after I had spoken to you. We had this powerful phone conversation. He was in LA, I was in New York, on the phone, and we have ... we've fostered a better relationship since then, and it's been neat that we could look back. It's unfortunate that it had to take something like this, but since then, our relationship has been great ever since that day.

Eric: One person who is in the studio today is your fiancée (now wife) Elena. I remember being on the phone with her, and she was equally worried, obviously. Elena, you being three thousand miles away ... First of all, let me say it's good that after all this time you are both still a happy couple, because a lot of couples could not handle the stress of that day. I would like you to talk about that day as somebody who was here in LA but had a direct emotional connection to Kevin. What was that day like, and how have the days been since as you plan your wedding?

Elena: Well, that definitely was the most difficult day I have ever experienced. We didn't know if Kevin was okay, and I automatically ... we hoped for the best, but didn't know if he was going to make it out. Like you, we made a million calls to the hotel. We both have family in the east coast, in Boston. We prepped them up, told them to get in their cars and drive toward New York. We weren't sure if Kevin would be in a hospital. Luckily Kevin was able to contact us two hours later. I then came to your office to tell you he was okay, and that was when I met you.

Since then, it has definitely made Kevin and I both kind of look at our lives differently. Every day is a day we should appreciate, and we appreciate each other, and our families, and our faith. We are excited about planning our wedding, and yeah, it was something tough to get through.

Eric: When is the wedding?

Elena: April 23.

Eric: Fantastic. I want to ask you, Kevin, how tough was it for you to go back to work and go back in the office when you came back? Here you've almost been killed. You're a rookie at the firm, and rookies in our industry, they eat dirt. They don't get paid a decent salary. You have to build a business from scratch. How are you able to just go to work?

Kevin: Well, Eric, I think when I got back to Burbank I felt this overwhelming sense of purpose. I felt I was given a second chance. I was so happy with how the firm treated me as a survivor from that disaster. They really did all they could to help me build the business. I teamed up with some partners in the Burbank office, and that really was a great decision for me. Three years later the business is strong and healthy. I really have learned a lot in that time. I am really happy with where I am at. I am happier to be marrying Elena, sitting next to me. She has been such an incredible force for me, she really is my best friend. That is going to help us as we get married. That will help my business, and we will be so happy together. Things are working out.

Eric: What did you do after you got to safety, after you got to the hotel? What did you do? Did you watch the news? What was going through your mind? How did you get through the next few hours just dealing with an incomprehensible situation?

Kevin: After the streets, and the smoke, and the debris, and the dust settled, we all got back to the hotel and met in the lobby. It was an incredible experience, because every time a member of our group walked in we all cheered. We all had to sign in and they would then send a wire to our branches to let them know that I had checked in. Then we went immediately to the bar.

(laughter)

We were in the bar, watching CNN, and really just hung out as colleagues, hugged each other, embraced each other, cried with each other, and we actually that night were missing twenty trainees. They never checked in. Like anybody would, we thought the worst, that these people died in the tower. I had said before that everybody made it out.

There is actually one funny story. Most of the people, some lived in New York and New Jersey, they just went home. They never checked out, they just went home to their families. They were accounted for. One guy, a funny story, he exited the World Trade Center that morning, found the nearest taxicab, said, "take me to North Carolina."

(laughter)

The cabbie just drove him to North Carolina. So that guy was unaccounted for for a few days, but eventually he did ... he was fine. He put the cabbie up for a night or two.

(more laughter)

The guy then went back to New York City.

So, it's just amazing that all these people from all walks of life, we all came back, we all made it out. Our company actually lost seven people out of five thousand. We were the largest tenant in the South Tower, and it's amazing that so many were saved.

Eric: Given that you were not from New York, and that was your first experience, what was your impression of New Yorkers throughout that whole tragedy? How did you find them as human beings?

Kevin: Well you know, going out there, everyone said that the typical New Yorker is brash, and abusive, and all this stuff ... and I'll tell you, those people, when the chips are down, those people are at their best. I don't know how I would have gotten back to my hotel if it wasn't for the New York people telling me which Shelbourne was, to go left, to go right, and extending helping hands to me as I traveled from the World Trade Center ruins up to my hotel, which was actually fifty blocks north from the towers. I had this overwhelming feeling that this group of people, that these people were united. What a great sense of unity amid so much tragedy that these people were there to help me.

Some guy from Burbank, from LA, and they extended a helping hand. They were tough, and they really were willing to help me, and that is something I will never forget. Elena and I have actually talked about going back to New York for the groundbreaking of the new tower, and it would be great for us to be there and see all the strides that the city has made. I have nothing but great things to say about the New York people.

Eric: What is your faith in terms of your relationship with God before and after the tragedy? Did something like this reaffirm your faith, did it shake your faith, was there no change? Have you felt any spiritual connections since that day and those events?

Kevin: Well, obviously during the attacks, I remember going down those stairs and praying to God that we would all be saved. I mean, there was a moment there when I was on the fifty-fifth floor, the fiftieth floor, the fortieth floor, when I felt I was never going to get out of there. We knew that the building got hit pretty hard by the cracks in the walls and everything else, so yeah, I prayed and said, "Please, it's not my time. I don't want to go. There is so much more I have to do." As I got out of the tower and I knew I was safe there was still this sense that, you know, was there another building that was going to be hit? I remember walking up the streets and thinking that maybe another building was going to be hit by an airplane, and was I safe at that point? Looking back three years later I think my faith is stronger. It's hard not to think about getting a second chance, that it wasn't my time. I think, gosh, I was on fifty-five, and that plane hit on around seventy-nine or eighty. Twenty-plus floors below, I probably wouldn't be sitting here today. I have a lot to be thankful for. Elena and I are so blessed. I think our faith is so much stronger since that day.

Eric: I can tell you that I issued a meaningless proclamation in our office that day. Because I knew that there was no teeth to it. Whenever somebody in my family would get sick, my grandfather would say, "Nobody is dying in this family." He will take care of it. Somebody in the family gets cancer, something will happen to take care of it. He finally died when he felt that everybody in the family could take care of themselves.

I remember in our office when one of the sales assistants was thinking the worst, I said to her, I must have snapped at her, "Nobody is dying in this office. Not in my office." Now I'm aware that there was nothing I could do about it, but I kept telling everybody "Not today. Nobody in this office is dying." I remember when we got the news. I went over the loudspeaker and announced that you were alive. People were high-fiving, they were hugging, because we realized that even though that there was going to be a lot of pain and suffering, and there was going to be plenty of time for that, "Not in our family."

Kevin: Right.

Eric: You were a member of our family. You were a new member, and it was good to know that you were okay.

One thing that I really would like to ask you is how do you feel in terms of justice? Do you seek vengeance? Do you have hatred in your heart toward the people who did this? Do you feel that maybe there is something the United States did? Are we too arrogant a country? Did we do anything at all to deserve what happened, or was this just evil at its worst? Expand on that if you can.

Kevin: Well, Eric, I've said many times, initially after the attacks, the anger was very obvious. I remember my cousin Lincoln and I were out in Boston, because I actually took a train to Boston after the attacks and stayed with family for five days. We wanted to sign up and join the military. We obviously after a couple of beers had this epiphany that we were going to be these soldiers that were going out to fight this war that we thought was justified.

You know, I think that I can't believe that human beings would do this to other human beings. You know, whether it's the West vs. the East, or us vs. them, I'm not sure about that, but all I can say is, God- loving people don't seek to harm other people. This was obviously a blatant attack on human lives. That's the part I don't understand and makes me angry, and how would people want to inflict such harm on other people?

Our course of action has been very strong, and I think it needed to be strong. I fully support our president. I think it's justified, and we need to protect ourselves here on our own country's soil. The ultimate idea is how human beings could do this to other human beings. That is the issue, I think.

Eric: Now, three years since this tragedy, on the anniversary of this tragedy, you are going to be doing what any normal person, what any decent person should be doing today. You are not only going to be going to a football game, but a USC football game.

(laughter)

So, is today completely normal for you, or in the back, little down deep, is it not?

Kevin: Well, you know, I think that I couldn't imagine anything else better than being at a sold out ninety-two thousand-plus USC football game at the Coliseum on 9/11, especially three years after the anniversary, and yes, I have had many phone calls this morning from friends and family, and Eric, I want to thank you for the opportunity to be here. It was great to hear your voice yesterday. I think that is what is special for me, connecting with my loved ones on this day. They will always remember how it felt, and how worried they were for me, and I'll always remember connecting with them and saying that I was okay. That will always be what this day reminds me of. It'll be great to see … to be with my friends here at the game, and also think what a great country we have. So it's a special day for us. It's also great that we're here with all the other USC fans as well.

(laughter)

Eric: What would make the perfect day for you one year from today? What would make September 11, 2005, a fabulous day?

Kevin: While I think, a couple things. If there is another USC game a year from now, that would be fine.

(laughter)

I'm okay with that. Like I said before, if Elena and I can get back to New York, and if it's on the four-year anniversary, that would be awesome. Just to think back four years from that day that what a tragic experience, and yet here we are, four years later, married, doing so well, and that's something that we'll always remember.

Either being in New York or being with other USC Trojan fans, I think, would be a great thing for us.

Eric: Well, I can't thank you enough, Kevin. You've been very generous with your time. We can continue on if you'd like to, if you have other places you need to be we can bring it short. I have a million questions I could ask you, but I want to make sure I am not taking it out of your tailgating time because I know how important that is.

(laughter)

Kevin: Well I know that my cellphone keeps ringing, so we probably have to get back to the tailgate. I do want to thank you for having us here. It was a wonderful time. It was great to see you as well. Again, Eric, my family speaks highly of you and how you handled that situation that day. They all called the office and said, "Eric took care of it." So I wanted to thank you again.

Eric: Well, I paid them handsomely to say that.

(laughter)

All I can say is that it's impossible for me to think of September 11 without thinking of you, and even though you and I probably hadn't talked in eleven months and twenty-nine days …

Kevin: Sure.

Eric: September 9 and 10 roll around, and I'm calling your office what seems like every four hours, desperate to get a hold of you …

Kevin: Absolutely.

Eric: Now that we've got this archived on cassette, and soon on CD, from now on, the world is going to hear your story.

Kevin: Absolutely.

Eric: I just want to say that on a day like this when we think of so many tragedies, and I don't want to minimize the tragedies, because we have had Spain on 3/11, we've had Russian schoolchildren … there is a positive message that I think comes out of it. Correct me if I am wrong, but that positive message is that we are stronger than they are.

Kevin: Right.

Eric: We are tougher than they are. The fact that you are here, that you are able to talk about it, and the fact that you're able to go to a game and you're able to laugh and joke, that you're not having nightmares every night … is it fair to say that even though they won that battle that day that we've won the war of civilization?

Kevin: I think so, because I think I'll never forget the picture of the firemen that were in the rubble that held up the American flag. There were three of them that day. Even though there were burning buildings behind them, they realized that our country is going to continue and go on. I think that is what the terrorists didn't realize. Our buildings might have been knocked down, and people died, but this country is so strong and our people are so united, and so that will never change. I think that this was a wakeup call for a lot of people to say, "We need to look at ourselves and look at the world and make sure that we are unified, and really unified for the causes of freedom."

Eric: Kevin, one of the reasons this country is so strong is because it has people like you. I appreciate you taking the time to tell your story. Thank you very much.

Elena: Thanks Eric.

Kevin: Thanks Eric.

Eric: Be well and God bless.

Kevin is now a successful stockbroker and a happily married man. Most years I still go about eleven months and twenty-nine days without calling him. Then 9/11 rolls around, and he dominates my thoughts. Neither he nor I will ever forget that day.

Rather than end on a heavy note, I will say that my way of healing is by flying.

On September 11, 2005, I broadcast my final radio show on the USC campus.

I then vowed to fly every 9/11. It was my way of fighting back.

On September 11, 2006, I flew from Los Angeles to Oakland to sit fifty-yard line, front row, as the San Diego Chargers took on the Oakland Raiders on Monday Night Football. It was the first week of the season, and the jets flew on high and proud before the game.

On March 11, 2007, the three-year anniversary of the Madrid bombing and the exact midpoint from 9/11, I began blogging.

On September 11, 2007, I was in Chicago on business. I flew that morning to New York. It was the first time since 2001 that 9/11 fell on a Tuesday. I made my way to Six Flags Great Adventure in New Jersey for Sean Hannity's Freedom Concert featuring Lee Greenwood. The audience used their cellphones to light up the night sky during the song "God Bless the USA."[95]

On September 11, 2008, I have a flight from Los Angeles to Chicago. 9/11 is a day to hug your loved ones. Hug them, and get on a plane. When we fly, we win.

eric

Permanent Flame—9/11/7

I began blogging on March 11, 2007. On my six-month anniversary, I decided to replay "Permanent Flame." A final verse was added.

At 8:46 AM on 9/11/7, I will be on a plane to New York. This flight was arranged deliberately. I wear the red, white, and blue of America on my t-shirt, and these colors don't run.

Permanent Flame—In memory of the United 93 Heroes

(Originally written 7/30/6 PERMANENT FLAME)

**Chorus: NEVER FORGOTTEN...PERMANENT FLAME
NO LONGER HERE, BUT YOU'LL ALWAYS REMAIN
THREE THOUSAND GONE...BUT NEVER IN VAIN
HONOR THEIR MEMORY...TAKE BACK THE PLANE**

1a) September 11, 2001
Started so normal, ended so wrong
American airplanes, turned into guns
Fired on our towers, that stood proud and strong

1b) Black clouds from New York ... to the Pentagon
Sixty years after 1941
American steel ... will never yield
Look at the hole, in the Pennsylvania field

1c) Beamer and company, saw America attacked
Our Capitol saved, because they fought back
Ordinary people ... scared but so bold
Rose to the challenge ... told the world "let's roll"

Chorus

2a) Some blamed the US, but nothing we did
Justified the murder of innocent kids
Since then we've had Bali, London, and Madrid
We try to save the world across the global grid

2b) 2002 ... Afghanistan
Liberated a nation, routed the Taliban
2003 ... war in Iraq
Saddam in jail ... democracy on track

2c) September 11, 2004
Thirty-six months since the start of the war
Less people airborne, scared to the core
What can we do … we must do more

Chorus

3a) An ordinary man … I see in the mirror
But now I understand … the picture is clearer
Only total victory … in the war on terror
Will make America … for all our children better

3b) Our soldiers fight … because the cause is right
So our children are safe … when tucked in at night
Donate your dollars to police … and those who firefight
Money left over … go book that flight

Chorus

4a) September 11, 2006
Chargers vs. Raiders … I got my tix
From LAX … To OAK
Don't worry Mom and Dad, I'll be okay

4b) I need to do this, it helps heal the pain
I'll get home safely, so don't be afraid
I'm only one link in an American chain
If others join me, we can take back the plane

4c) So call up United, Delta, and Southwest
Show all the world our American best
Take back our freedom … take back the sky
For our fallen heroes … American Eagles let's fly

Chorus (sing twice)

May God Bless the USA … again … Let's roll.

September 11, 2007
En route to New York … I point to the heavens
The war we will win … and evil we'll sever
September 11, 2000—forever

eric aka the Tygrrr Express

America forever!

eric

I Don't CAIR

I had the pleasure of attending a presentation by attorney Reed Rubenstein on the danger that the Council on American-Islamic Relations, or CAIR, poses to Western civilization. CAIR is not, as it claims, the "Muslim NAACP." CAIR is a terrorist organization.

I was informed of the event by Richard Baehr of *American Thinker*. One reason Richard Baehr and I are under attack is because Republican Jews are hated for their religion and ideology. This hatred is also directed at non-Jewish Republicans and Jewish liberals. Many on the far left see real threats where none exist. More importantly, they see no threat where a significant one exists. This brings things back to CAIR.

Reed Rubenstein was the attorney for Andrew Whitehead for the case of CAIR vs. Whitehead. A similar case of significance was U.S. vs. Holy Land Foundation. Part of Mr. Rubenstein's presentation included a CD that contained documents in abundance. Mr. Rubenstein did not want us to take his word for what he had to say. He challenged the audience in attendance to view every piece of documentary evidence.

He started by pointing out that the *Jayson Blair Times*, in an article on March 14, 2007, wrote that "CAIR is partially funded by donors closely identified with Persian Gulf governments." The *JBT* also incorrectly stated that "Chapters of CAIR are franchises."[96]

The Justice Department sees it differently. Their documents states that, "Moreover, from its founding, CAIR conspired with other affiliates of the Muslim Brotherhood to support terrorists."[97]

Additionally, the evidence in the case led Mr. Rubenstein to logically conclude that the National CAIR controls the branches.

The case that led to this lecture began when Andrew Whitehead, a retired military man enraged over 9/11, started a Web site called "anti-CAIR."[98]

CAIR then sent Whitehead a cease and desist letter, demanding he take his site down. To his credit, Whitehead refused to back down. He published the letter, and then CAIR sued Whitehead for defamation.

For those who have not figured it out, terrorist organizations try to use America's tolerant laws against us. Yet in this case, the terrorists have miscalculated. Their strategy worked in Britain because England's defamation laws put the burden of proof on the defendant. In America, the plaintiff must prove their case. The process of discovery allows those accused to turn the tables and bury plaintiffs in document requests.

Mr. Whitehead's lawyer, Mr. Rubenstein (whose firm took the case pro bono), sent three hundred document requests to CAIR, asking for detailed information about every aspect of their operation. CAIR then filed an amended motion for judgment, which dropped most of the claims. The only claims remaining were those that claimed CAIR was a terror supporting front group, and that CAIR sought to overthrow the constitutional government of the United States.

When asked why CAIR quotes directly from the Hamas charter, they stated this was not true. When asked to prove this, CAIR stated that they could not find a single copy of the charter. Apparently CAIR does not know how to use the Internet. They also denied that Hamas murdered innocent civilians, and that it was a "foreign jurisdictional issue."

When CAIR was faced with a motion to compel them to produce more documents linking them to terrorism, they quickly decided to settle the case. Mr. Whitehead's Web site is allowed to stay up, and he is not required to apologize for or retract any of his comments. It was a victory for Andrew Whitehead and a defeat for CAIR.

So what did the case turn up that CAIR is so desperate to keep out of court?

CAIR was set up as a cell of the Muslim Brotherhood. They have been intertwined with the Islamic Association for Palestine (IAP), which is closely allied with the Muslim Student Association. The Holy Land Foundation (HLF) played a key role. CAIR encouraged people to donate to the HLF. The HLF then sent the money to Hamas.

The IAP has since been shut down, and the HLF was shut down after 9/11. CAIR handled the media, law, and politics. The IAP were the public relations people, handling education and organizing. The HLF were the money people, bankrolling the organizations. These organizations all have logos with crossed swords, not typical of groups truly committed to peaceful activities.

CAIR has top-level people who have expressed that "The loss of Palestine in 1948 is second only to the loss of the Caliphate." The rationale for CAIR was expressed in October of 1993, that being to "advance the brotherhood agenda, reduce Jewish influence, and mobilize all Muslims to join in anti-Israel activity." On June 12, 1995, a *New Republic* article described a meeting where a young holy warrior asked for a legal ruling with regards to killing

Jews. The homicidal elder responded that "Killing Jews is a good deed, and does not require a legal ruling. Just bring the dead body."

CAIR's Web site on September 17, 2001, listed three Web sites through which people could donate to help 9/11 victims. One link was to the Red Cross. This link was legitimate. Another link was the NY/DC Emergency Relief Fund. No such fund existed. Clicking on that link took people straight to the HLF Web site. On September 26, 2001, slight changes were made to CAIR's site. The link listed as the fictitious NY/DC Emergency Relief Fund was replaced with a direct listing of the HLF site. The Red Cross site was still linked, as was another site labeled the Global Relief Fund. That link led to a place where people could make contributions, which went straight to funding Al Qaeda and the Taliban.

CAIR rallies include people waving Hezbollah flags and CAIR leaders wearing the Keffiyah (head covering) with the insignia of the Al Aqsa Marty's Brigade.

The way to convict such terrorists living in America is usually by getting them on visa fraud. Many terrorists come here legally but then overstay their visas. Visa fraud is the mobster equivalent of tax evasion.

Also, as part of their aspirations, CAIR on one occasion offered a doctored photo outside the Capitol during their press conferences. Blondes become brunettes, and Muslim women without head coverings are given head coverings. Perhaps they do know how to use the Internet, or at least Photoshop.

CAIR claims that they condemn terrorist attacks, but they never once condemned Hamas, Hezbollah, Saudi Arabia, Iran, Sudan, the Taliban, or any Muslim country.

CAIR has sued David Frum, *National Review Online*, and uses liberal media outlets to further their cause. They normally go through the *JBT*, the ACLU, and the National Council of Churches.

Whenever anybody criticizes any Muslim with either terror connections or suggestions that Jews immolate themselves through "dialogue" with terrorists, those on the wrong side claim anti-Muslim bigotry. For example, Congressman Keith Ellison wants Jews to "talk to CAIR."

In 1993, worried about being recorded (which they were), CAIR people stated that, "We cannot support Samah." Samah is Hamas spelled backwards. In 1999, the head of CAIR endorsed suicide bombers in the name of Islam.

In 2007, CAIR criticized "right wingers and 'Neozionists.'" Neozionists is a way of confirming that "Neoconservatives," or "Neocons" for short, are just Jews.

CAIR Action Alert #508 is a false denial by CAIR that they wish to destroy the holy shrines of other faiths.

Also, CAIR plays the victim card to perfection when they are the ones promoting hatred, bigotry, and intolerance. Examples include Muslim cab drivers in Minneapolis refusing to accept blind people with guide dogs as passengers because it violates their faith.

CAIR is also insecure. They feel compelled to compete with Jews and non-Muslims on every level. Since there are six million Jews in America, CAIR claims there are seven million Muslims. This is not true. Pew research reflects only two-and-a-half million Muslims. Yes, there are Persians in Los Angeles, and plenty of Arabs in Dearborn, Detroit, and Minneapolis, but the two-and-a-half million number is accepted by reputable sources such as Pew.

FBI statistics from 2006 reflect that in that calendar year, there were 156 anti-Muslim crimes and 967 anti-Jewish crimes. CAIR claims that Muslims are simply scared to report their crimes. CAIR claims fifty thousand members on their Web site, but only lists seventeen hundred members for IRS reporting purposes. It is unlikely that they are lying to the IRS, since the IRS can punish them in ways the media cannot. If the IRS digs, their operation crumbles. In 2000, CAIR reported $732,000 in dues. In 2007, dues were $58,000. In Maryland, gigantic mosques are being built. The mosques are empty. There are no parishioners inside. The mosques are for appearances, and the illusion of strength in numbers. The bottom line is that CAIR is media savvy but not a grassroots organization. They are a top-down operation.

The problem in America is getting people to face the truth and act on it. The U.S. government sends conflicting information. They label terrorist organizations as such, but then invite CAIR leaders to the White House under the banners of diversity and multiculturalism. The media ignores CAIR entirely. The *JBT* reporter that wrote the initial erroneous story about CAIR was offered to view the evidentiary documents, but refused. He was "uninterested in a civil issue." The *Washington Post* was uninterested in the story.

Media diversity guidelines require referring to Muslim harassment victims in the same vein and proportion as purveyors of overt terrorist attacks that are Muslim. Terrorists are to be compared similarly to white supremacists and anti-abortionists. In keeping with a left-wing agenda, environmentalist terrorists such as ELF are exempt from this.

Approximately 65 percent of Muslims in America are first generation; most of them having arrived since 1990. This is not foreign infiltration. Homegrown terrorists are living among the Muslims that love America and Western values. The bad have blended in with the good so that an attack on CAIR is an attack on all Muslims. One organization helping this along is the North American Islamic Trust. This organization is a Saudi front that finances 45–70 percent of the mosques in America.

"The big problem is political correctness and multiculturalism. In short, we do not have to respect CAIR's beliefs. The fact that they may have an educational wing that is not into terror is irrelevant. If the Klan wanted to work with people on a clean streets initiative, we would refuse their help because they are still the Klan. This is not about stifling their right to speak. It is about preventing them from stifling the right of others to have free speech and criticize them." They will use the power of American courts to sue people, hoping that once enough people roll over and surrender, CAIR will gain more power.

"They cannot win, but we can lose. We must demand accountability. We must hear Muslim voices for freedom. We must speak the truth."

One questioner asked about the Michael Savage case, but Mr. Rubenstein differentiated the cases. Mr. Savage made comments about CAIR. CAIR pressured his advertisers, and the advertisers caved. From a moral standpoint this is what we must try and prevent, but Mr. Savage's suit against CAIR was tossed out because advertisers have a legal right to be cowards. Another questioner asked about the Mark Steyn case, but that was more a human rights case.

"The burden is on moderate Muslims to find us, not the reverse. We must stop the Western guilt. Immigrants today, like all immigrants in decades past, must leave their baggage in the old country.

The Muslim per capita income is greater than the average per capita income of other Americans.

Jews, especially liberal ones, are part of the problem. They want to keep quiet on this issue. They want no part of it for fear of a backlash." So CAIR threatens to silence all Jews, and Jews respond by staying silent.

"The Klan, Communists, Nazis, and CAIR are all heinous but legal. The goal is not to get CAIR shut down, but to get the facts out. It is tough to shut down people who support terrorists because it is tough to define the word support. It is illegal to support terrorists financially, but not emotionally."

Mr. Rubenstein offered some final thoughts.

"CAIR is *The Sopranos* equivalent of the *Bada-Bing Club*.

The Patriot Act without a doubt has saved American lives.

There is a media war, but only one side is fighting."

Mr. Rubenstein's presentation is sobering and disturbing, but less sobering and disturbing than the fact that many people will remain ignorant of the facts, in some cases through willful blindness.

CAIR does not represent all Muslims. All Muslims are not terrorists.

CAIR are terrorists. For those who offer excuses … I just don't CAIR.

eric

Tea With Mussolini, Columbian Coffee With Armageddonijad

For the sake of full disclosure, no, I have never watched the movie *Tea with Mussolini*. I also have never seen *Beaches, Steel Magnolias,* or *Fried Green Tomatoes*. If I did I would have to kick my own @ss, or have my friends come over and kick it for me. I am a heterosexual, red meat eating, football watching alpha male. Feminists call me a Neanderthal. I refer to myself as a guy. For those of you who are passionate about the right of homosexual vegetarians to watch frisbee golf on TV, leave me alone. I have nothing against your causes. I just want to get home without being bombarded with leaflets.

If I wanted to watch something about airhead women babbling, jabbering, and yammering about nonsense, I'd watch, *The View*. I don't, so I don't. Yet *Tea with Mussolini* was merely a movie. "Columbian Coffee with Armageddonijad" is real life.

I used to think as an uneducated teenager (I did go to public school after all.) that Colombia was a nation known for coffee, cocaine, cartels, and corruption. I now know as an adult that Columbia is a place for tree huggers, treason, terrorism, and thoughtlessness.

In the real world, 9/11 was a tragedy of unmatchable proportions. We lost policemen, firefighters, medics, fathers, sons, daughters, mothers, and loved ones everywhere. The memorial resides in the state of New York.

In the *Tea with Mussolini* world of Columbia, 9/11 is an anachronism. Despite the fact that the university is located in New York, it intellectually resides in the state of oblivion.

In the real world, Lee Bollinger is a terrorist sympathizer and America hater who preaches diversity, but bans ROTC from the Columbia campus because United States soldiers are the villains and Armageddonijad is a freedom fighter.

In the *Tea with Mussolini* world of Columbia, Lee Bollinger is an academic, aka a man that possesses knowledge, which apparently distinguishes book smarts from street smarts.

In the real world, Armageddonijad is a terrorist who should be shot on sight. Let those who orgasm over the Geneva Convention criticize us after we put two bullets right in his murderous heart. The Geneva lovers do not seem to be concerned with his hundreds of violations of this worthless rule preventing political assassinations. Those who argue that it could lead others to try and murder George W. Bush should admit that those terrorists are constantly plotting this. The way some liberals talk, I am not sure that this even troubles them, given their warped view of good and evil.

In the *Tea with Mussolini* world of Columbia, Armaggedonijad is A-Jad, a celebrity often confused with A-Rod, J-Lo, Skee-Lo, K-Fed, C-Span, or Brangelina.

In the *Tea with Mussolini* world of Columbia, everyone has a right to free speech.

In the real world, free speech does not entitle anybody to be allowed to address a college campus. I could demand the right to give the commencement address at Columbia. I would implore the students to go to work at McDonald's, because that is all their Poison Ivy League degrees would be worth. After all, toilet paper is not a rare enough commodity to get rich selling.

In the *Tea with Mussolini* world of Columbia, valuable insight can be gained engaging in dialogue with a genocidal madman. In fact, one of the deans of Columbia would have invited Hitler. Granted this would have been before the Holocaust, when Hitler was a nice guy and wonderful painter.

In the real world, Armageddonijad should be captured, cuffed, and then drawn and quartered. Perhaps he could be the prequel to the Kentucky Derby. Actually, quartering him should be done at the Belmont Stakes because that is in New York (sorry Maryland Preakness fans).

On the subject of the Holocaust, in the real world, it did happen. The sun rises in the east, two plus two actually is four, and my father did not make the whole thing up to scare me straight.

In the *Tea with Mussolini* world of Columbia, debates about the Holocaust are important because diversity of ideas is valid. Next week the Flat Earth Society will address the crowd to adoring throngs. If only Lee Bollinger could have gotten Ed McMahon to introduce Armageddonijad like he was Johnny Carson, it would've been a perfect show.

In the *Tea with Mussolini* world of Columbia, there are no homosexuals living in Iran. Being gay is a phenomenon unique only to the United States, such as In 'n' Out Burger or Dairy Queen.

In the real world, there may not be many gays in Iran because Iran is such a wonderful democracy that gays have the freedom to choose whether to be shot, stoned, or burned to death (as opposed to universities where students are merely bored to death).

In the real world, one would think that left-wing activists from groups such as gay rights, civil rights, animal rights, environmentalists, feminists, and others would protest against regimes such as Iran that believe that peace and harmony can exist in a nation when dissenters are beaten, raped, tortured, and killed by savage baboons such as the Ayatollah Khomonkey and Armageddonijad.

In the *Tea with Mussolini* world at Columbia, peace activists fly into violent rages. They protest that they are being censored at the top of their lungs. They despise American soldiers, adore left-wing and other murderous "freedom fighters," and demand legislation to address their oppression at being forced to live in an imperfect but amazingly noble nation. They also seem to think that those that worry about illegal immigration think in both directions. Nobody will stop them from leaving. I would guarantee this in writing.

In the *Tea with Mussolini* world of Columbia, everybody has something valuable to offer (except conservative Republicans and American soldiers). Civility and respect of opposing views is important (except when throwing pies at Ann Coulter or storming the stage against the Minutemen).

In the real world, New York City has a hole in the ground. Armageddonijad has a hole in his head, although his is figurative. It needs to be made literal. One day I will stand before God, and I will absolutely stand by my willingness to advocate the killing of this bloodthirsty thug. He should be wiped off of the map as if he never existed. At the very least, we should use "enhanced interrogation techniques" until he breaks down and sobs his love for America and Israel. Perhaps we can torture ... excuse me, enhance ... him into surrendering by blaring rock music so he cannot sleep, like we did with Noriega. We can force him to listen to Def Leppard's *Hysteria* album, from, "Pour Some Sugar On Me," to the new Mullah theme song, "Armageddon It"[100] (yes, that is a real rock song).

Given how angry and enraged I am about this, I should just go completely off the rails. That way I will be mistaken for either a leftist protester at a peace rally or a genocidal, maniacal, third-world dictator. Either way, that would qualify me to lead a *Tea with Mussolini* discussion, enlightening the students getting a Poison Ivy League education.

Then again, I enjoy being an intelligent and productive member of society. I support efforts to strip Columbia of all government funding. That is sanity, not censorship. The Patriot Act bans aiding and abetting terrorists. It would be fabulous if students turned on their hippie parents and stormed Bollinger's office and demanded their right to a quality ideologically free education. I do not encourage violence, but think about how wonderfully delightful it would be to have students actually protesting for something useful, such as the right to learn.

Maybe they can protest for the right to have the National Rifle Association address the campus to teach the students about responsible gun ownership and the appropriate usage of firearms to defend the USA and its citizens.

After all, one never knows what threats may show up to cause Ground Zero … or to try and lay a wreath at Ground Zero after enjoying tea or Columbian coffee with Bollinger.

eric

Live From Tel Aviv—Beaches, Disco, and BMX Terrorism

The woman and I prepared an Israel trip involving tourism, beaches, and discos. We were not prepared for the most bizarre form of domestic terrorism the world has ever seen. This will not make the newspaper. In the world of beaches and discos, Israel, BMX terrorism is upon us.

We did not make it to the discos on Saturday night. However, the beach was gorgeous. The restaurant bar on the beach was paradise. We had the Mediterranean Sea in front of us. We stayed until almost 4 AM. The woman and I were sitting at our table when glass and metal went flying. We did not fear for our lives. However, this was BMX violence at its worst.

The young boy was about twelve, and while the bicycle he was riding may not have been BMX, I only know them, Schwinn, and Huffy. BMX sounds best.

Our table was the closest one to the bike path, and this boy veered toward us. He was quite inebriated. When his bike hit our table, our glasses spilled all over us. My black jeans were covered either in beer or Diet Sprite. The woman got doused as well. The boy somehow managed not to fly across our table. He was polite, slurring the words "excuse me" in Hebrew, which the woman translated.

I got up and rushed over to him just before he fell down. I held his bicycle up. This kid was blitzed. Another guy said, "He may be drunk." I replied, "You think!" The boy then laughed, unaware of anything that had occurred. The man walked the boy away as we all laughed, since everybody was okay. We moved over to the next table, and the waitress made it clear that "we are not going to be bombed here."

Maybe so, but I am not sure we were totally safe, either! The people in nearby tables said that they had never seen that before. Some of them wanted to make sure that I did not blame Israel for this one boy. I told them that I prayed that the boy was not American, since I did not want all Americans to be blamed either. Everyone laughed.

Had we been in the Gaza Strip, and had the boy been Arab or Palestinian, perhaps the table would have exploded as soon as the boy made contact. I sure wouldn't be laughing. On a more serious note, I hope this boy's parents discipline him, since in four years he might be driving a car.

Otherwise, the land of milk and honey is not bad so far, although I have not tried any milk or honey. I do look forward to the discos. They are indoors, which means the BMX Palestinian Hamas Hezbollah Cabal will not get to us inside. Also, we were charged for our drinks anyway. Several shekels should be taken from this boy's allowance. All is well, and I will be riding a bicycle tomorrow. If I see this boy, I will bike over to him and steal his ice cream while yelling "Allah Akbar."

No, not really.

eric

Colonel David Hunt and the JFK Plot—They Still Just Don't Get It

I have done everything I can as a private citizen to help America in my own small way win the War on Terror. In his book, *They just don't get it*,[100] retired Fox News military analyst Colonel David Hunt outlines the problems we face and what we can do about them. His book, like his personality, is a battering ram, a needed belt to the chops. This gruff former marine puts aside political correctness and tells us exactly what we need to do to eventually win this war.

First of all, we have to get mad. Then we have to stay mad. Many people turn off the television when they see images of 9/11, preferring to watch Paris Hilton or Anna Nicole Smith coverage. I still well up with rage when I see 9/11 coverage. Who the hell did these animals think they were? How dare they try to blow up my nation! If we do not love and desire to protect our nation as we would our family, is it no wonder our nation would weaken? We need to be part of the solution. It starts with getting fired up about fiercely cherishing and protecting our homeland.

The American military does a spectacular job. We need to let them do it, and without restrictions or touchy-feely politically correct concerns. Unless one has boots on the ground or lived in a foxhole, there is nothing to carp about. When I need somebody to drive a Humvee over a bridge and into a lake or ditch, I will consult Ted Kennedy, since that seems to be his area of expertise. Nancy Pelosi needs to spend more time in San Francisco and less time in Damascus. When I hear liberals say they support the troops and want to bring them home, I want to scream, Colonel Hunt style, "You just don't get it." Until liberals realize that Islamofacism is the enemy, and not George W. Bush, they won't get it.

I talk to soldiers. My travels to places with military presences such as Honolulu and San Diego allow me to ask soldiers what they think. Many have been to Afghanistan and Iraq and support and believe in their mission by an overwhelming margin. On Memorial Day, a young man just back from his third tour of duty was asked in front of his mother what Americans can do to help. He said that while care packages were nice, the best gift the American people could give the soldiers was their unwavering support and total belief in the mission. That is not ambiguous. Unwavering support and total belief do not add up to withdrawal, retreat, and defeat. "These colors don't run," is not a slogan. It is how our troops behave. Civilians need to back them.

We need to stop fighting polite wars. We need to stop apologizing just because the *JBT* hates President Bush more than they love our troops. Abu Gharaib and Haditha were nothing. That's right ... nothing. Rougher hijinks can be found at college fraternity initiation ceremonies. The enemy beheads people. We make them feel bad and hurt their feelings, and we get criticized.

We need to harshly, verbally slap down San Francisco protesters. San Francisco-style anti-war protesters want us to pull out of Iraq, end all war, and stop imposing American imperialism on a world that just wants to be left alone to live in peace. Until San Francisco is bombed, they will not understand ... anything.

I am absolutely not wishing San Francisco get firebombed. It would not be fair to the twelve to fourteen Republicans who would be collateral damage. I fiercely disagree with liberals, but I do not want them to die. I think they are hopelessly misguided, but the reason I want to defeat their world view is because I want them to live ... and remain alive myself. I try to crush their world view so that they can live in peace. Wrong, free, and alive is better than wrong and dead.

We need to name the enemy. The War on Terror is a war on Islamofacism. It is a religious war. Those who wage jihad have been bitter since the Crusades. They should be humiliated worse this time. We do not need to fight a more sensitive war, as John "anti-war protester" Kerry would prefer.[101] We need to fight a more ruthless, cutthroat war.

When our soldiers have the chance to take out an entire town, we cannot have politicians fear that collateral damage would look bad on the nightly news. If people want to avoid being collateral damage, get the hell out of the war zone. We are afraid to blow up mosques because that would be seen as anti-Muslim. Wrong. Under the Geneva Convention, which terrorists do not seem to abide by anyway, a mosque used for criminal activity loses its protected status. If terrorists are holed up in a mosque with weapons and battle plans, blow up the mosque and save innocent lives. We can always rebuild another one. The goal is to kill the terrorists. Most decent Muslims understand that terrorists who seek refuge in mosques do damage to the mosques anyway. Guns are forbidden in mosques to begin with.

Also, is there any city in Iraq that is not a holy city? When we damage enough holy cities, these monsters might decide to stop thinking that they can hide in the remaining holy cities and fire at us indiscriminately. New York City was a holy city to me. We should have pounded Fallujah the first time and stopped worrying about public relations.

We must immediately commence profiling. Now, while sending the ACLU to Guantanamo Bay until this war ends is tempting, a simpler solution would be to overpower them. Stop donating money to them until they get it. Slash their budget. Then commence profiling. Not all Arabs and Muslims are terrorists, but virtually all terrorists are Arab Muslims, mostly young, single, male Arab Muslims. Do we really need to delay my plane flight so that we can search eighty-six-year-old Etta Mae Johnson, retired librarian from Hattiesburg, Mississippi? Does her knitting apparel really need to be confiscated? As a Jewish man, I am asked to remove my black hat sometimes (consistency would be nice), yet Arab Muslims are not required to remove their turbans. This is nuts.

We need to stop being politically correct. The Danish cartoons were deadly accurate. They should be published repeatedly. Will it anger Arab terrorists? Yes. So what? Water is wet. Everything angers Arab terrorists. We need to give them repeated helpings of "get over it."

We need to understand that this is not a battle far away. Arab Muslims tried to blow up JFK. For those who still don't get it, they tried to reduce a major American airport to rubble, just as they did the World Trade Center towers. These animals were homegrown. However, they needed help from overseas. The plot was foiled, but how many plots need to be foiled before we realize that they still want to kill us?

Colonel Hunt, I will do my part. On 9/11 of 2006, I flew from LAX to Oakland. One week before that I flew to New York. On 9/11 of 2007, a Tuesday, I will be flying straight into JFK. I will be in the airborne at 8:46 AM. This is my way of telling the terrorists to go f*ck themselves. They cannot stop me from getting on that plane. All I ask is that everybody else fulfill their responsibilities as well. Airport security needs to step it up. Military leaders need to support their soldiers. Politicians need to shut up and get out of the way. Those disgusted by anti-war protesters need to shout down these bullies. When hit between the eyes, they will retreat. That is what separates them from American soldiers, who conduct themselves with dignity on and off the battlefield.

What can we do to win the war on Islamofacism? As Colonel Hunt says, we have to start by "getting it." We have to know who the enemy is. Our soldiers have to go after them with overwhelming brute force. Our politicians and military leaders have to support them. Private citizens have to get mad, stay mad, and provide unwavering support. When you see soldiers, thank them.

Tell them, "Thank you, and welcome home." Tell them you support their mission. Those who don't will never get it.

I get it, Colonel Hunt. The war on Islamofacism reached JFK Airport. Luckily, the plot was foiled. This will be a long, hard struggle, and we must be prepared to either win all out or go home. Our military needs to be allowed to do what it does best … kill terrorists, destroy their hideouts, burn their villages, and break their wills. Force works. The only solution is a military solution. The troops have my overwhelming support. They will get the job done, and get it done right, provided that those in the way get out of the way and get it.

I am burning with rage over 9/11 and the JFK plot. I will be angry until I get on that plane to JFK on 9/11 of 2007. When I touch down, I will go to Ground Zero and drive a stake through the pictures of the bad guys' hearts, and pray that American soldiers do the same in real life. I know they eventually will. They clearly get it.

eric

Chapter 17: The Republican Jewish Coalition

As a Jewish person, 99 percent of the world is different from me. Many of these people hate me. As a Republican, many people disagree with me, and true liberals despise me. As a Jewish Republican, I encounter more bigotry from people than perhaps Pygmy Nazis. Short people get no breaks, and Randy Newman did not help matters.

I initially became a member of the Republican Jewish Coalition because I wanted to meet hot Republican Jewish brunettes. Unfortunately, the one good dichotomy is that many people have political lives that match their moral lives. Finding a woman politically conservative and morally liberal proved to be more difficult than finding a woman at the NOW willing to shut up and cook me dinner without any backtalk.

I have the scars, and until *Playgirl* magazine compensates me, they will remain hidden.

Somewhere along the line, I accidentally began developing substance on issues. This is not to be confused with substance abuse. Substance itself is positive.

The Republican Jewish Coalition is an organization of fine human beings that are helping to improve the world through grassroots organizing. They are like many left-wing organizations, except their contributions are positive and they lack corruption.

May the RJC continue to do good work.

Now that we have finally elected a Jewish president in George W. Bush, the only thing left is to spread the Zionist Crusader Alliance For World Domination.

For the less ambitious, there are social mixers with ice cream.

Ideological Bigotry Part XVII—Obama Attacks the Republican Jewish Coalition

Barack Obama has decided that his quest to become dictator and king for life has run into a snag. Apparently disagreeing with his holiness is still legal.

Unfortunately for democracy, dissent of the anointed one may not be permissible for long.

Barack Obama has decided to wage war on the Republican Jewish Coalition, whose only sin seems to be supporting Republican candidates for office, including John McCain.

Before getting to this specific incident of left-wing bullying, some brief contextual background is necessary.

Democrats are not the party of free speech. The left is not about tolerance. Free speech and tolerance are for those that agree with them ideologically. Those that do not, aka conservatives, are subjected to ruthless ideological bigotry.

It is the left that removes lawn signs and keys cars containing GOP bumper stickers. It was a Democrat that ran over Florida Secretary of State Katherine Harris with his car due to his displeasure over the 2000 election. It is the left that feels the need in every GOP administration to find one bogeyman to hate. First it was Ronald Reagan. President George H. W. Bush was considered moderate, so Dan Quayle was savaged. When Clinton and Gore were in power, the left demonized Speaker of the House Newt Gingrich. Nobody went after Tom Foley in that manner.

In the beginning of the presidency of George W. Bush, he and Vice President Cheney received some abuse, but not as much as now. Speaker of the House Dennis Hastert was considered moderate and therefore likable. The left had to go down the list to Attorney General John Ashcroft to find someone they could loudly detest. I do not remember a liberal attorney general getting that treatment. When he left, the liberals had to search and search, and they finally found John Bolton, the ambassador to the United Nations. Does anybody remember who the last liberal U.N. ambassador even was?

Now Sarah Palin is in the crossfire. The left wears t-shirts that say, "Abort Sarah Palin."[102] I guess they ran out of "Kill Bush,"[103] and "Bush = Hitler"[104] t-shirts.

The purpose of such rabid frothing at the mouth is to silence and intimidate those on the right. Conservatives disagree with liberals. Liberals despise conservatives. They want to take Republicans and destroy them, rip their insides out, and grind them into dust.

Some will say that it is wrong to blame all liberals for a few million lunatics. Fair enough. However, when the leaders of an entire political party become hijacked by the basket cases and start engaging in the same tactics, they must be called out.

Sarah Palin is hated on the left for being politically conservative and existing. That is it. A rally to condemn Iranian President Armageddonijad became political when Sarah Palin was disinvited. Disinvited? For what reason? Does she not have the right to be against a terrorist murderer and proclaim loudly how awful Armageddonijad is? When did free speech only become allowable for those on the left?

This free speech angle is important, because there are so many chilling attempts by the left to simply ban the right of those on the right to voice their opinions.

Liberals lament about how the debate is coarser than it used to be. They blame talk radio, Fox News, and Rush Limbaugh in particular. What they are really lamenting is that the right has any voice at all. The left has ABC, NBC, CBS, PBS, NPR, The *JBT*, the *Los Angeles Times*, the *Washington* (com)*Post*, and virtually all the cultural institutions in America ranging from public schools to libraries.

The left is angry that it can no longer get liberals elected by drumming up "fake but accurate"[105] memos or by breaking drunk driving scandals just before an election.

This is why the left wants to bring back the Fairness Doctrine. There is nothing fair about it. What the Fairness Doctrine means is that for thirty minutes of conservative programming, there has to be thirty minutes of liberal programming to balance it. Whether or not the station makes any money is irrelevant. The reason conservative talk radio flourished was because the right had no voice at all until it existed. The marketplace had an opening. Additionally, Rush Limbaugh did not succeed because of his political views alone. He is genuinely entertaining.

Liberal talk radio fails because it is boring. Also, it is politically correct. Humor cannot succeed when virtually every constituency is off limits or apologies have to be rendered after every joke. Also, liberals are terrible at making fun of themselves. Ronald Reagan was self-deprecating. Liberals from Michael Dukakis to John Kerry never learned this.

Yet as awful as it is that the left is going after conservative institutions, they are getting more and more hateful. The left is now going after private citizens.

Joe the Plumber is the latest example. All this man did was ask a potential leader a question. Barack Obama, who has been very disciplined, slipped up. He said that we should "spread the wealth around."[106] That phrase breathed new energy into conservatives. Instead of analyzing Barack Obama, the left decided to provide scrutiny to Joe the Plumber. This is what they do. Anybody on the right knows that if they speak up, they can be destroyed. Being on the right is not even necessary. Challenging anyone on the left is enough to become a public enemy. Just ask Paula Jones, the only person I know making $35,000 per year that was audited by the IRS after speaking up about being sexually harassed.

Not all private citizens have the money or power to fight back. Students get bullied by leftist professors, although a well-placed tape recorder gives them a slim fighting chance.

This brings me to the newest victims of Barack Obama's attempts at censorship, the Republican Jewish Coalition.

(Full disclosure: I am a member of the RJC leadership. All this means is that I attend their events, and occasionally make donations. I am not employed by them, nor is my blog in any way affiliated by them. I do not take orders from them, but am proud to have many RJC members as my friends. Any columns I write about them are solely my choice.)

The Republican Jewish Coalition is the preeminent organization in America for those that are politically right of center and members of the Hebrew faith.

Jews are not monolithic in the same way blacks, women, and other minorities are not monolithic. One of the great traditions of Judaism is the notion of debate. For those that have ever sat at a Jewish dinner table, the discussions are lively. Senator Barbara Boxer, no friend of Republicans, has publicly praised the notion of debate.

Given the election of 2008, several synagogues have been holding Jewish debate forums. The left has been represented by congressmen such as Adam

Schiff and Howard Berman, former congressman Mel Levine, and Andrew Lachmann, who heads up Democrats For Israel. The right has mainly been represented by the Republican Jewish Coalition. Larry Greenfield does most of the debates on the west coast, while other RJC executives have done others on the east coast. Richard Baehr, an RJC member who writes at *American Thinker*, crisscrosses America, debating and making the case for the GOP. I have even recently gotten into the act myself, sparring with Democratic strategists.

These debates were lively, informative, and mostly civil. Then I noticed that something began to change. The competitors on the left began getting angry, snarky, and downright hostile towards the RJC. In one debate, Mel Levine attacked the RJC about fourteen times.

I will put my personal integrity on the line and say that I would never belong to an organization that traffics in hate speech. I would not sacrifice my principles for career advancement. I challenge anybody to find anything on the RJC Web site or in any RJC printed publication that crosses the line. Like other politically right of center organizations, we focus on policy distinctions, not personal attacks.

Mel Levine[107] and Ira Forman[108] began accusing the RJC of engaging in hate speech, lies, and smears. When asked to produce one solid example, they failed to do so.

What really began to bother those on the left was that the younger Jewish community, not wed to FDR and JFK, was thinking for itself. The older Jewish community was also having doubts. The normally 80 percent of the Jewish community that votes on the left was being reduced to as little as 60 percent. It could reach parity in a decade. Some will say this is because Obama is being smeared. The truth is that many Jews privately like George W. Bush, supported Rudy Giuliani, and are very comfortable with John McCain. Joseph Lieberman has gravitas in the community, and that helps as well.

The days when liberal Jewish politicians could walk into a synagogue and automatically receive a standing ovation are gradually lessening. So instead of honest debate, the left tries bullying tactics. Congressman Robert Wexler of Florida has made comments about Sarah Palin that cannot be printed in a blog that abhors such language.

The bottom line is that Jewish debate audiences were no longer stacked against the right. The crowds were sharply divided. One recent forum I attended was actually majority Republican!

The Obama campaign, basically trying to run out the clock on the election, saw that the strategy of debating the issues was not working in a Jewish community that is becoming less and less reflexively liberal. He therefore gave a directive *banning* his surrogates from engaging in any debates with anybody from the RJC.

The incredibly weak excuse his campaign proffered was that since his surrogates were "official", they would only debate "official" surrogates from the McCain campaign.[165]

This is nonsense. These are Jewish debates. The RJC is every bit as important to right of center Jews as the NAACP is to many blacks and the Catholic League is to many Catholics. Will the Obama campaign ban debates about gay and lesbian issues from including anyone from the Log Cabin Republicans?

Mel Levine and others followed their marching orders and pulled out of several debates at various synagogues at the eleventh hour. This was rude, abrasive, and dishonest. The goal of these boycotts was to force the synagogues to cancel the events. After all, partisan events could jeopardize their tax-exempt statuses. With nobody on the left, the speaker on the right could not debate, and the events would be canceled.

Yet Jewish Republicans learned from what happened when John McCain recommended skipping a debate for noble reasons. Barack Obama threatened to show up alone. That is exactly what members of the RJC did. Thankfully, the synagogues did not give into the blackmail. They excoriated the participants who canceled at the last minute. The synagogues reiterated their non-partisan status, but explained that canceling events would cost them money and anger their congregations. In some cases, last minute surrogates filled in.

This is not an alleged conspiracy. Mel Levine and others have publicly stated that the Obama campaign will not let them debate the RJC. Mel Levine has debated with Larry Greenfield on several occasions, as have other surrogates on the left. For the Obama campaign to try to get these debate forums canceled is pure thuggery.

The Obama campaign has no right to decide who the other side chooses to offer as debate opponents. The only criteria should be if they are legitimate opponents. Mel Levine even sniveled that he did not want to debate Larry Greenfield again because he "did not want to elevate him in importance."[110]

I have a news flash for Mel Levine. He already debated Larry three times. Mel Levine is also somebody who was a congressman back when *Dallas* was on television. He came in fourth place in a 1992 senate race. I am not saying he is unimportant, but most people on the street would not recognize him.

Those on the left who are dropping out of these debates at the last minute are engaging in nothing but cowardice. They are also offending many Jewish people who gave up their evening, and in some cases money, to see actual debates representing various viewpoints.

Is this how Barack Obama would govern? Would he try to pressure synagogues to ban RJC members from speaking at all?

If anybody thinks this is fear mongering, investigate Robert Wexler. He is the "Bully of Boca," pressuring synagogues into silencing his opponents. It is already happening.

This needs to be dealt with immediately. Barack Obama is going to learn one way or another that you cannot bully your opponents into submission in the United States of America. We may have a media that would rather investigate private citizens than a potential world leader, but private citizens are fighting back.

Republicans are tired of ideological bigotry. We demand an honest discussion of issues. We are not scared of foreign attackers, so we will certainly not be scared by leftist Jewish bullies taking their instructions from somebody who wants to silence those who point out his shaky credentials on Jewish issues.

It is these obscene tactics that only add to the many justified questions surrounding Barack Obama on Jewish ... and non-Jewish ... issues.

Senator Obama can bring the hammer down, but he cannot hit every nail. The questions will be asked, and Jewish Republicans will continue to speak out.

Senator Obama, you are out of line. You have some explaining to do. We will get to the truth. We will be heard. This, and only this, is beyond any debate.

Hineni. Here I am. Republican, Jewish, and proud.

eric

RJC in DC—Meeting Sir Charles of Krauthammer

At a Republican Jewish Coalition leadership meeting, I insisted months earlier that I would not attend. I did not want to fly from Los Angeles to Washington DC for one day. To spend money on airfare and use up one vacation day was a non-starter. I thoroughly enjoy RJC events, but I was absolutely not attending this meeting. My time is valuable, and short of getting Charles Krauthammer as a speaker, I was skipping this one.

Several days later, an e-mail arrived in my inbox. The featured guest at the next RJC Leadership meeting would be none other than Sir Charles of Krauthammer himself. I shook my fist to the sky, said, "D@mn you Larry Greenfield!" (my dear friend at the RJC in Los Angeles, who keeps letting me know about such spectacular events) and immediately made plans for Washington. The event was directly next door to the White House. Except for President Bush and Vice President Cheney, there is nobody that I desired meeting more than Charles Krauthammer.

The word gets overused, but he is a genius. God has restricted him physically. He is confined to a wheelchair and therefore rarely leaves Washington DC. The rare times he has, the events were sold out to capacity. This was another reason I made the trip. As for limitations on his physical mobility, God compensated by simply giving him one of the finest minds on earth.

The man is one of my intellectual heroes, and I do not have that many. I count the list on one hand. Rather than offer any more well-deserved effusive praise for this intellectual giant, I will let his words speak for themselves. With that, below is the wit, warmth, and wisdom of Solomon, or as he is known on earth, Charles Krauthammer.

"I have gone in a quarter of a century from covering Walter Mondale to appearing on Fox News. My defense for my past is that I was young once.

I am a licensed psychiatrist. I have been a psychiatrist in remission for twenty-five years.

The world of psychiatry and the world of Washington both involve dealing with people that have delusions of grandeur. Washington is more dangerous because the people with delusions of grandeur have access to nuclear weapons.

Either God is a Republican, or God has a good sense of humor. The Democrats have nominated their weakest candidate. The Republicans, by complete accident, have nominated their strongest candidate.

The Republicans got lucky. First, Mike Huckabee had to defeat Mitt Romney in Iowa. Then John McCain won New Hampshire. Then Fred Thompson siphoned off just enough support in South Carolina to allow McCain to defeat Huckabee. In addition, heavy snowstorms affected the part of the state that was strongest for Huckabee. In addition, the Giuliani strategy benefited McCain. Rudy Giuliani was his main competition. With John McCain, the Republicans nominated the one guy who can win. None of the others could have won. Only McCain can.

Winning three straight elections is difficult. Only Ronald Reagan in the modern era won a third term, in the form of George Herbert Walker Bush."

Mr. Krauthammer's analysis of Barack Obama was equally brilliant.

"Obama may not believe the words of Pastor Jeremiah Wright, but Wright is correct when he says that Obama is just a politician.

It is interesting regarding the timing of Obama's denunciation of Wright. He had twenty years to be offended, but only objected when he himself was attacked as a pandering politician by his former pastor. Insulting the United States of America is one thing. Insulting Obama himself really offends him.

Obama is not unpatriotic. He is a leftist academic, not a radical. He loves America, but he is an academic.

Obama has never expressed a gut position on Israel.

Pastor Wright said that 'Zionism, not Judaism, is a gutter religion.' This is quite the bizarre statement.

At the ABC debate, George Stephanopoulos asked a clear question. 'Is an attack on Israel an attack on the USA, requiring retaliation in line with the NATO Alliance?' (Stephanopoulos was not stating that Israel was a member of NATO. The question remains valid.) Hillary Clinton remarked that obliterating Iran would be the response.

'Obliterating' Iran was a 'moderate' way to put it (the crowd laughed hysterically), and an effective way to put it.

If we can make Persian history a memory, Iran might think twice.

Obama calls an attack on Israel 'unacceptable.' Now that is tough talk.

Obama is a rookie. He gave a non-answer to a new question. His answer was ignorance and prudence. Diplomacy with Iran on the nuclear issue is nonsense and totally useless. We had three useless UN resolutions, then the EU 3 of Britain, France, and Germany offered nothing. Obama is prepared to fly to Tehran, and tell them what? Is he naive or cynical? Unacceptable? That will scare the hell out of the mullahs. Negotiation is an excuse to do nothing. He does not accept the premise that Iran is trying to go nuclear. Aggressive diplomacy? That has meant nothing and been tried for the last six years.

Candidates spend time preparing for every possible question in debates, and Obama was simply confronted with an unexpected and new question. He chose what he thought was a safe, inoffensive answer, which is his general strategy.

President Bush has the legal authority to attack Iran. However, having the moral authority is tough with a 28 percent approval rating.

If we attack the Strait of Hormuz, oil will skyrocket to $200 to $300 per barrel, and Hezbollah will attack from Lebanon. In October of 2006 ... (When the NIE report came out and was manipulated to hurt the case for an attack), ... President Bush was resigned to no attack.

Some say Israel should attack Iran. Israel might not have the physical capacity to do it. This is not like attacking the Osirak reactor in 1981 or Damascus in 2007. Iran is further away from Israel. Refueling might be an issue. In September of 2007, Israel hit Syria through Turkey. Turkey allowed Israel to hit Syria. They might not be willing to do so again. Iran is not a one day operation. It might take a couple of weeks.

The mullahs will be overthrown. Half the population is under twenty-five. They hate the mullahs. The USA must simply have a 'nuclear umbrella' over Israel.

Israel at sixty is one of the great historical acts of all time. Israel is now in a stable situation from terror. In 2002 there were fifty-nine homicide bombings. In 2007 there was one.

President George W. Bush is the best on Israel since President Truman.

The Gaza withdrawal was a good thing, but Israel should have declared an immediate policy of deterrence. One rocket attack should have yielded one hundred in response.

Why does Israel supply the Palestinians with electricity and food? Prime Minister Ehud Ohlmert botched the war in 2006, and Bibi (former and hopefully the next Prime Minister of Israel) would not tolerate such nonsense.

We must stay and succeed in Iraq. We have our general. The war is the most important issue for the United States and Israel.

Anti-Semites are pathological. We've gone from having no Holocaust at all to saying it was induced by the Zionists. Try understanding that one.

There is a certain psychosis in liberal Jews backing Obama, yet saying that they love Israel.

In April of 2002, President Bush gave Ariel Sharon free reign, not forty-eight hours. Yet liberal Jews see President Bush as the Antichrist."

Mr. Krauthammer was at his very best when discussing the meetings at Annapolis, Maryland. Many staunch backers of President Bush wondered if the man who supported Israel fiercely for six-and-a-half years was beginning to waver. Was he so desperate for a peace agreement the way his predecessor was that he was willing to pressure Israel?

No, he was not. Annapolis meant nothing, and I personally was never worried. I kept telling my friends to calm down. Annapolis was just feel-good symbolism. President Bush every once in awhile needs to offer the mildest of criticism toward Israel to make it look like he is neutral. He has been a friend of Israel and will remain so. One only needs to see Palestinians burning him in effigy with the passion of modern liberals to realize that he had not changed his views.

I was thrilled when Mr. Krauthammer offered the same assessment I have offered since Annapolis. For a brief moment I felt like I was on his intellectual level. That disappeared when he expressed those sentiments in a much more eloquent manner.

"Do not worry about Annapolis. Annapolis is meaningless. It is a great photo opportunity, not a sellout. It looks great and accomplishes nothing. It was completely useless. By diplomatic standards it was a total and complete success."

The crowd howled with laughter.

"Jews support Obama over McCain by about 80 percent to 20 percent. Liberal Jews see voting in their own self interest to be a violation of a moral principle. This is insane."[111]

As thrilling as his remarks were, meeting him was more of a thrill. I asked him before his speech if I could give him a gift. He said, "Not right now; afterwards is fine."

It quickly occurred to me that if everybody placed gifts in his lap, it would make steering his wheelchair more difficult! He was appreciative, but wanted anyone offering gifts to wait until after his speech, when it would be easier for him to navigate from the lobby to his car. He did so after his speech with several gifts sitting in his lap, including mine.

After his speech, I had my picture taken with him and patiently waited my turn to speak to him. I allowed others to cut in front of me because I wanted more time, which comes to those who wait for the crowd to disperse. He was not pressed for time, allowing me to be gracious about it. He was being treated like a rock star, which I more than understood.

Then I finally spoke to him. I asked him if he had been knighted yet, and if he was now known as "Sir Charles of Krauthammer."

He warmly responded, "I haven't yet. I haven't found a nation that has been willing to do it. That would be nice though."

I then asked him a more serious question.

"Mr. Krauthammer, on a more serious note, given all the recent European leaders that are very friendly to Israel, such as Sarkozy (Nicolas, President of France), Berlusconi (Silvio, Prime Minister of Italy), and Harper (Stephen, Prime Minister of Canada), ... isn't now the best time for Israel to attack Iran? Isn't this a brief window of time with world leaders that would be okay with such a strike?"

Mr. Krauthammer empathized but reiterated an earlier point of his.

"It would be great, but I just don't know if Israel has the physical capacity to do it."

Lastly, I gave him my gift.

"Mr. Krauthammer, I am a Republican blogger. Every day I take verbal brickbats to the Daily Kossacks and others." (He thanked me for that.) "You are the model of how I want my column to be. I like that you raise the level of discourse while keeping your convictions. Forgive me, but my gift to you is more an attempt at shameless self-promotion than a gift." (He laughed.) "I hope you like some of my better columns." (I gave him an envelope with some of those columns and a very nice note.) "I hope they are up to your standards. If they are, I would be honored to interview you one day."

He genuinely thanked me and did not commit to a timetable for an interview. I certainly was not going to press the issue. I was concerned that even giving him the columns might be too aggressive. Nevertheless, I was not too concerned to refrain. I hope he found me polite about it. When I went to shake his hand, he offered me a closed fist, which is what he did with everybody. I gently clasped his hand, and made sure not to accidentally hurt him. When he wheeled away with his gifts sitting in his lap, he seemed genuinely happy about receiving such a warm reception from the conference attendees.

This was justifiably expected. The Republican Jewish Coalition would naturally offer extreme warmth to one of the greatest Jewish Republicans in this country. In addition, he is a proud Neocon. Of course we love the guy.

Meeting an intellectual titan was a thrill that even his words might not describe. Maybe his could. Mine cannot. He is a hero of mine, and I wish him well always. I just hope that the Queen of England or some other dignitary finally takes my advice through osmosis and knights this man already.

I am absolutely not going to the next DC meeting. I don't want to go. Short of getting Nicholas Sarkozy or Silvio Berlusconi, I am definitively, positively not going. Given what high caliber people go to these meetings, the RJC will most likely make me eat my words again. After all, I was absolutely not attending this past meeting.

Then again, as a proud member of the (Republican) Zionist Crusader Alliance (For World Domination), it was a privilege to meet our unofficial leader, the honorable Sir Charles of Krauthammer.

eric

Chapter 18: From Smokey and the Bandit to Blue Moon of Kentucky

From Burt Reynolds and Jerry Reed (rest his soul) playing the Bandit and the Snowman to Vince Gill as Boomhauer on *King of the Hill* singing "Blue Moon of Kentucky," America is filled with great people everywhere.

Lee Greenwood sang "The Bandit Express," which is how I became known as "The Tygrrrr Express."

You see, only eighteen chapters in, and I am already revealing more about myself. I could jump up and down on Oprah's couch, but the restraining order prevents this. One time I hit on Monique, and next thing you know every beautiful plus-sized black woman in America thinks they are next. They might be, but that is not the point.

The point is that America has some magnificent human beings. I make fun of liberals, but without them conservatives would not look so comparatively wonderful.

We are stuck with each other, so we might as well get along.

As Stone Cold Steve Austin said on MTV's *Celebrity Deathmatch*, "That's the bottom line, because Stone Cold said so."[112]

So while we joke around and advance arguments, let's not mix the political with the personal. I am not saying we should all go out and hug trees, but liberals hug trees, so perhaps we can go hug a liberal.

Besides, at worst we can scrub ourselves with lava soap afterwards. At best we may have just made a new friend, or even a new concubine.

Now that is worth crossing party lines, and something I prefer in liberal doses.

2008 Republican Convention Day One—Magnificent Minneapolis Mayhem

The Tygrrrr Express is partying in Minneapolis. It has been a thrill ride a minute.

Yes, this has been an unorthodox start to the convention, but there are so many things to see and do. Memories to last a lifetime are the rule, not the exception.

First of all, I am sleeping at a sportsbar in downtown Minneapolis known as "Centerfield." Brad is the owner, Josh is his son, and they make fabulous pizza. If sleeping in a sportsbar sounds fun … it is.

http://www.linwoodpizzamn.com/

As for the convention itself, it appropriately turned into a fundraiser for the victims of Hurricane Gustav. After that, some more adventures occurred, including clashes with leftist protesters and a police escort home for me and a friend.

There was universal praise for Louisiana Governor Bobby Jindal, who for obvious reasons did not have time to tape a statement. There was also widespread praise for President Bush. The federal government and the states affected have been in close cooperation and coordination.

No Republican governors announced that they were "so overwhelmed." They got down to business. These Republican governors are capable, competent, and on top of things.

I interviewed radio hosts Hugh Hewitt and Armstrong Williams and many other politicos. Even though I had interviewed her by email, I finally met Townhall.com reporter Amanda Carpenter in person. I briefly met Mitt Romney again. He was his usual gracious and friendly self. Other events included a blogger event with Fred Thompson as well as meeting some Republican governors.

Before leaving the convention center, I ended up accidentally stumbling into a meeting of Catholics for McCain. They knew I was Jewish, but we are all good Republicans. Heck, they fed me. I had not had an ounce of food until 5:30 PM, and the bread of affliction tasted delicious. Later today I'll be attending a Jewish party in one of the luxury boxes in the XCEL Convention Center, and I look forward to seeing my new Catholic friends again.

After the convention, the protesters were out not in full force, but in quarter force at best.

I had fun with them. I even offered to bring a razor to the convention to shave the beards of the men and the underarms of the women. This was after they said mean words my mother would not condone.

One protester complained that we were in a police state that used military tactics on civilians. I told them that they were wrong, because I pleaded with the police to use brute force, and they refused. They would not use tear gas or rubber bullets. So I guess democracy is alive, even for scum. The protesters continued to yell about fascism, and the police still would not validate their opinions. I was hoping they would have the sequel to Kent State just long enough for protesters to grasp what freedom means.

I told one protester, "You have the right to speak. I have the right to say that you are full of garbage. Notice I did not curse. That is civilized discourse."

As for the anti-Semites that make up Code Pink, I pointed out that Jews are leftists for the most part, and to engage in anti-Semitic rhetoric was stupid.

When asked by Ron Paul supporters about him, I explained that I did not care about black transvestites.

I even offered to give leftist protesters hugs. Most refused. I asked them if they were for peace, and they said they were. They explained they could not hug a Republican. When I explained that peace has to mean everybody, they tried to protest, since they are protesters. However, I loudly announced that my feelings were hurt, and that they would not hug for peace.

Some of my escapades were videotaped. YouTube infamy awaits. My poor parents may have to return to hiding.

One leftist protester made a remark about Sarah Palin's daughter getting pregnant at age seventeen. I refuse to cover this non-story the same way I refused to cover Al Gore's son committing actual crimes. I told the protester that the media should leave Sarah Palin's daughter alone, and the same goes for Al Gore's son, the Bush twins, and Chelsea Clinton (until she entered the arena). I told him it was a disgrace to go after Mary Cheney. The man agreed, and we shook hands. I told every protester that they were my opponent, not my enemy. Some of them got it. Others are what they are.

At the end of the night, the inability to figure out the bus schedule had us asking police officers for cab information. Instead, they offered to drive us back to Centerfield Sportsbar. It was awesome. We had our own convoy.

The good news was that they gave us a ride. The bad news, in their words, was that "it would be in a minivan." They felt bad for us. They know we wanted the whole police officer squad car with the sirens blaring type of thing. It was not to be. We would have taken pictures of us in the back of the squad car. Instead we just took photos of us with the officer. He reminded is that he was not a member of Minnesota's finest, but Minneapolis's finest. Other cities were to get no credit.

More thrills abound. On to the next adventure.

eric

Thank You, Lee Greenwood, From a Misty-Eyed American

One misconception about conservative Republicans is that when we wave that flag loudly and proudly, we heap scorn on those who don't. While I disagree with Alan Colmes on most issues, I trust that he is sincere when he claims to be "Red, white, and liberal." I will not criticize others who choose to show their patriotism in a calm, silent, stoic manner. I only hope that my right to be over the top in all things positive about America is not seen as nationalism, ethnocentrism, or jingoism. If it is, so be it. I get angry when I see 9/11 footage. I beam with pride when I see firefighters, EMTs, and police officers rescuing people. I still get charged up watching highlights of the 1980 Olympic hockey game where we beat the Russians and Al Michaels asked us all if we "believed in miracles." Yes! This is America. Of course we do. America is a miracle.

To this day, nothing gets me as misty eyed as listening to Lee Greenwood sing "God Bless the USA." As I hear the words, I picture sports highlights as well as my own journeys. I travel all across this land. The song and the people amaze me.

"From the lakes of Minnesota ..." (The Mall of America is a destination ... I met Governor Pawlenty and Senator Coleman, and look forward to meeting Jesse Ventura.)

"... to the hills of Tennessee ..." (From the Titans Adelphia Miracle 'Tennessee has pulled off a miracle! There are no flags!' to the wonderful Jewish community of Chattanooga, to the most romantic horse and buggy ride I have ever been on.)

"... across the Plains of Texas ..." (Dallas has where JFK was shot, plus where JR Ewing was shot. I apologize for the good people of Dallas for "Standing on the Star" outside a Cowboys Preseason game. Deion Sanders has an awesome house.)

"... from sea to shining sea ..."

"...from Detroit... (Northwest has a large airport hub) ... down to Houston ..." (Fat Robert made my Mardi Gras. Thank heavens Sister Mary and the nuns had no idea what happened in that hotel banquet hall five hours earlier. Bikers know how to party, and they worry about the public school systems.)

"... and New York (Brooklyn born, Long Island raised, Mark Messier made 1994 a sports season for the ages, and Rudy Giuliani remade Gotham into a world class city ... and 9/11 is seared into me forever.) to LA ..." (Randy Newman is right; I love living here.)

"... There's pride in every American heart, and it's time we stand and say ..."

"... I'm Proud to be an American, where it least I know I'm free

I won't forget the men who died, who gave that right to me

I'll gladly stand up next to you, defend her still today

Cause their aint no doubt I love this land, God bless the USA."

It is more than a flag. It is a story of fifty noble kingdoms, each one with their own special story. There was Mom's Diner in South Carolina, to that quiet hotel in Fort Payne, Alabama, to that record store in Pocatello, Idaho, where I finally found a cassette that no one else in America seemed to have.

In 2006, I finally made it to Hawaii and the Pro Bowl. Holding back tears, I touched the ground at Canton, Ohio, the home of the National Football League Hall of Fame. In the future I will make it to Green Bay, Wisconsin. I was told to go to Brett's Restaurant and have the ribs. I have partied in Miami, celebrated Passover in Chicago, and kissed the forehead of a troubled but sweet girl in Scranton, Pennsylvania. I have danced sweetly with one in a hotel room in Salt Lake City, Utah, and more suggestively in Gulfport, Mississippi. From "Sweet Home Chicago (Baby Dontcha Wanna Go)"[113] to the "Louisiana Boogie (Baby wontcha slide on down),"[114] every city has a hamlet that is unique.

Brasstown, North Carolina has the "Dropping of the Possum"[115] (it is harmless; no animals get hurt), and there are no songs for pure fun like "Blue Moon of Kentucky" or the "Alabama Jubilee" (Hail hail, the gang's all here).

Brooklyn has the Boardwalk and the original Nathan's Hot Dog restaurant, and Oakland has my friends of the Raider Nation.

I love what Lee Greenwood sings because I love seeing for myself who the people are that make up this land. I look forward to meeting every single one of these people and shaking their hands, and of course, hearing their stories.

The people add to the beauty of the song. May we all have the privilege of experiencing what Lee Greenwood writes about.

"There ain't no doubt I love this land ... God bless the USA."

President Bush said after 9/11 that, "The entire world has seen the state of our union, and it is strong."[116]

I hope you all get to see for yourselves.

Time to throw darts at the map and see which people I will be lucky enough to befriend next.

eric

Lack of Conclusions

When all is said and done, I might be the simplest guy on earth. I can often be found with a soda and a burger, which is what I recommended to all of you before this adventure began.

I laugh when my team wins, cuss for a few moments when they lose, and am lucky enough to have had the same friends my whole life. Watching football is about being with friends. I have the best friends a guy could ask for.

I have no children of my own that I know of, but my close friend adopted a baby boy. Every time I look in that little boy's eyes, it crystallizes what matters in life.

Yet life is often deeper than what we see on the surface, and my burning desire is to rid the world of ideological bigotry forever.

God created me. God loves me, accepts me for all of my many flaws, and will not judge me any more or less harshly based on my politics. If I am good enough for God to create and let roam around this earth, then I am good enough for liberals, Palestinians, and even feminists to acknowledge my existence.

Besides, the best feeling in the world is when people who think they would not like each other meet and become lifelong friends. If that does not improve the world, I have no idea what does. I hope to defeat the left at the ballot box, but still always invite them into my home. I hope they harbor the same attitude toward me.

The death of ideological bigotry will have life affirming results.

So if you see me, no matter what your beliefs, approach me. Say hello. Offer a handshake or a hug. Pull up a chair and tell me your story. It is the least I can do since I shared with you glimpses of mine.

As for me, my battle cry remains the same. *Hineni.* Here I am. Jewish, proud, politically conservative, and morally liberal.

So what next?

I'll be flying down the highway headed West ...

In a streak of black lightning, called the Tygrrrr Express.

On to the next adventure. God bless.

eric

Acknowledgements

My grandparents are gone, but with me always. My parents were never wealthy, but I was raised right.

Without love, there is no life. The love of my life is the current romantic administration.

My friendships are lifelong friendships. They are listed in alphabetical order by last name to avoid any possible (insert nightmare scenarios here).

Seth Arkin, Brian Arnold, Richard Baehr, Billy Beene, Michael and Ann Benayoun, Lara Berman, Arno Berry, David Blumberg, Johnny Ceng, Ligang Chen, Lisa and Bob Cohen, Nim Cohen, Chaim and Tova Cunin, Seth Edelman, Brian Elfand, Jason Elman, Uri Filiba, Ken Flickstein, Deron Freatis, Eric and Jennifer Goldberg, Steve Goldberg, Eugene Grayver, Molly and Leonard Grayver, Meri Green, Elyse and Aaron Greenberg, Larry Greenfield, Steve Grill, Danny Halperin, John Heller, Julia and Marc Jaffe, Jason Kenniston, Tarik Khan, Jonathan Klein, Jamie Krasnoo, Jerry Krautman, Jeff Kuhns, Lisa Macizo, David Marcus, Jason Margolies, Margie and Tom Mergen, Carl Merino, Mike Monatlik, Andrew Nelson, Izzy Newman, Greg Neyman, Erica Nurnberg, Terry Okura, Mare Ouellette, Mike Patton, Harold and Sharon Rosenthal, Jeanie and Bernie Rosenthal, Ron Rothstain, Michael Rubinfeld, Daniel Savitt, Evan Sayet, Alan Schechter, Alicia and Josh Stone, Ryan Szackas, Ruth and David Tobin, Dov and Runya Wagner, Adam Wasserman, Hilarie Wolf, Laura Wolfe, Nate and Janna Wyckoff, Oliver Young, Marc Zoolman.

My extended family includes the Arzillos, the Diels, the Katzs, David Malakoff, the Mouradians, the Rossis, and the Weitzs.

Lara Berman convinced me to start a blog. Jamie Krasnoo provided the technological advice. Eliot Yamini of Hotweazel developed it. Hugh Hewitt,

Armstrong Williams, Ward Connerly, Evan Sayet, and Larry Greenfield all have helped my blog expand. Chabad, USC Hillel, the Republican Jewish Coalition, and the Zionist Crusader Alliance have all nourished and inspired me.

I never met Ronald Reagan, but feel his presence. May God bless him always.

George W. Bush and Dick Cheney have faced more ideological bigotry than I ever will, and they have done so with dignity. Their inner strength inspires me.

Almighty God, your patience with me is always appreciated.

eric, aka the Tygrrr Express   http://www.tygrrrexpress.com

Endnotes

I am not the *Jayson Blair Times*. Fabricating stories is for liberals. Many of my sources are from liberal sites. While I loathe to promote leftists in any way, listing the typical conservative sites would just open me up to charges of less thorough research. I want the world to see that evidence of left-wing ideological bigotry can be found at horrid, wretched excuses for "sources."

(1) Malkin, Michelle. *Unhinged*, Page 97, 2005.

(2) Krauthammer, Charles. Bush derangement syndrome. Townhall. com, December 5, 2003.

(3) Seeley, Katharine Q. Gore says Bush betrayed the U.S. *Jayson Blair Times*, February 9, 2004.

(4) Allen, Mike. Reid calls Bush a loser. *Washington Post*, May 7, 2005.

(5) Goodwin, Mike. "Howard and Hillary sing the same tune." *New York Daily News*, June 12, 2005."

(6) West Virginia Senator Robert Byrd. Senator Byrd calls for Secretary of Defense Rumsfeld to resign. Byrd.Senate.Gov/Speeches, September 13, 2006.

(7) Massachusetts Senator John Kerry. White House misleading public on prewar Iraq intelligence. Kerry.Senate.Gov/Speeches, November 14, 2005.

(8) Crowley, Candy, and Snow, Mary. Clinton's 'plantation' remark draws fire. CNN, January 18, 2006.

(9) Gramm, Phil. Lexington on Alan Greenspan. *The Economist*, January 6, 2000.

(10) Ekelund, Robert B. More awful truths about Republicans. Mises. org, September 4, 2008.

(11) Imus, Don. *Imus in the Morning,* April 4, 2007.

(12) Valley Beth Shalom, Hanukkah sermon, December, 2007.

(13) Calder, William. UCLA Hillel, Yom Kippur, October, 2008.

(14) Morris, Dick. Berger rolls for Bill and Hill. *Pittsburgh Tribune-Review,* April 9, 2005.

(15) Hot Chocolate. "You Sexy Thing (I Believe in Miracles)", 1975.

(16) Jacoby, Jeff. Al Sharpton, The Democrats' David Duke. *Capitalism* magazine, February 26, 2003.

(17) Hoenig, Jonathan. Carbon credit trading is ultimate rigged game. SmartMoney.com, June 26, 2008.

(18) Peters, Ralph. In Gaza's shadow. *New York Post,* June 14, 2007.

(19) *Ali Baba Bunny,* 1957.

(20) Sheppard, Noel. Dennis Miller stumps for Democrat president in 2008. *NewsBusters,* December 30, 2006.

(21) Dennis Leary, *Glenn Beck,* June 13, 2007.

(22) John C. McGinley as character Dr. Perry Cox, *Scrubs.*

(23) Camper Van Beethoven, "Take the skinheads bowling." Camper Van Beethoven.com, 1985.

(24) Beastie Boys, *Licensed to Ill,* 1987.

(25) Friedman, Thomas. 9/11 is over. *New York Times,* September 30, 2007.

(26) Israel raids into Gaza leave at least six dead. *Los Angeles Times,* December 21, 2007.

(27) Free our Talib. *Los Angeles Times,* July 29, 2007.

(28) ACLU defends Nazis' right to burn down ACLU headquarters. *The Onion,* October 14, 2003.

(29) Clinton, Hillary. Modern progressive vision: shared prosperity. HillaryClinton.com, May 29, 2007.

(30) 110 people who are screwing up America. Bernard Goldberg, p. 297, 2005.

(31) Finkelstein, Daniel. An open letter to readers of the *New York Times*. *Times of London*, January 17, 2008.

(32) Sowell, Thomas. See I told you so. *Rush Limbaugh*, 1993.

(33) Ben Affleck, *Boiler Room*, 2000.

(34) *South Park*, "Mr. Hankey the Christmas Poo," December 17, 1997.

(35) Looney Tunes, "One Froggy Evening." December 31, 1955.

(36) *Sesame Street*, Mr. Snuffleupagus, debuted 1971.

(37) *South Park*, "Manbearpig," April 26, 2006.

(38) George Wendt as character Norm Peterson, *Cheers,* debuted 1982.

(39) Aerosmith, "Full Circle," *Nine Lives,* 1997.

(40) Stevie Nicks, "Rooms on Fire," *The Other Side of the Mirror,* 1989.

(41) Sting, "Be Still My Beating Heart," *Nothing Like The Sun,* 1987.

(42) *Stocks and Blondes*, 1985.

(43) Jim Carrey, *The Truman Show*, 1998.

(44) *Showgirls*, 1995.

(45) *Redeye*, debuted 2007.

(46) Angie Harmon as character Abby Carmichael, *Law and Order,* 1998.

(47) Koppel, Ted. Encyclopedia.com, April 9, 2006.

(48) Berman, Chris. *ESPN NFL Primetime,* debuted 1987.

(49) *Monday Night Football* intro, Falcons vs. Saints, September 25, 2006.

(50) *Football Shorts,* Glenn Liebman, p. 161, 1997.

(51) Bret Michaels, Poison, "Something to Believe In," *Flesh and Blood,* 1990.

(52) The Cowsills, "Hair," 1969.

(53)   *Fraggle   Rock*   Theme,   1983.
(54) Malamud, Allan. "Notes on a scoreboard." *Los Angeles Times,* debuted 1963.

(55) Dave Chapelle, "I know black people." March 10[h], 1984.

(56) Monique, *Showtime at the Apollo,* debuted 2004.

(57) Gloria Gaynor, "I Will Survive," Love Tracks, 1978

(58) Kevin Kline, *In & Out,* 1997.

(59) Barry Manilow, "Copacabana," 1978.

(60) Reagan, Ronald. Tear down this wall. ReaganLibrary.com, June 12, 1987.

(61) Gamble, Doug. Funnyman Reagan. *National Review,* June 7, 2004.
(62) *Batman: The Dark Knight,* 2008.

(63) President George W. Bush, at Ground Zero, September 14, 2001.

(64) President George W. Bush, "History offers lessons on Iraq." RealClearPolitics.com, August 22[d], 2007.

(65) Winston Churchill, Thinkexist.com.

(66) Vice President Dick Cheney, speaking before the Republican Jewish Coalition in Florida, 2007.

(67) Texas Governor George W. Bush, upon landing in Israel, 1998.

(68) Simmons, Andy. Robin Williams grows up (a little bit). *Readers Digest,* 2005.

(69) McCain taps Alaska Governor Palin as vice president pick. CNN, August 30, 2008.

(70) Fleckenstein, Bill. "Is the Fed a short sale?" November 14, 2004.

(71) Van Halen, "Right Now." *For Unlawful Carnal Knowledge*, 1991.

(72) Maryland Lt. Governor Michael Steele, GOP convention, September 3, 2008.

(73) Hawaii Governor Linda Lingle, GOP convention, September 3, 2008.

(74) Beaker, a character on *The Muppet Show*, debuted 1976.

(75) Larry Hagman as character J.R. Ewing, *Dallas*, debuted 1977.

(76) President George H W Bush, speech from the Oval Office, January 16, 1991.

(77) Vice President Dan Quayle, "Dan Quayle vs. Murphy Brown." *Time Magazine*, June 1, 1992.

(78) Fred Thompson, *Die Harder*, 1990.

(79) Fred Thompson as character Arthur Branch, "Ain't No Love." *Law and Order*, 2005.

(80) *King of the Hill*, debuted 1997.

(81) "Dilbert," Created by Scott Adams, debuted 1989.

(82) *American Dad*, debuted 2005.

(83) Massachusetts Governor Mitt Romney, speaking at the California Republican Party Convention in 2007.

(84) The Police, debuted 1977.

(85) Sean Paul, "Temperature," *The Trinity*, 2005.

(86) Ron Paul and Rudy Giuliani, GOP presidential debate, May 16, 2007.

(87) Karl Rove, speaking at American Jewish University, February 28, 2008.

(88) Ol' Dirty Bastard, Wikipedia, 1998.

(89) David Letterman, *Late Night With David Letterman*, 2003.

(90) Voltaire, QuotationsPage.com, eighteenth century.

(91) Jack Nicholson as character Colonel Nathan R. Jessup, *A Few Good Men*, 1992.

(92) Colonel Bill Cowan, speaking to the David Horowitz Freedom Center, May 30, 2007.

(93) Chaka Khan, "I Feel For You," *I Feel For You*, 1984.

(94) Steve Winwood with Chaka Khan, "Higher Love," *Back in the High Life*, 1986.

(95) Lee Greenwood, "You've Got a Good Love Comin'," *God Bless the USA* 1984.

(96) "Scrutiny increases for a group advocating for Muslims in U.S." *Jayson Blair Times*, March 14, 2007.

(97) Reed Rubinstein, speaking to the Republican Jewish Coalition in Chicago, March 17, 2008.

(98) Andrew Whitehead, Anti-CAIR-net.org, debuted 2003.

(99) Def Leppard, *Hysteria*, 1987.

(100) Hunt, Colonel David. *They Just Don't Get It*, 2005.

(101) Dan Balz and Mark Leibovich, GOP assails Kerry's call for 'sensitive war.' *Washington Post*, August 13, 2004.

(102) Malkin, Michelle. 'Abort' Sarah Palin. September 29, 2008.

(103) WorldnetDaily.com, 'Kill Bush' t-shirt for sale. April 13, 2005.

(104) Attacking President Bush with Nazi symbol. *Atlantic Review*, August 16, 2006.

(105) Memos on Bush are fake but accurate, typist says. *New York Times*, September 15, 2004.

(106) Illinois Senator Barack Obama, speaking to Joe "the Plumber" Wurlezebacher, while stumping in Ohio, October 13, 2008.

(107) Levine, Mel. Putting politics above Israel. Jews 4 Obama, October 2, 2008.

(108) Forman, Ira. The shamelessness of the Republican Jewish Coalition. *Huffington Post*, October 2, 2008.

(109) Greenberg, Brad. Obama campaign halts debates with RJC. The God Blog, *Jewish Journal*, October 15, 2008.

(110) Greenberg, Brad. Obama campaign halts debates with RJC. *Jewish Journal*, October 15, 2008.

(111) Sir Charles of Krauthammer, speaking to the Republican Jewish Coalition in Washington DC, May 7, 2008.

(112) Stone Cold Steve Austin, *MTV's Celebrity Deathmatch*, debuted 1998.

(113) James "Kokomo" Arnold, "Sweet Home Chicago," 1934.

(114) J B Lenoir, "Louisiana Boogie," 1950.

(115) Keep your ball. We've got the possum. *New York Times*, December 31, 2003.

(116) President George W. Bush, address to Congress, September 20, 2001.